THIRD EDITION

# Nursing & The Law

Mary W. Cazalas, R.N., J.D.

An Aspen Publication

Aspen Systems Corporation
Germantown, Maryland
1978

Library of Congress Cataloging in Publication Data

Main entry under title:
Nursing and the law.

Includes index.

1. Nursing—Law and legislation—United States.
I. Cazalas, Mary W.
KF2915.N8N87      1978      344'.73'041      78-24253
ISBN 0-89443-075-0

9c176

Library of Congress Catalog Card Number: 78-24253
ISBN: 0-89443-075-0
*Printed in the United States of America*
3 4 5

# Table of Contents

# Foreword

Often I am told that I have an unusual and unique background since I have two professions— nursing and the law. I am frequently asked: which was first and why the second?

I guess I'd have to say I inherited my interest in medicine from my grandfather, Dr. George Slappey, who was a physician, back in the horse and buggy days in Jeffersonville, Georgia. (He never paid medical malpractice insurance premiums, nor was he ever in danger of suit for malpractice.) Although he discouraged my mother from a nursing career because he thought the profession too difficult, she passed her ambitions along to me.

When I graduated from high school in 1945, my mother encouraged me to enter the Cadet Nurse Corps. Even though World War II was over, the government extended the Corps— established to fund education for nurses during the war years— for one more class. Thus did I enter a profession that has since rewarded me with both independence and a challenging career.

My first position as a general duty nurse paid me $180 per month for a six-day week, eight hours a day. Because there was a shortage of nurses, we often were required to work double shifts. In those days, nurses were taught to stand with respect when a physician approached the desk. This was in 1948 and the American Nurses Association and the National League for Nursing Education were planting the seeds for higher education for nurses. I considered my future and decided to return to college and eventually enter medical school.

I received by B.S. in pre-med in 1954 (all the while working as a registered nurse) and my M.S. in anatomy in 1960. At one time during this period, I recall voting at a faculty meeting to accept the first male students into the nursing school.

Later, I worked in the Urology Department at the School of Medicine at Tulane University and attended evening classes at the School of Law at Loyola University, where I subsequently received my Juris Doctor degree.

In my new profession I learned legal research and writing as a law clerk, and also had a small private practice that provided practical experience in the courtroom. My next position was Assistant United States Attorney. Since entering the legal profession I have written and argued more than 250 criminal appeals in the Fifth Circuit Court of Appeals in Louisiana.

My knowledge of medicine is an invaluable asset when I handle malpractice and personal injury cases; working with malpractice cases enables me to remain current in medical practices.

Since I am a part of both worlds, I feel that I can justifiably criticize both. Unfortunately, in the legal profession there are shysters, and in the medical profession there are quacks. However, even the most competent medical practitioner can make a mistake.

Prior to attending law school I never considered having malpractice insurance. Today, I would not work one moment without it. The nurse may not be at fault, but a judgment may be rendered in favor of the plaintiff. Even if the nurse is successful in proving the defense, the cost of litigation must be paid. Insurance pays for the legal costs and any judgment rendered up to the limits of the policy. A young nurse once told me that since she had just graduated she could not afford insurance. My answer was: you cannot afford *not* to have insurance.

Once I was told by a judge that my law had ruined my nursing because it instilled in me fear of a law suit for malpractice. I say that law has *improved* my nursing, for it makes me aware of the value for continuing education, and of the necessity for extreme care in practicing the art of both my professions.

We must never make our professions immune to suit for damages we cause by our negligent acts for two reasons. If we cause harm we must pay, and the fear of a suit serves as a deterrent to negligence and causes us to strive toward at least the standard of the reasonable nurse under the circumstances.

Mary Williams Cazalas
December, 1978

# Introduction

The purpose of this book is to present an introduction to the law. "Introduction to Law," Chapter 1, explains the sources of the law and which law applies. The Anatomy of a Trial traces a case from the filing of the complaint to the judgment. Nurses should have knowledge of wills so that they can advise the patient who may die. They may be witnesses in cases that are not malpractice suits— patients suing for personal injury may call their nurse to testify; or the nurse may be the plaintiff seeking redress of a wrong.

Chapter 2, "Principles of Nursing Liability," defines malpractice. Who can be sued, the basis for suits, and the defenses available are also discussed.

What is consent? Who should obtain the consent; from whom should it be obtained; in what form should the consent be; what is informed consent; and what can be done if no consent is obtained? These are the questions raised and answered in Chapter 3, "Consent to Medical and Surgical Procedures."

In Chapter 4, "Medical Records," the importance of properly maintained records is emphasized. There is a discussion of the content of medical records, use in legal proceedings, confidentiality of communications, and right to subpoena, introduce and use such records in court proceedings.

Although regulations may seem burdensome, they are necessary for protection of the consumer. Chapter 5, "Drugs and Medications," gives a cursory review of state and federal regulations of drugs, medications and devices.

Chapter 6, "Intentional Wrongs," defines the torts, or civil wrongs, that result from intentional wrongs rather than negligence, for which the nurse may be sued. These include assault and battery, false imprisonment, invasion of privacy and defamation.

Provisions and recent changes in nurse practice acts, and a discussion on licensing procedures and methods of regulating and controlling the nursing profession in order to assure safety for the consumer, are brought to your attention in Chapter 7, "Licensing Laws and Scope of Practice." The changing role of the nurse has necessitated a change in the definition of nursing to grant authority for the nurse to perform tasks which only physicians have been permitted to perform in the past.

"The New Nursing Professionals," Chapter 8, summarizes recent studies by the United States Department of Health, Education and Welfare on the role of nurse practitioners and physician assistants— referred to as mid-level professionals— and the current status of education, regulation, licensing and reimbursement of these practitioners. If their joining the medical team improves the quality of medical care and reduces the costs, malpractice suits may decrease. If educational programs are poor and their practice is not competent, malpractice suits may increase and the consumer will be harmed.

The relationship of the nurse as an employee, and who may be responsible for the nurses' acts of negligence under the doctrine of *respondeat superior* is explained in Chapter 9, "The Nurse as an Employee."

Establishment of unions in hospitals has occurred in recent years. Chapter 10, "Labor," gives a cursory review of the labor laws which affect medical care facilities. Consideration is given to the effects of unionization in hospitals.

"Insurance," Chapter 11, describes the insurance contract and medical professional liability coverage. Some alternatives through state legislation are discussed. These include arbitration agreements and availability of state malpractice insurance coverage. "Appendix C" is the Louisiana statute which is similar to statutes in some other states.

Employees and patients have a right to be free from discrimination. Chapter 12, "Civil Rights," defines their civil rights. The Constitution of the United States guarantees equal protection of the law, due process, and freedom from cruel and unusual punishment. This chapter discusses the American Hospital Association's Patients' Bill of Rights, and rights of the mentally ill. Patients' knowledge of their rights and patient advocacy groups bringing litigation before the courts may cause an increase of actions for malpractice.

Chapter 13, "Legal Reporting Obligations," enumerates what matters must be reported according to statutory requirements. "Appendix E" is a summary of the statutes requiring reporting of child abuse. This is a widespread and very grave problem, and all states have amended their statutes to expand reporting requirements.

Chapter 14 and "Appendix F" summarize the "Good Samaritan Laws."

Legislation and judicial decisions pertaining to the right to an abortion and the degree of regulation a state may exercise are reviewed in "Abortion," Chapter 15. This topic is still controversial.

"Sterilization and Artificial Insemination," Chapter 16, points out the medical care provider's liability when the desired results of sterilization are not obtained. The ethical, moral and legal implications of artificial insemination are interesting, but there has been only minimal litigation involving this.

Chapter 17, "Autopsy and Donation," deals with liability that can occur from autopsies being performed without consent from the one with authority to give consent, or if not performed in accordance with the consent given. State statutes regulate donations of bodies and parts of bodies for medical use. A summary of the Uniform Anatomical Gift Act is included. Unclaimed dead bodies are generally buried at public expense, and a public official has the duty of burying or otherwise disposing of such bodies.

This book is written so that nonlawyers will understand the legal terminology, and to give to you concisely and clearly the most current information on the subject matter discussed. The research sources and case citations are in the body of the text for those who wish to read additional material.

This book will make nurses aware of what they can be sued for and how they can protect themselves from suits for malpractice. In summary, always keep informed by reading medical and nursing journals and books; attend continuing education programs; never undertake to practice in an area in which knowledge and ability are lacking; always use extreme care; whenever in doubt request that the person with authority give advice and assistance; and be considerate, kind and understanding to all. Always have adequate malpractice insurance coverage in the event of a suit so that costs of defense and any judgment for damages rendered against you will be paid.

# Part I

# Nurses and Their Patients

# Chapter 1

# Introduction to Law

This Chapter is designed to provide nurses with some basic information about the law, the workings of the legal system, and the roles of the branches of government in creating, administering, and enforcing the law.

## NATURE OF LAW

According to most definitions, law is, in essence, a system of principles and processes by which people who live in a society deal with their disputes and problems, seeking to solve or settle them without resort to force. Law governs the relationships of private individuals and organizations to other private individuals and to the government, which is the paramount authority of the society. Law that deals with the relationships between private parties is termed private law, whereas public law deals with the relationships between private parties and government. The increasing complexity of society and life in the United States has necessitated a broadening of the scope of public law, and the regulation of private persons and institutions has become pervasive.

One important segment of public law is criminal law, which prohibits conduct deemed injurious to the public order and provides for punishment of those found to have engaged in such conduct. A crime is the performance of the proscribed act, and the government enforces criminal law against alleged perpetrators of crimes. Public law consists also of countless regulations designed to advance societal objectives by requiring private individuals and organizations to adopt specified courses of action in their activities and undertakings. Much of the public law contains criminal provisions that are applicable when individuals and organizations do not abide by the regulations. The thrust of most public law is to attain what are deemed valid public goals.

Private law is concerned with the recognition and enforcement of rights and duties of private individuals and organizations. Legal actions between private parties are of two types, tort and contract. In a tort action one party asserts that wrongful conduct on the part of the other party has caused harm, and seeks compensation for the harm suffered. In a contract action one party asserts that, in failing to fulfill an obligation, the other party has breached the contract, and seeks either compensation or performance of the obligation as remedy.

Law serves as a guide to conduct. Most disputes or controversies that are covered by legal principles or rules are resolved without resort to the courts. Thus, each party's awareness of the law and of the relative likelihood of success in court affects its willingness to modify its original position and reach a compromise acceptable to both sides.

## SOURCES OF LAW

Law encompasses principles and rules derived from several sources. The principles and rules of enacted law emanate from legislative bodies and are set in hierarchical order. Law is also generated by the decisions of courts and the decisions and rules of government agencies.

The Constitution of the United States which was adopted at the Constitutional Convention in 1787 and ratified by the states, together with the duly ratified amendments, is highest in the hierarchy of enacted law. Article VI of the Constitution declares: "This Constitution, and the Laws of the United States which shall be made in Pursuance thereof; and all Treaties made, or which shall be made, under the Authority of the United States, shall be the supreme Law of the Land . . . ." The clear import of these words is that the Constitution, federal law, and treaties take precedence over the constitutions and laws of the several states. The position of a court or agency relative to other courts and agencies determines the place assigned to its decision in the hierarchy of decisional law. The decisions of the U.S. Supreme Court are highest in the hierarchy of decisional law; however, because of the parties or the legal questions involved, most legal controversies do not fall within the scope of the Supreme Court's decision-making responsibilities.

In addition to enacted and decisional law, an extensive body of law is issued by administrative agencies created by legislatures. This law takes the form of administrative rules and regulations valid only to the agency which has promulgated them, provided that they are not in conflict with the federal Constitution and federal legislation. State agency regulations and rules must also conform to federal law and must not conflict with the particular state's constitution and legislation.

Many of the legal principles and rules applied by the courts in the United States are products of the common law developed in England and, subsequently, in the United States. The law in Louisiana, however, derives from the civil law of the French, Spanish, and Romans. The Louisiana Civil Code had as its model the Napoleonic code. The term "common law" is applied to the body of principles which evolves from court decisions and is continually adapted and expanded. During the colonial period, English common law applied uniformly; however, after the Revolution each state adopted all or part of the existing English common law, then added to it as needed. Thus, the common law on specific subjects may differ from state to state. Statutory law has reenacted many legal rules and principles that initially were established by the courts as part of the common law. However, many issues, especially in private law disputes, are still decided according to common law. The rules of common law in a state may be changed by enactment of modifying legislation; they may also be changed by later court decisions which establish new and different common law rules.

With regard to the law applicable to specific controversies, courts for the most part adhere to the concept of *stare decisis,* or following precedent. In other words, by referring to a similar case previously decided and applying the same rules and principles, a court arrives at a comparable ruling in the current case. However, slight factual differences may sometimes provide a basis for recognizing distinctions between precedent and the current case. And sometimes, even when such differences are absent, a court may conclude that a particular common law rule is no longer in accord with the needs of society and may depart from precedent.

It should be understood that all principles of law are subject to change, whether they originate in statutory or common law. Statutory law may be amended, repealed, or expanded by action of the legislature; common law principles may be modified, abrogated, or created by new court decisions. Thus, the law affecting nursing, including not only statutory and common law but governmental administrative regulations and decisions of administrative agencies, is not static; it is in a continuing process of growth and modification.

## GOVERNMENTAL ORGANIZATION AND FUNCTION

The foregoing sections have introduced the legislative and judicial branches of government and touched on their functions in regard to the nature and sources of law. Now the focus is upon the structure of the three branches of government and the manner in which the functions of one branch relate to the functions of the other two. A vital concept in the constitutional framework of the government, both federal and state, is that of the separation of powers. Essentially, this means that no one branch or government is clearly dominant over the other two; however, in the exercise of its functions, each may affect and limit the activities, functions, and powers of the others.

The concept of separation of powers, which may be referred to as a system of checks and balances, is illustrated in the relationships between the branches in regard to legislation. On the federal level, when a bill to create a statute is enacted by Congress and signed by the President it becomes law. If the President should veto the bill, it would take a two-thirds vote of each house of Congress to override the veto. Or the President can prevent a bill from becoming law by not taking any action while Congress is in session. This procedure, known as a pocket veto, can prevent a bill from becoming law temporarily and may prevent it from becoming law at all if later sessions of Congress do not act favorably on it.

A bill that has become law may be declared invalid by the U.S. Supreme Court, an agency of the judicial branch of government, because the Court decides that the law is in violation of the Constitution.

Individuals nominated by the President for appointment to the federal judiciary, including the Supreme Court, must be approved by the U.S. Senate. Thus, in the course of time both the executive and legislative branches can affect the composition of the judicial branch of government. In addition, even though a Supreme Court decision may be final with regard to a specific controversy, Congress and the President may generate new constitutionally sound legislation to replace a law that has been declared unconstitutional. The processes for amending the Constitution are complex and often time-consuming, but they too can serve as a method of offsetting or overriding a Supreme Court decision.

Each of the three branches of government has a different primary function. The function of the legislative branch is to enact laws, which may amend or repeal existing legislation or may be essentially new legislation. It is the legislature's responsibility to determine the nature and extent of the need for new laws and for changes in existing laws. By means of a committee system, legislative proposals are assigned or referred for study to committees with special concerns or interests. The committees conduct investigations and hold hearings, at which interested persons may present their views, in order to obtain information to assist the committee members in their consideration of the bills. Some bills eventually reach the full legislative body, where after consideration and debate they may be either approved or rejected. The Congress and all state legislatures are bicameral (consist of two houses) except for *Nebraska,* which has a unicameral legislature. In a bicameral legislature both houses must pass identical versions of a legislative proposal before it can be brought to the chief executive.

The primary function of the executive branch is to enforce and administer the law. However, the chief executive, either the governor of a state or the President of the United States, has a role in the creation of law through the power to approve or veto a legislative proposal. If the chief executive accepts the bill through the constitutionally established process it becomes a statute, a part of the enacted law. If the chief executive vetoes the bill, it cannot become law unless the legislature overrides the veto; this usually requires the vote of two-thirds of the legislators.

The executive branch of government is organized on a departmental basis. Each department is responsible for a different area of public affairs, and each enforces the law within its area of responsibility. Most federal law pertaining to nurses is administered by the Department of Health, Education and Welfare. Most states also have separate departments for health and welfare matters, and these departments administer and enforce most state law pertaining to nurses. It should be recognized, however, that other departments and agencies of government may also affect nursing. On the federal level, for example, laws relating to wages and hours of employment are enforced by the Department of Labor; these laws and their enforcement may have substantial impact upon nurses.

The function of the judicial branch of government is adjudication: it resolves disputes in accordance with law. When a patient brings suit against a hospital, seeking compensation for harm allegedly suffered as the result of wrongful conduct by hospital personnel, the suit is decided by the courts.

Many disputes and controversies are resolved without resort to the courts, by arbitration, for example. However, sometimes there is no way to end a controversy without submitting to the adjudicatory process of the courts. A dispute brought before a court is decided in accordance with the applicable law; this application of the law is precisely the essence of the judicial process.

## ANATOMY OF A TRIAL

In a trial, the judicial procedure is designed to ascertain facts by hearing evidence, determine which facts are relevant, apply the appropriate principles of law, and pass judgment. The judgment determines the conduct to be followed. The many technical procedures in a lawsuit can be divided into six major steps: commencement; pleading; pretrial; trial; appeal; and execution.

## Commencement of the Action

Lawsuits must be brought within a certain time limit that has been prescribed by law in a statute of limitations. For example, in many states, a suit to recover damages for personal injury caused by negligence must be brought within two years of the occurrence of the injury. If a case is not brought within the prescribed time, the action will be forever barred.

The first step in the trial process is to determine what kind of legal action must be instituted. If the controversy has to do with the performance of a contract, the proper action is for breach of contract, whereas if one person alleges to have been injured by the negligent actions of another, the correct action would be in negligence.

The choice of a trial court where the case will be presented depends upon two things: which court has jurisdiction over the subject of controversy, and which geographic district includes the area where one of the parties resides or where the action causing the complaint occurred. For example, a person claiming damages for negligent injury could not file suit in a court which is authorized to hear only divorce matters.

The parties to the controversy are the plaintiff and the defendant. The plaintiff is the person who brings the action and makes the complaint; the defendant is the person against whom the suit is brought. Many cases have multiple plaintiffs and defendants. For example, a husband and wife may sue a hospital and several employees, charging that the employees were negligent in doing their jobs. Or the plaintiff may sue a hospital and a person who is not an employee (a physician, for example, or perhaps the manufacturer of an elevator). These nonemployees are called independent contractors. They may be joined in the suit as parties defendant because the plaintiff alleges that they all contributed to the injury suffered.

When the preliminary items have been taken care of by the attorney, in consultation with the client, the suit will begin. There are two major methods by which a lawsuit may be formally initiated. First, in some courts an action is commenced by filing an order with the court clerk to issue a paper, called a writ or summons, to the sheriff. This summons orders the sheriff to inform the defendants that they must appear before the court on a particular date. Many states and the federal courts use a second method in which suits are commenced by filing and serving the complaint itself.

Upon delivery of the summons or complaint, prompt notice to the defendant's attorney or insurance company is necessary. The defendant's attorney will need to investigate the matter, decide on strategy, identify and talk to witnesses, and prepare a defense. Notice by the defendant to the appropriate insurance company is also important because a malpractice insurance policy generally requires prompt notice of a suit so that the company can make an early investigation of the facts. When notice to the insurer is required, failure to provide it promptly generally bars any right of the insured person under the policy.

## Pleading

Once the action is commenced, each party must present a statement of facts, or pleadings, to the court. The modern system of pleading requires a setting forth of the facts, which serves to notify the other party of the basis for the legal claim. The first pleading filed in an action is the complaint. In some states the complaint may have been filed as a means of commencing the action. However, if the action did not begin in this way, the plaintiff must file a complaint.

After the complaint is filed, a copy is served on the defendant, who must ordinarily make some reply within 15 or 20 days. If the defendant fails to answer the complaint within the prescribed time, the plaintiff will win the case by default and judgment will be entered against the defendant. However, in certain instances a default judgment will be lifted if the defendant can demonstrate valid reasons for failure to comply.

Upon receiving a copy of the plaintiff's complaint, the defendant also has the right to file preliminary objections before answering the complaint. In the preliminary objections, the defendant cites possible errors that would defeat the plaintiff's case. For example, the defendant may object that the summons or complaint was improperly served, that the action was brought in the wrong county, or that there was something technically incorrect about the complaint. The court may permit the plaintiff to correct the mistakes by filing a new or amended complaint. However, in some instances the defects in the plaintiff's case may be so significant that the case is dismissed.

At this time the defendant may also present a motion to dismiss, alleging that the plaintiff's complaint, even if believed, does not set forth a claim or cause of action recognized by law. If the objection is sustained, the plaintiff's case will be dismissed. The plaintiff does have the right to amend the complaint or appeal the lower court's action to an appellate court. If the court rules against the defendant's preliminary objections and motions, the defendant is then required to file an answer to the plaintiff's complaint.

In some cases, the defendant also has a claim against the plaintiff and would now file a counterclaim. For example, the plaintiff may have sued a hospital for personal injuries and property damage caused by the negligent operation of the hospital's ambulance. The hospital may file a counterclaim on the ground that its driver was careful and that it was the plaintiff who was negligent and is liable to the hospital for damage to the ambulance.

When the defendant has filed an answer, the plaintiff can generally file preliminary objections to that answer. The plaintiff may urge that a counterclaim cannot be asserted in the court in which the case is pending, that the answer is defective in form, that the counterclaim is not legally sufficient, or that the new matter is not legally sufficient. The objections are disposed of by the court and the case moves on.

The pleading may raise questions both of law and of fact. If only questions of law are involved, the judge will decide the case on the pleadings alone. If questions of fact are involved, there must be a trial to determine the facts. When questions of both law and fact are involved and the trial is before a jury, the determination of facts will be made by the jury. The judge decides questions of law and instructs the jury as to the law it is to apply. Parties have a right to waive a jury trial. When the trial is before a judge only, questions of fact and law will be determined by the judge.

## Pretrial Procedures

A number of procedural steps that occur before the trial are specifically classified as pretrial proceedings. After the pleadings are completed, many states permit either party to move for a judgment on the pleadings. When this motion is made, the court will examine the entire case and decide whether to enter judgment according to the merits of the case as indicated in the pleadings. In some states the moving party is permitted to introduce sworn statements showing that a claim or defense is false or a sham. This procedure cannot be used when there is substantial dispute concerning the matters presented by the affidavits.

In many states a pretrial conference will be ordered at the judge's initiative or upon the request of one of the parties. The pretrial conference is an informal discussion in which the judge and the attorneys eliminate matters not in dispute, agree on the issues, and settle procedural matters relating to the trial. Although the purpose of the pretrial conference is not to compel the parties to settle the case, it often happens that cases are settled at this point.

In federal courts as well as most state courts, the parties have the right to discovery—the examination of witnesses before the trial. The usual manner of conducting the discovery is by presenting interrogatories or depositions to the opposing parties. Interrogatories are questionnaires that are answered under oath, usually in writing, concerning the facts in the case. When the interrogatories are presented orally by an examiner, the answers under oath are called depositions. Either party may obtain a court order permitting the examination and copying of books and records such as medical records, as well as the inspection of buildings and machines. A court order may also be obtained allowing the physical or mental examination of a party when that condition is important to the case.

In certain instances, it may be desirable to record a witness' testimony outside the court before the time of trial. In such a case one party, after giving proper notice to the opposing party and to the prospective missing witness, may require the witness to appear before someone authorized to administer oaths in order to answer questions and submit to cross-examination. The testimony is recorded stenographically and filed with the court, and it is entered in evidence as the testimony of the missing witness if, when the trial arrives, the witness is in fact unavailable. This procedure may be used when the witness is aged or infirm and may die or be too ill to testify by the time of the trial.

## The Trial

At the trial the facts of the case are determined, the principles of law relating to those facts are applied, and a conclusion as to liability is reached. If the case is argued before a judge and jury, it is the jury's function to determine the facts; however, if the case is presented to a judge sitting alone, the judge determines the facts and applies the law.

Evidence given at a trial consists of testimony or answers to questions put to witnesses on direct examination or cross-examination. Evidence may also include real evidence such as equipment, instruments, devices, and other tangible items which have a bearing on the issues or questions in the case. Generally, witnesses are persons who have a direct connection with some part of the case. They may have seen certain events take place or heard one of the parties say something. In highly technical cases, where the ordinary layman is not qualified to appreciate or properly evaluate the significance of the facts, witnesses who qualify as experts in their particular fields are called. The expert witnesses state opinions in answer to hypothetical or theoretical questions asked at the trial.

At the start of the trial, a jury is selected. A number of apparently qualified people will be selected as a panel, and from that panel the jury will be chosen. After the jury is selected and sworn, the attorneys make opening statements. This practice may vary slightly from state to state, but usually the statement indicates what each attorney intends to prove as the trial proceeds.

After the presentation, the attorney for the plaintiff calls the plaintiff's first witness, and direct examination begins. When the direct examination is completed, the opposing attorney may cross-examine the witness in an effort to challenge or disprove the testimony. After cross-examination the plaintiff's attorney may ask the same witness additional questions in an effort to overcome the effect of the cross-examination. When the examination of the plaintiff's first witness has been concluded, each of the plaintiff's other witnesses is questioned in the same manner. The plaintiff's attorney also introduces other evidence such as documents and real evidence.

After the plaintiff's entire case has been presented, the defendant may make a motion for a directed verdict on the grounds that the plaintiff has failed to present sufficient facts to prove a case or that the evidence is not a legal basis for a verdict in the plaintiff's favor. If the motion is overruled, the defendant's witnesses are then subjected to direct examination and cross-examination, and the defendant's documentary and real evidence is introduced.

After all the evidence has been presented, either party may ask the judge to rule that the claim has not been proved or that a defense has not been established and direct the jury to render a verdict to that effect. If these motions are overruled, the attorneys make oral arguments to the jury and then the judge instructs the jury on the appropriate law. This practice varies widely from state to state and even from judge to judge. Some judges marshal the facts, integrate them with the applicable legal principles, and comment on the evidence as well. Other judges merely state the controlling legal principles. Following the reading of instructions, the jury retires to a separate place to deliberate and reach a verdict. When they have done so, they report to the judge, who then renders a judgment based on the verdict.

At the time the judgment is rendered, the losing party has an opportunity to move for a new trial. If the new trial is granted, the entire process is repeated; if not, the judgment becomes final, subject to a review of the trial record by the appellate court.

## Appeals

An appellate court reviews a case on the basis of the trial record as well as written briefs and short oral arguments of the attorneys. After argument, the court takes the case under advisement until the judges consider it and agree upon a decision. An opinion is then prepared explaining the reasons for the decision. Appellate court decisions and opinions are a source of continuing legal information for lawyers, who can prepare themselves by referring to earlier cases that are similar to the case they are considering.

When a case is decided by the highest appellate court in the state, a final judgment results and the matter is ended. The instances when one may appeal from the ruling of a state court to the Supreme Court of the United States are rare indeed. A federal question must be involved, and even then the Supreme Court must decide whether it will hear a case. A federal question is one involving the Constitution of the United States or a statute enacted by Congress. Thus, it is unlikely that a negligence case arising in a state court would be reviewed and decided by the Supreme Court.

## Execution of Judgments

Generally, in lawsuits naming hospitals, physicians, and nurses as defendants, a party will seek to recover money damages. Other forms of relief are available, such as an order or injunction requiring the defendant to perform or refrain from performing an act. The jury decides the amount of damages, subject to review by the higher courts.

If, after the trial and the final appeal, the defendant does not comply with the judgment in the suit, the plaintiff may cause the judgment to be executed. If the judgment is an order that the defendant perform or refrain from performing an act, the failure to obey will be regarded as contempt of court and will result in a fine or imprisonment. If the judgment is for the payment of money, the plaintiff may cause the sheriff or other judicial officer to sell as much of the defendant's property as is necessary to pay the plaintiff's judgment and court costs.

## THE EXPERT WITNESS

In court, the general rule is that witnesses must testify as to facts. Their opinions and conclusions are inadmissible. It is the jury's function to receive testimony presented by the witnesses and to draw conclusions in the determination of facts. These functions are the exclusive province of the jury. But the law recognizes that the jury is composed of ordinary men and women and that some of the fact-finding they will be asked to perform will involve subjects beyond their knowledge. When the jury cannot otherwise obtain sufficient facts from which to draw conclusions, an expert witness who has special knowledge, skill, experience or training is called upon to submit an opinion.

Laymen are quite able to render an opinion about a great variety of nonscientific and general subjects, but for technical questions the opinion of an expert is preferable. For example, no jury of laymen could be expected to know whether an injury to the sciatic nerve would cause permanent or temporary damage. Therefore, a physician with training and experience in neurology would be asked to review the medical information relating to the patient and offer an opinion about the permanence of the damage.

The question of how much and what type of training or experience qualifies a person to be an expert is a difficult one. The American Law Institute, an organization of lawyers and judges, suggests the following definition:

> A witness is an expert witness and qualified to give expert testimony if the judge finds that to perceive, know or understand the matter concerning which the witness is to testify requires special knowledge, skill, experience or training, and that the witness has the requisite special knowledge, skill, experience or training.

In practice, when it becomes evident that expert testimony is required, the attorneys for both sides will secure the services of an expert. When testifying, the expert's training, experience, and special qualifications will be explained to the jury. Then the expert will be asked to give an opinion concerning hypothetical questions based on the facts of the case. It is then up to the jury to determine which expert opinion to accept.

Nurses, especially nurses with supervisory or teaching experience, may be asked to testify in court as an expert. Supervisory nurses may be called to describe the standard of nursing care in the community when another nurse is being sued for negligence. The jury will then have a standard against which to measure the defendant nurse's conduct. If a nurse is accused of injuring a patient by an improper injection, a nursing instructor might be called to testify about the usual way of giving injections. When a supervisory or teaching nurse is not available, an experienced registered nurse may be asked to testify as an expert.

After answering questions for the party that called in the expert witness, the witness may be questioned and challenged by the attorney for the opposing side. The attorney who requested the expert witness' services is expected to object to improper questions by the other attorney. In the event of an objection, the witness refrains from giving testimony until the judge decides to uphold or deny the objection and directs that the witness answer or the attorney withdraw the question. The witness may not be able to answer every question; an honest "I don't know" often helps convince the jury of the witness' competence.

Whether a witness who is not directly involved in a case is required to testify depends upon the rules of the particular state. A witness who fails to appear in court after being subpoenaed may be fined.

It is important to remember that expert witnesses perform a service for the court. They aid the judge and jury by providing information from which realistic conclusions can be drawn and upon which sensible and fair judgments can be made.

## WILLS

### Definition

A will is a legal declaration of a person's intentions upon death. It generally relates to the disposition of property, the guardianship of children, or the administration of an estate. A will enables a person to express a choice as to the direction which his property and interests will take after death. A will is called a testamentary document because it takes effect after the death of its maker.

Every state has certain specific requirements for the making of wills. If these requirements are not met, a will is considered invalid and is not probated—in other words, validated by a special court. Nurses need to be knowledgeable about wills because they are sometimes asked to act as witnesses.

## Written and Oral Wills

With one exception, all wills must be in writing. The person who makes a will, called the testator, must sign in front of witnesses who are not named as beneficiaries in the will. If the testator is unable to sign, a third person may sign at the direction and in the presence of the testator. Witnesses must be present and must sign the document. The number of witnesses required varies from state to state.

In some states a will that is entirely handwritten by the testator, known as a holographic will, may be valid. But the will must meet all the legal requirements: it must be in the testator's handwriting, it must be dated, and it must bear the testator's signature. Unless a specific law requires otherwise, a holographic will does not need to be witnessed.

The one exception to the requirement that all wills be in writing is the oral or nuncupative will. A nuncupative will is stated orally by the testator in contemplation of death and before a sufficient number of legally competent witnesses, and it must be reduced to writing as soon as possible. Since most states have either eliminated nuncupative wills or limited them to soldiers and sailors, it is advisable to check the law in each state to determine the applicability of this type of will.

Nurses attending a patient who has expressed the intention to make an oral will should write down their recollections as soon as the patient's statement is completed. They should then send the written memoranda, signed and dated, to the hospital administrator so that the patient's family and representatives may be notified. A patient may declare several wills during a last illness. On each occasion, a witnessing nurse and anyone else who attends the patient should complete the same procedures.

## Signatures of Witnesses

Most states require that a will be attested to and signed by witnesses in order to be valid. Attestation is the act of bearing witness or vouching that all the required formalities have been complied with. The witnesses must have personal knowledge that the will was signed by the testator and that, to the best of their knowledge, the testator was of sound mind and memory at the time of the signing. It is also the witnesses' duty to insure that the testator is acting freely and voluntarily.

Each state specifies the number of witnesses required to sign the will. Usually from one to three witnesses are required. When a state does not require that witnesses sign the will, it usually requires that they testify, at the time the will is probated, that the testator's signature is authentic.

A witness need not read or be familiar with the contents of a will, except in the case of a nuncupative will. But the witness is required to confirm that the testator declared the document to be a last will, that the testator signed the document in the witness' presence, and that all witnesses signed in the presence of each other.

A nurse who is requested to witness a will may refuse gracefully and suggest to the patient that it might be better to have a lawyer present and to ask friends and relatives who are not beneficiaries to be witnesses. However, when a dying patient tries to make an oral will, the nurse may need to participate because such circumstances require that the dying patient's words be recorded. Obviously, a nurse may then be asked to testify when the will is probated.

# Chapter 2

# Principles of Nursing Liability

Professional nurses, like everyone else, are liable for any harm that results from their personally negligent acts. They are held to a standard of care expected of reasonably competent nurses. The fact that they provide services to patients in a hospital as employees of the hospital does not relieve them of personal legal responsibility to the patients in their care.

## DEFINITION OF MALPRACTICE AND NEGLIGENCE

Malpractice is the term for negligence or carelessness of professional personnel. To determine what is and what is not careless, the law has developed a measuring scale called the standard of care. Usually, the standard of care is determined by deciding what a reasonably prudent person acting under similar circumstances would do. A judge or jury, the finder of facts, makes this determination. The parties have a right to a jury trial but may prefer a trial without a jury present. If a nurse or physician employed by the federal government is sued, the United States substitutes itself for the person sued (the defendant) and the trial is always before a judge under the provisions of the Federal Tort Claims Act.

This reasonably prudent person is a legal fiction— in other words, a hypothetical average person with average skills and training in the relevant field and with a hypothetically average amount of judgment and good sense. What this person would do is the yardstick for measuring what others should do in similar circumstances. Once the determination is made as to what the reasonably prudent person would have done, the actual performance of a person who is charged with negligence is measured

17

against that standard of care. Just as the nursing profession has Mrs. Chase, so the legal profession has the reasonably prudent person under the circumstances.

If the action of the defendant meets or surpasses the standard, there has been no negligence or carelessness, just an unavoidable occurrence. But if the defendant's actions fail to meet the standard, then there has been negligence, and the judge or the jury must make two determinations: First, was it foreseeable that harm would follow the failure to meet the standard of care? Second, was the carelessness or negligence the proximate or immediate cause of the harm or injury to the plaintiff (the person who is bringing suit)? A nurse who fails to meet the standard of care will be liable for negligence if that failure results in harm to another.

The four elements of negligence are: (1) a standard of due care under the circumstances; (2) a failure to meet the standard of due care; (3) the foreseeability of harm resulting from failure to meet the standard; and (4) the fact that the breach of this standard proximately causes the injury to the plaintiff.

Negligence may be an act of omission such as failure to give a medication that has been ordered. It may be an act of commission such as giving the wrong medication or an incorrect dosage.

One may not be negligent but liability may be imposed by statute. This is strict liability which is based on public policy. For example, there is a prohibition against serving adulterated foods. Regardless of the care exercised by the dietary department and the nursing staff, serving broiled fish with a worm inside may result in a judgment for the patient who sues.

A nurse may be negligent and still not incur liability if no injury to another person results. The term "injury" includes more than mere physical harm. In some states it may include mental anguish and other invasions of rights and privileges. For example, a wife whose husband has been hospitalized as a result of a third person's negligence may sue that third person for loss of marital services. Nominal and punitive damages are awarded in some states.

To establish what the reasonably prudent nurse would do, the courts utilize the services of an expert witness, a person trained in nursing or medicine who can testify to what the professional standard of care is in the same or similar communities. This testimony is necessary because the judge or jury is not trained or qualified to determine what the reasonably prudent nurse's standard of care would be under the circumstances. The testimony of the expert provides the standard by which the actual conduct of the nurse is measured. Procedure manuals and well-recognized textbooks may also be introduced as evidence to assist in establishing the standard of care. If the actual conduct falls below the standard established, the nurse will be found to have been negligent.

In the performance of professional duties, every nurse is required to exercise reasonable care so that no harm or injury comes to any patient. The law measures the reasonableness of the care by the performance of other nurses in the community. Thus, the standard of care for nurses is that degree of care ordinarily exercised by nurses of similar training and experience in the same or similar localities.

Some courts have moved away from the community standard of care and have applied what might be called a national standard. In this situation, the expert witness testifies as to what any reasonably prudent nurse anywhere would have done. The theory is that the standard of care should not vary according to the locale where the individual receives care.

The accompanying guidelines on negligence summarize the concepts of negligence and malpractice and the standard of care to be met in a particular situation. (See chart on page 20.)

## STANDARDS OF CARE

### Nurses

Professional nurses, in providing care to patients, are held to the prevailing standard of care. Thus, when injury has been suffered by a patient, in order to hold the nurse liable for negligence it must be shown that the nurse failed to meet the standard. The fact that injury is suffered, without proof that the nurse deviated from the practice of competent members of the nursing profession, is not sufficient for imposing liability upon the nurse.

Whether a nurse adhered to a standard of care generally practiced by the nursing profession in the community was a question raised in *Norton v. Argonaut Insurance Co.,* [144 So. 2d 249 (La. Ct. App. 1962)]. That case involved the entry of an erroneous or ambiguous order upon a patient's chart by the attending physician and focused on the responsibility of a nurse to obtain clarification of the medication order.

The nurse in the *Norton* case, familiar only with the injectable form of the medication and unaware of the elixir form which was far less potent, believed the order to be incorrect. The nurse asked two physicians present in the ward whether they recommended giving the medication as ordered by the attending physician. The physicians did not interpret the

## GUIDELINES ON NEGLIGENCE
### PROFESSIONAL NEGLIGENCE IS MALPRACTICE

| ELEMENTS OF LIABILITY | EXPLANATION | EXAMPLE GIVING MEDICATION |
|---|---|---|
| 1. Duty to use due care (defined by the standard of care) | The care which should be given under the circumstances (what the reasonably prudent nurse would have done) | A nurse should give medications:<br>• accurately and<br>• completely and<br>• on time |
| 2. Failure to meet standard of care (breach of duty) | Not giving the care which should be given under the circumstances | A nurse fails to give medications:<br>• accurately or<br>• completely or<br>• on time |
| 3. Foreseeability of harm | Knowledge that not meeting the standard of care will cause harm to the patient | Giving the wrong medication or the wrong dosage or not on schedule will probably cause harm to the patient |
| 4. Failure to meet standard of care (breach) *causes* injury | Patient is harmed because proper care is not given | Wrong medication causes patient to have a convulsion |
| 5. Strict Liability | Liability imposed by statute based on public policy although no one may be negligent | Some courts have upheld and others rejected a strict liability theory in administration of blood transfusions |
| 6. Injury | Actual harm results to patient | Convulsion or other serious complication |

order in the way that the nurse did and therefore did not share the nurse's concern. They told the nurse to follow the attending physician's instructions. The nurse did not contact the attending physician, and the medication was administered according to the nurse's understanding of the order. The patient died as a result of the administration of the medication in the injectable form rather than the elixir form.

The court found that the nurse had been negligent in failing to contact the attending physician before giving the medication. In its opinion the court specifically discussed the requisite standard of care applicable to the nurse. Given the facts of the case, this standard required that the nurse call the prescribing physician when in doubt about an order for medication—a standard that the court considered most reasonable and prudent. In its opinion the court stated that the same rules which govern the duties and liabilities of physicians in the performance of professional services to their patients applied to nurses as well.

This articulation of the standard of care applicable to nurses was followed by the same court in *Thompson v. Brent,* [245 So. 2d 751 (La. Ct. App. 1971)]. In this case the medical assistant of the defendant physician removed a cast from the plaintiff's arm with an electrically powered saw known as a Stryker saw. While sawing through the cast, the assistant cut the plaintiff's arm, thereby causing a residual scar almost the length of the cast and the width of the saw blade. Following the *Norton* case, the court held that, in determining whether the physician's assistant was negligent in the use of the saw, it was necessary to consider the degree of care which would have been demanded of the physician if he had removed the cast himself. Applying this standard, the court found the assistant's conduct negligent and the physician liable for the negligence under the doctrine of *respondeat superior.*

It may well be that the statement of the court in the *Norton* decision meant no more than that, as physicians are measured against the standard of competent medical performance, so nurses are measured against the standard of competent nursing performance. However, even with this latter interpretation, a basis for liability could be found in the *Thompson* case.

Underlying much of the litigation concerned with the liability of nurses for negligence is the determination of what constitutes the standard of good nursing practice. In *Mundt v. Alta Bates Hospital,* [35 Cal. Rptr. 848, 223 Cal. App. 2d 413 (1963)], a *California* court was faced with conflicting testimony concerning a nurse's responsibilities after observing increasing swelling and redness in the area of a "cut-down." The patient had been seriously injured as the result of excessive infiltration from an intravenous infusion over a long period of time. The attending physician testified that a nurse who observes swelling or redness at the site of a cut-down must either notify the attending physician or turn off the intravenous infusion. He further testified that if the nurse had stopped the flow of the intravenous solution when the swelling reached a critical point, serious injury would have been averted. There was other testimony from nurses to the effect that a nurse who observes swelling or other danger signs in the area of a cut-down should notify the attending physician, but without an order from the physician, the nurse could not cut off the flow of the intravenous solution. These standards differed on the issue of whether a nurse should stop the flow of the solution without an order, and the court did not decide which standard should be applied to determine whether the nurse was negligent. The case was sent back for a new trial, and the court recognized that selecting the standard to be applied would be left for the jury to decide. If the standard allowing a nurse to halt an intravenous infusion without an order were applied, it would be much more likely that the nurse who failed to take such action would be held negligent. Of course, if the other standard were accepted by the jury and applied, the nurse probably would not be held liable.

Although sometimes, as in the *Mundt* case, there may be inconsistent evidence of the standard of nursing practice by competent nurses, often there is little difficulty in determining the standard against which the allegedly negligent nurse is to be measured. Thus, in *Weinstein v. Prostkoff,* [23 Misc. 2d 376, 191 N.Y.S. 2d. 310 (1959)], the nurse was held liable for negligence in the administration of an anesthetic. Information had not been obtained as to whether the patient had partaken of food within an unsafe period of time before nitrous oxide was administered, and the nurse did not check the mask, as is customary, to watch for signs that gastric contents were coming up. The patient was found to have been asphyxiated because the breathing passages were blocked with vomitous material.

When a nurse failed to read all the entries in the patient's record pertaining to the administration of a particular medication, such failure was found to be negligence. The case of *Larrimore v. Homeopathic Hospital Association,* [54 Del. 449, 181 A.2d 573 (1962)], concerned a female patient who had been receiving a drug by injection over a period of time. The physician wrote an order on the patient's order sheet changing the mode of administration from injection to oral administration.

When the nurse on the unit, who had been off duty for several days, was preparing to give the medication to the patient by injection, the patient objected and referred the nurse to the physician's new order. The nurse, however, told the patient she was mistaken and gave the medication by injection. Perhaps the nurse had not reviewed the order sheet after being told by the patient that the medication was to be given orally, or perhaps the nurse did so in a negligent manner and did not notice the physician's entry. Either way, the nurse's conduct was held to be negligent. The court went on to say that the jury could find the nurse negligent by applying ordinary common sense to establish the applicable standard of care.

Two Canadian cases demonstrate how the standard of care is applied in similar situations. Both involve nurses who left their posts to take coffee breaks. In one case the nurse was not found negligent and in the other case the nurse was found negligent.

In *Child v. Vancouver General Hospital*, [71 W.W.R. 656(1969)], the nurse left for a coffee break after the physician in charge had seen the patient who, as the physician later testified, appeared "much improved." In deciding that the nurse was not negligent to leave such a patient unattended, the court emphasized that the question of liability should be determined in the light of the circumstances as they existed at the time. When the nurse left the patient, it was not foreseeable that an increased risk to the patient would be created.

However, in *Laidlaw v. Lions Gate Hospital*, [70 W.W.R. 727 (1969)], the court held that the nurse who left on a coffee break and the supervisor who allowed the nurse to leave might reasonably have anticipated needs for nursing care that could not be met during the nurse's absence. When the nurse left, there were two patients in the recovery room with only one nurse to attend to them. Within a very brief time three other patients arrived, including the plaintiff, Mrs. Laidlaw. This meant there were now five patients and only one nurse in the recovery room. Because the one nurse did not have sufficient time to minister properly to her, Mrs. Laidlaw suffered extensive, permanent brain damage as the result of insufficient oxygen while still under the anesthetic after surgery.

A nursing supervisor testified at the trial that there usually were two nurses present in the recovery room and that the nurses were expected to take their coffee breaks before any patients arrived. There was also testimony that the nurses on duty in the recovery room knew the operating schedule and, therefore, should have anticipated the need for both to be present to meet the needs of patients who would be arriving at the unit. The court found that the nurse who took the coffee break and the supervisor who authorized the nurse's absence were negligent in leaving the recovery room with only one nurse in attendance.

Evidence of the standard of care applicable to nursing activities may also be found in regulations of a state governmental agency or of the federal government, as well as in the standards of the Joint Commission on Accreditation of Hospitals. The personnel of a hospital subject to such regulations or standards are responsible for meeting that prescribed standard of care, and the failure of a nurse to do so provides a basis for finding the nurse liable for negligence.

Changes in the standard of care for nurses reflect new kinds of duties which are being imposed upon the practice of nursing by statutes, regulations, hospital rules, and court cases. These duties include not only those directly related to nursing techniques and procedures, but also duties affecting the way in which nurses work with others in the hospital. In the *Illinois* case, *Darling v. Charleston Community Memorial Hospital,* [33 Ill. 2d 326, 211 N.E. 2d 253 (1965)], a minor sued a hospital and a physician for allegedly negligent medical and hospital treatment which necessitated the amputation of his right leg below the knee. A judgment in favor of the plaintiff was affirmed by the Supreme Court of *Illinois*.

On November 5, 1960, the 18-year-old plaintiff in the *Darling* case broke his leg while playing in a college football game. He was taken to the hospital's emergency room and treated by the physician who was on emergency call that day. With the assistance of hospital personnel, the doctor applied traction and placed the leg in a plaster cast. A heat cradle was applied to dry the cast. Not long after the cast was applied the plaintiff complained of great pain in his toes, which protruded from the cast. The toes became swollen and dark, and eventually they became cold and insensitive. On the evening of November 6, the physician "notched" the cast around the toes, and on the afternoon of the following day, he cut the cast approximately three inches above the foot. On November 8, he split the sides of the cast with a Stryker saw. The plaintiff's leg was cut on both sides while the cast was being removed. Blood and other seepage were observed by the nurses and others, and a great stench filled the room.

The plaintiff remained in the hospital until November 19, when he was transferred to a hospital in St. Louis and placed under the care of an orthopedic specialist. The specialist found that the fractured leg contained a considerable amount of dead tissue. In his opinion, this resulted from interference with blood circulation when the leg swelled or hemorrhaged against the cast. The specialist performed several operations in a futile attempt to save the leg, but ultimately it had to be amputated eight inches below the knee.

The plaintiff contended that in this case, it was the duty of the nurses to watch the protruding toes constantly for color, temperature, and movement, as well as to check circulation every 10 to 20 minutes. According to the evidence in the case, these things were done only a few times a day. The plaintiff also argued that the hospital was negligent in failing to have, for bedside care of all patients at all times, a sufficient number of trained nurses capable of recognizing the progressive gangrenous condition of the plaintiff's right leg and of bringing it to the attention of the hospital administration and the medical staff.

The court held that on the basis of the evidence, it could reasonably conclude that the nurses did not test for circulation in the leg as frequently as necessary, whereas skilled nurses would have promptly recognized the conditions that signal a dangerous impairment of circulation and would have known that the condition would become irreversible in a matter of hours. It was the duty of the nurses to inform the attending physician of the prevailing conditions and, if the physician failed to act, to advise the hospital authorities so that appropriate action could have been taken.

The *Darling* case was not the first instance of a court's finding it a nurse's duty to bring appropriate matters to the attention of the physicians in charge of a case or to alert the hospital authorities. In *Goff v. Doctors General Hospital,* [166 Cal. App. 2d 314, 333 P.2d 29 (1958)], the court held that nurses who attended a mother, and who knew she was bleeding excessively, were negligent in failing to report the circumstances so that prompt and adequate measures could be taken to safeguard her life.

Nursing procedures have become more complicated; nurses work in closer connection with physicians in the performance of medical and surgical procedures; and it has recently been recognized as a duty of nurses to bring appropriate matters before the proper authorities. Failure to exercise that duty will lead to liability not only of the nurses, but also of the hospital under the doctrine of *respondeat superior.* However, court recognition of this duty has not gone so far as to provide guidance to nurses on the proper manner of fulfilling this duty. Thus, in order to live up to this duty, nurses will have to be aware of the many problems involved and will also have to make careful decisions about when to report and when not to report to their superiors. A safe rule to follow is: when in doubt, always report.

## Student Nurses

As part of their educational program, student nurses are entrusted with the responsibility of providing certain kinds of nursing care to patients. When liability is being assessed, a student nurse serving at the hospital in a patient care unit is considered an employee of the hospital. This is true even if the student is on affiliation and is not a student of the hospital's school of nursing. The nursing student will be personally liable for negligence if injury results, and under the doctrine of *respondeat superior,* the hospital will be personally liable for any harm suffered.

Although this may seem a harsh rule at first, student nurses are held to the standards of competent professional nurses when performing nursing duties. In several decisions, the courts have taken the position that anyone who performs duties customarily performed by professional nurses is held to the standards of professional nurses. Every patient has the right to expect competent nursing services, even if the care is provided by students as part of their clinical experience. It would be unfair to deprive patients of compensation for injury because the hospital has undertaken to utilize students to provide nursing care.

What if the student nurse's negligence occurs while performing a task the student was not yet capable of performing in a manner consistent with the standards of competent professional nurses? In this situation, the supervisor, whether a designated clinical instructor or the nurse in charge of the unit where the student is working, can be found to have deviated from the standard of competent nursing practice applicable to a supervisor and can be held liable.

Until it is clearly demonstrated that student nurses are competent to render nursing services without increasing the risk of injury to patients, there must be more supervision than is ordinarily provided for professional nurses.

## Nursing Supervisors

The legal issues arising from nurses' supervisory responsibilities affect both supervisory nurses and staff nurses who have no supervisory titles but who, nevertheless, direct personnel in the performance of their duties. A nurse with supervisory responsibility is not liable merely because one of the persons to whom duties have been assigned or delegated is negligent and thereby causes harm to a patient. The supervisor is liable only for negligence in carrying out supervisory duties. The supervisor's liability should be clearly distinguished from the liability of the employer—the hospital—for negligence under the doctrine of *respondeat superior.* The nurse with supervisory responsibilities is not the employer; the hospital is the employer and the supervising nurse is another hospital employee who has administrative responsibility for the performance of subordinate personnel.

Thus, if a nursing supervisor assigns a task to an individual who the supervisor knows or should have known is not competent to perform the particular task, and if a patient suffers injury because of incompetent performance of the task, the supervisor can be held personally liable for negligence as a supervisor. The hospital will be liable, under the doctrine of *respondeat superior,* as the employer of both the supervisor and the individual who performed the task in a negligent fashion. The supervisor is not relieved of personal liability even though the hospital is liable under *respondeat superior.*

In determining whether a nurse with supervisory responsibilities has been negligent, the nurse is measured against the standard of care of a competent and prudent nurse in the performance of supervisory duties. If charting a patient's fluid intake were assigned to a nurse's aide who had not been instructed in performing this task, and if such an assignment is not usually made until the supervisor personally ascertains that the aide knows how to chart fluids satisfactorily, this departure from the standard of care would constitute a basis for imposing liability for negligence if a patient were harmed as a result.

A supervisor may ordinarily rely upon the fact that a subordinate is licensed or certified as an indication of the subordinate's capabilities in performing tasks within the ambit of the license or certificate. But where the individual's past actions have led the supervisor to believe that the person is likely to perform a task in an unsatisfactory manner, assigning the task to the person can lead to liability for negligence because the risk of harm to the patient is increased.

### DEFENSES

### Contributory Negligence

Once the plaintiff has established that a defendant has been negligent, the defendant may raise defenses to the claim for damages. The most common defense in a negligence action is contributory negligence, that, when established, constitutes a complete barrier to the plaintiff's damage claim.

When contributory negligence is raised, the defendant claims the conduct of the injured person to be below the standard of care that a reasonably prudent person would exercise for his or her own safety. The two elements of contributory negligence are: (1) that the plaintiff's conduct is below the required standard of care; and (2) that there is a connection between the plaintiff's careless conduct and the injury. Thus, the defendant contends that the plaintiff contributed to the plaintiff's injury.

The rationale for contributory negligence is based on the principle that people must be both careful and responsible for their acts. Therefore, the plaintiff is required to conform to the same broad standard of conduct, that of the reasonable person of ordinary prudence under like circumstances, and the plaintiff's negligence will be determined and governed by the same tests and rules as the negligence of the defendant.

Contributory negligence is a defense to negligence *only*. It is not a defense if the defendant's conduct actually was intended to inflict harm upon the plaintiff, such as, an intentional wrong of battery or false imprisonment.

## Assumption of Risk

The second most commonly used defense is assumption of risk. This defense simply means that the plaintiff has expressly given consent in advance, thereby relieving the defendant of an obligation of conduct toward the plaintiff and taking the chances of injury from a known risk arising from the defendant's conduct. For example, a private duty nurse who agreed to care for a patient with a communicable disease, and who contracted the disease, would not be entitled to sue the former patient for loss of earnings. In taking the job, the nurse agreed to assume the risk of infection and thereby released the patient from all legal obligations.

In this case, if the nurse were to bring suit, the patient could invoke the doctrine of assumption of risk as a defense. This is because the nurse's conduct meets the two requirements necessary for the defense: first, that the plaintiff must know and understand the risk that is being incurred; and second, that the choice to incur the risk must be entirely free and voluntary.

## Unavoidable Accident

The defense of an unavoidable accident may be raised where an injury has occurred but the elements necessary to constitute negligence are not present. If a patient's ankle turns and *only* this causes the patient to fall in the hospital corridor, the hospital would not be liable where elements of negligence are absent.

## Comparative Negligence

Comparative negligence is recognized in only a few states. This doctrine relieves the plaintiff of the hardship of losing an entire claim when the defendant has entered a plea of contributory negligence. In many cases of negligence, there has been carelessness on the part of both parties. If the plaintiff is guilty of minor carelessness, whereas the defendant has been more grossly careless, forcing the plaintiff to lose the entire claim is considered too harsh a result in jurisdictions that recognize comparative negligence.

The doctrine provides that the degree of negligence or carelessness of each party be determined by the finder of fact, and that each party be responsible for the appropriate proportion of the injuries. For example, where the plaintiff suffers injuries of $10,000 from an accident, and the plaintiff is found 20 percent negligent and the defendant 80 percent negligent, the defendant would be required to pay $8,000 to the plaintiff. Thus, with comparative negligence, the plaintiff can collect for 80 percent of the injuries, whereas an application of contributory negligence would deprive the plaintiff of any money judgment.

## Statute of Limitations

The statute of limitations is "a statute prescribing limitations to the right of action on certain described causes of action." No suit can be maintained on such causes of action unless brought within a specified period after the incident occurred. The correct legal terminology is that "the statute of limitations has run."

Whether a suit for personal injury can be brought against a nurse often depends upon whether the suit has commenced within a time specified by the applicable statute of limitations. Generally, the statutory period begins when an injury occurs, although in some cases, usually involving foreign objects left in the body during surgery, the statutory period commences when the injured person discovers, or should have discovered, the injury.

There are many technical rules associated with statutes of limitations. Statutes in each state prescribe that malpractice suits and other personal injury suits must be brought within fixed periods of time, but court decisions and specific statutes in many states have extended the limitation periods substantially. For example, the fact that the injured person is a minor or is otherwise under a legal disability may, under the laws of many states, extend the period within which an action for injury may be brought.

Actions for malpractice may be brought in tort or in contract. A tort is a civil wrong which includes negligence. Most malpractice actions are in tort as the amount of damages is greater. The plaintiff would not be able to obtain a judgment awarding pain and suffering if the suit were in contract. However, since a contractual relationship does exist, a suit may be brought for breach of contract. If the statute of limitation has run for bringing an action in tort, but it has not run for a suit in contract, then the action can be brought in contract.

Some states have passed special statutes setting statutes of limitation or prescriptive periods for bringing malpractice suits. In 1975 Louisiana added a new statute, LA R.S. 9:5628, which provides that no action for damages arising out of patient care brought against any physician, dentist or hospital licensed under Louisiana laws shall be brought unless filed within one year from the date of the alleged act, omission or neglect, or within one year from the date of discovery of the alleged act, omission or neglect, provided, however, that as to claims filed within one year from date of discovery, such claims must be filed at the latest within a period of three years from the date of the alleged act, omission or neglect. In Louisiana, tort actions not based on malpractice must be brought within one year from discovery and actions in contract within ten years from the breach of the contract. This statute places a maximum of three years from the act that suit can be brought. Nurses are not included in this act. However, suits brought against parties named in the act are frequently based on alleged malpractice by nurses who are employees of these parties. Therefore, the act indirectly applies to nurses. Nurses may wish to bring before legislatures the necessity of including nurses in legislation involving medical malpractice.

# Chapter 3

# Consent to Medical and Surgical Procedures

Before any medical or surgical procedure can be performed on a patient, even a procedure involving the simple movement of a patient's limb, consent must be obtained from the patient or from someone authorized to consent on the patient's behalf. Consent is required because the intentional touching of another without authorization to do so is a legal wrong called a battery. In a case of emergency, the consent requirement may be said not to apply or consent may be held to be implied.

Not every touching results in liability. When a person voluntarily enters a situation in which a reasonable person would anticipate a touching, consent is implied. Thus, consent is not required for the normal, routine touchings and bumpings that occur in life. But the law does require consent for the intentional touchings which occur in health care situations.

The question of liability for performing a medical or surgical procedure without the patient's consent is separate and distinct from any question of negligence or malpractice in performing the procedure. Liability may be imposed for a nonconsensual touching of the patient even if the procedure improved the patient's health.

## NATURE OF CONSENT

Consent is an authorization, by the patient or a person authorized by law to consent on the patient's behalf, that changes a touching from nonconsensual to consensual. Although most consent cases involve physicians, the principles of law concerning the nature of consent are equally applicable to hospitals and to nurses. In many cases, it is the nurse who actually procures the consent.

A patient has a right to be secure in his person from any touching, and is free to reject treatment which medical advisers deem necessary. Therefore, before treatment is begun, the patient's consent to treatment and substantial proof of that consent are needed so as to guard against liability because of an allegedly unlawful touching of the patient.

An authorization from the patient without a full understanding of what is being consented to is not effective consent. The patient must be given sufficient information to exercise freedom of choice. In other words, each patient has the right to make an intelligent choice from among the various courses of treatment possible, as well as the right to refuse or reject a specific course of treatment. State courts are in wide disagreement as to the proper test for determining whether the information furnished to the patient was sufficient to provide a basis for effective consent.

Two basic tests to determine the adequacy of disclosure have emerged. The first, an objective test, requires the physician to provide as much information about a contemplated procedure as is ordinarily provided by other physicians in the community. This test was used in a *Wyoming* case, *Govin v. Hunter,* [374 P.2d 421 (Wyo. 1962)]. According to the patient, the surgeon should have advised her that multiple incisions would be necessary in a vein stripping procedure and that scars and disfigurement of her leg would result. The court recognized that in some circumstances a physician has a duty to reveal any serious risks involved in a contemplated procedure, and it stated that the manner in which a physician chooses to discharge this duty is primarily a matter of medical judgment. The court denied the patient's claim because no proof was presented that the patient's physician departed from the practice of other competent physicians in informing patients about this procedure. In saying that the proper standard was the practice of other competent physicians performing the same procedure, the court utilized an objective test. Thus, the patient had the burden of proving that the physician departed from the standard practice. Because the patient failed to do this, she lost her case.

The second test, a subjective test, relies upon the patient's understanding of the physician's explanation of risks and probable consequences of the procedure. Thus, a physician may be held liable if a jury finds that the information given the patient was not enough for informed consent. An example of this test is the *Florida* case, *Russell v. Harwick,* [166 So. 2d 904 (Fla. 1964)]. The patient had signed a consent form authorizing the physician to perform any operation he deemed advisable to repair her fractured hip. But the patient asserted that if she had been better informed about the procedure that was going to be used, she would not have authorized it and would instead have sought an orthopedic consultation. Expert testimony at the trial indicated that, in electing to remove the head of the femur and replace it with a metallic prosthesis, the physician had used the most satisfactory and most successful method of treating such a fracture. However, the patient had not been told that the leg would be shorter. The jury found the physician liable for malpractice, and the verdict was upheld by a higher court on the ground that the patient had a right to know the likely consequences of the contemplated treatment before deciding whether to give consent. It should be noted that the procedure itself was performed with care and was successful by medical standards.

Several recent cases indicate that the subjective test may evolve into a "reasonable person" standard to be applied by the judge or jury as the finder of facts. In *Canterbury v. Spence,* [464 F. 2d 772 (D.C. Cir. 1972)], the *District of Columbia* Circuit Court of Appeals said that whether the physician's disclosure was reasonable depends on what the physician knows, or should know, to be the patient's needs for information. Whether any danger in the proposed treatment must be disclosed depends upon whether it could be material to the patient's decision to accept or reject such treatment. The court explained that a risk is material when a reasonable person would be likely to attach significance to the risk in making the decision for or against treatment.

When a physician informs a competent adult patient that a procedure is necessary, and the patient assents, an express consent has been obtained. Consent can also be implied, even though there is no explicit oral or written expression of consent. There is implied consent where the intention to consent is not manifested by explicit or direct words, but is determined by implication or necessary deduction from the circumstances, the general language, the actions or conduct of the parties. A patient may voluntarily submit to a medical procedure by implied consent without any explicit spoken or written expression of consent.

In the *Massachusetts* case, *O'Brien v. Cunard S.S. Co.,* [154 Mass. 272, 28 N.E. 266 (1891)], a ship's passenger who joined a line of people receiving injections was held to have implied his consent to a vaccination. The rationale for this decision is that an individual who observes a line of people and notices that injections are being administered to those at the head of the line should expect that if he joins and remains in the line, he will receive an injection. Therefore, the voluntary act of entering the line, along with the opportunity to see what was taking place at the head of the line, was accepted by the jury as a manifestation of consent to the injection. The *O'Brien* case contains all the elements necessary to imply consent from a voluntary act: The procedure was a simple vaccination; the proceedings were at all times visible; and the plaintiff was free to withdraw up to the instant of the injection.

Voluntary submission itself does not always imply consent. In *Woods v. Brumlop,* [71 N.M. 221, 377 P. 2d 520 (1962)], a patient sustained injuries as the result of electroshock treatment. Although the patient had voluntarily submitted to the treatment, she contended that her physician's failure to provide her with sufficient facts about the procedure rendered ineffective any consent implied from the voluntary submission. The court found that the patient was in the right. Thus, voluntary submission constitutes implied consent only if the patient is fully informed and apparently understands the nature and seriousness of the procedure—in other words, if actions and words, taken together, would cause a reasonable person to believe the patient was consenting to the procedure.

Whether the patient's consent can be implied is a frequent question when the condition of the patient requires some deviation from the procedure which was selected by the surgeon and discussed with the patient. If a patient is apprised of the nature of the contemplated extension and its possible risks and results, the authorization of the extension is effective. However, if a patient expressly prohibits a specific medical or surgical procedure, consent to the procedure cannot be implied. The same consent rule applies if a patient expressly prohibits a particular extension of a procedure, even though the patient has voluntarily submitted to the original procedure.

## HOSPITAL LIABILITY FOR FAILURE TO OBTAIN CONSENT

Hospitals may be liable if medical or surgical procedures are performed without consent of their patients. This liability is based on either of two theories: (1) the duty of hospitals to protect patients against injuries inflicted by third persons; or (2) the doctrine of *respondeat superior.* It is a hospital's duty to protect its patient when it has or should have knowledge of the patient's objections to the medical or surgical procedure and when the patient is legally or physically incapable of consent.

In *Fiorentino v. Wenger,* [280 N.Y.S. 2d 373, 223 N.E. 2d 46 (1967)], the plaintiff claimed that the hospital was liable because it failed to ensure adequate disclosure of the facts before its operating facilities were used. The patient, a minor, died of a hemorrhage subsequent to a novel surgical procedure designed to support the spine in a straight position.

The surgical procedure was developed by the defendant surgeon who was the only surgeon in the United States to use it. The court held that the hospital was not liable and did not have to verify whether an informed consent had been obtained. The court stated that the hospital was not required to intervene between the physician and the patient unless it knew or should have known that there had not been an informed consent, or unless the performance of the procedure itself would constitute malpractice.

Under the doctrine of *respondeat superior,* hospitals are responsible for the legal consequences of the acts of their employees while acting within the scope of employment. Therefore, according to this doctrine, a hospital will be held legally responsible for any battery by its employees while they are performing their duties. Since rendering medical or surgical treatment to a patient without consent is clearly a battery, if the treatment were performed by hospital personnel, the institution would be liable. Thus, a nurse who performs an act upon a patient to which the patient has not consented may create liability for the hospital. In these circumstances, the nurse may also be liable for battery.

## PROOF OF CONSENT

A written consent has one purpose only: to provide visible proof of consent. An oral consent, if proved, is just as binding as a written one, for there is no legal requirement that the patient's consent be in writing. However, an oral consent may be difficult to prove in court. A valid written consent must include these elements: (1) it must be signed; (2) it must show that the procedure was the one consented to; and (3) it must show that the person consenting understood the nature of the procedure, the risks involved, and the probable consequences.

Many physicians and hospitals have relied on consent forms worded in such general terms that they permit the physician to perform any medical or surgical procedure believed to be in the patient's best interests. This kind of form is usually signed by the patient at the time of admission, but it does not constitute valid consent. Legally there is little difference between a surgical patient who signed no authorization and one who signed a form consenting to whatever surgery the physician deems advisable. In both situations, testimony would be necessary to establish the extent of the patient's actual knowledge and understanding. It is possible for the patient, after treatment, to claim a lack of advance knowledge about the nature of the physician's treatment. And, it is possible that a jury will believe the patient and impose liability upon the physician or the hospital or both.

The most satisfactory way to prove that the patient has consented to medical or surgical treatment is to use two integrated consent forms. An admission consent form should be signed when the patient is admitted to the hospital. This records the patient's consent to routine hospital services, diagnostic procedures, and medical treatment. [For an explanation of an admission consent form, see Appendix A.] A signed special consent form should be obtained before every medical or surgical treatment except the aforementioned routine activities. [For an explanation of a special consent form, see Appendix B.]

State statutes may set forth specifically what is required for a valid consent. For example, Louisiana provides in Louisiana Revised Statute 40:1299.40 that written consent to medical treatment means a consent in writing to any medical or surgical procedure or course of procedures which sets forth in general terms the nature and purpose of such procedure, and the known risk, if any, of death, brain damage, quadriplegia, paraplegia, loss or loss of function of any organ or limb, or disfiguring scar. There must be acknowledgment that such disclosure of information was made and that all questions asked about the procedure were answered in a satisfactory manner. The consent is signed by the patient, or if the patient is a minor or lacks capacity to sign, it is signed by the person with legal authority to consent for the patient. This consent is presumed valid unless there is proof that the consent was induced by misrepresentation of material facts. If consent is not obtained as set forth, proof may be introduced, according to ordinary rules of evidence, to show that the required information was given and all the patient's questions were answered.

In *People v. Privitera,* [141 Cal. Reptr. 764 (Ct. App. 1977)], a provision in the California Health and Safety Code which prohibited the sale, prescription and administering of medication or devices for diagnosis and treatment of cancer unless first approved by a federal agency with authority to make such a determination, was held unconstitutional. The court reasoned that the right of a patient to be free from any governmental impediment in his or her choice of cancer treatment is "of such fundamental nature that its free exercise may be impinged upon or forbidden only by such state interest as may be a 'compelling interest.' " This right derives from the right to be let alone. The court held that "where informed consent is adequately insured, there is no justification for infringing upon the patient's right to privacy in selecting and consenting to the treatment." Furthermore, a physician has a right, constitutional in nature, to treat and treat by unorthodox modalities, as yet unapproved by the state board, when the patient has given informed consent. To hold otherwise would deny the physician's privacy interest in dispensing alternative modes of treatment and would suppress innovation by the person best qualified to make medical progress.

## WHO MUST CONSENT

Generally, a patient's consent is required before treatment is administered. However, when a patient is either physically unable or legally incompetent to consent, and no emergency exists, consent must be obtained from a person who is legally authorized to consent on the patient's behalf. A person who gives consent for treatment of another must have sufficient information to make an intelligent judgment, and must be aware of the risks involved in the procedure.

A patient at a United States Public Health Service Hospital died and the physician wanted an autopsy. One of the patient's visitors had told the nurses she was the patient's common law wife. The couple resided in Mississippi, and it was not known when they lived together or whether common law marriages were recognized during that time. The physician decided not to perform the autopsy since the visitor's authority to consent was questionable and it would be difficult to determine with certainty who did have authority to consent.

A hydrocephalic child was abandoned at the hospital by its mother. Surgery for shunting cerebrospinal fluid was indicated. A court order from the juvenile court was obtained to authorize the procedure.

Persons who have authority to consent may be given in a state statute. Louisiana Revised Statute 40:1299.53 provides that consent may be given by any person temporarily standing *in loco parentis,* whether formally serving or not, for the minor under his care and by any guardian for his ward. Any female, regardless of age and marital status, may consent for herself when such consent is given in connection with pregnancy or child birth. Any parent may consent for his or her child. In the absence of a parent, consent for a minor may be given by the minor's adult brother, sister, or grandparent.

The Louisiana Revised Statute 40:1299.56 provides that a person 18 years of age or over has a right to refuse treatment of his or her own person. Any married person may consent for his or her own treatment and for treatment of the spouse.

In *re Osborn,* 294 A.2d 372 (D.C. App. 1972), the court stated the factors for consideration in determining whether to compel medical care rejected by a patient on religious grounds is whether that patient validly and knowingly rejected the medical care and whether there is a sufficient state interest to override the individual's desire based on religious beliefs. The degree of state interest is a compelling state interest.

## Consent of Minors

The question of whether a minor's consent alone is sufficient and, if not, from whom must consent be obtained must be considered when a medical or surgical procedure is to be performed upon a minor.

When faced with this issue the courts have used as a point of reference the requirement of an adult's assent in order to make a minor's obligation binding in commercial matters. That obligation is binding on the responsible parent, not on the minor. The courts have held that, as a general proposition, the consent of a minor to medical or surgical treatment is ineffective, and the physician must secure the consent of the minor's parent or someone standing *in loco parentis,* or must risk liability.

However, a number of courts have held the consent of a minor to be sufficient authorization for treatment in certain situations. In any specific case a court's determination that the consent of a minor is effective, and that, therefore, parental consent is unnecessary, will depend upon factors such as the minor's age, maturity, marital status, and emancipation as well as on certain public policy considerations. An example of this more liberal view is the *Michigan* case of *Bishop v. Shurly,* [237 Mich. 76, 211 N.W. 75 (1926)]. The patient's mother contracted with the defendant doctor for the removal of her 19-year-old son's tonsils with the condition that ether, not cocaine, be used as an anesthetic. Testimony showed that the minor requested a local anesthetic upon entering the operating room, and cocaine was used. The boy died as a result of the anesthetic. In finding for the defendant, the court emphasized the contractual, rather than consensual, nature of the surgery. The court reasoned that since the deceased could have entered into a binding contract for necessaries, he could also modify a contract made on his behalf, as he did by requesting a different anesthetic. Although it is not clear that consent to surgery is a contract, it is clear that the court, in upholding the judgment for the physician, placed considerable emphasis upon the maturity of the patient and his ability to understand what he was consenting to.

The *Massachusetts* Supreme Court took into consideration a somewhat unusual factor in determining whether a minor's consent is effective. In *Masden v. Harrison,* [No. 68651 Equity Mass. (1957)], the court decided that a healthy twin, age 19, could give an effective consent to an operation in which one of his kidneys would be removed and implanted in his sick twin. After hearing a psychiatrist's report, the court found that the operation was to the healthy twin's psychological benefit, even though it might not be to his physical benefit. The court ruled that the healthy twin had sufficient capacity to understand the planned procedure and to consent.

Parental consent is no longer required in certain cases where the minor is married or is otherwise emancipated. Approximately half the states have enacted statutes making it valid for married and emancipated minors to consent to medical and surgical procedures. For example, *New Mexico* and *Arizona* statutes specifically provide for this. A *California* statute provides for the effectiveness of a married minor's consent. Statutes making the consent of minors effective for blood donations and obstetrical care under specified circumstances have also been enacted by the *California* legislature.

Louisiana Revised Statute 40:1095 provides that consent by a minor to all medical or surgical care or services is valid and binding as if the minor had achieved majority and cannot be subject to a later disaffirmation by reason of the person's minority. Consent of a spouse, parent, guardian or any other person standing in a fiduciary capacity to the minor is not necessary. Furthermore, it is within the discretion of the physician whether to inform the spouse, parent or guardian of the minor's treatment.

The safest course to follow is to obtain consent from the minor, when competent, and also from the parent, guardian or spouse. If in doubt as to who has authority to give consent, a court order should be obtained. If a patient has reached the age of majority and is competent, and the health care provider informs the spouse, parent or guardian of the patient's condition, this may be held to be an invasion of the patient's right of privacy.

Some state statutes specifically provide for the effectiveness of a minor parent's consent to treatment for a child. Even in the absence of such a statute, a married minor's consent to treatment would appear to be effective where emancipation through marriage is recognized or where the maturity of the individual minor is considered. It should be noted that there are no reported cases holding a married minor's consent to treatment of a child ineffective.

Many states have recognized by legislation, that provides for the effectiveness of a minor's consent, that there are conditions—specifically pregnancy, venereal disease, and drug dependency—for which a minor is likely to seek medical assistance without the knowledge of a parent. To require parental consent for the treatment of these conditions is to increase the risk that the minor will delay or do without treatment in order to avoid explanation to the parents.

The parents of a minor may refuse, for religious or other reasons, to consent to a medical or surgical procedure recommended for a child. Proceeding with treatment despite parental objections, in the absence of an emergency or specific statute exemptions, would almost certainly provide a basis for imposing liability. The physician could be liable for nonconsensual touching, and the hospital would be liable to the same extent as for any other battery.

The ultimate decision to treat children whose parents refuse consent is for the courts to make. There is no legal justification for the hospital to proceed with treatment unless a court orders it to do so. Procedural mechanisms exist in legislation for resolving the hospital's potential conflicting role in these situations, and the hospital must take the action as provided by legislation.

## Consent of the Mentally Ill

Persons found to be mentally incompetent have been considered unable legally to consent to medical or surgical treatment. For a person who has been declared legally incompetent by a judicial proceeding, the consent of the patient's legal guardian must be obtained. Where no legal guardian is available, a court that handles such matters must be asked to allow the procedure.

To comply with equal protection of rights, a person who is mentally ill should have the same right to choose treatment for his illness as does the person who is physically ill if the mentally ill person has the competency to so choose. A person may prefer not to undergo treatment because of stigmas placed on those who have been incarcerated in a mental institution and have lost their civil rights as a result.

In *Bell v. Wayne County General Hospital at Eloise*, 384 F. Supp. 1085 (E.D. Mich., 1974), the court held that chemotherapy may not be administered to an individual alleged to be mentally ill until after final adjudication that the individual is to be involuntarily committed because of mental illness, unless the individual consents to such therapy or unless the administration of such therapy is necessary to prevent physical injury to the individual or others, as when acts of the patient or other objective criteria clearly show to a physician that the patient is presently dangerous to himself or others.

Full-time, involuntary hospitalization should be ordered only as a last resort. Persons suffering from mental illness who are not alleged to have committed any crime are not to be totally deprived of their liberty if there are less drastic and less restrictive means for accomplishing the same basic treatment goals. To comply with constitutional guarantees of due process, equal protection of the law, and freedom from cruel and unusual punishment, legislative abridgement to fundamental personal liberties through involuntary civil commitment of the mentally ill must provide for use of the least restrictive alternatives to achieve the desired treatment.

In *Lessard v. Schmidt,* 349 F. Supp. 1078 (E.D. Wis., 1972), the court resolved that a person seeking to have someone committed to full-time, involuntary hospitalization should prove what other alternatives are available, what alternatives were investigated, and why the investigated alternatives were not deemed suitable. Such alternatives would be out-patient treatment, day treatment in a hospital, night treatment in a hospital, placement in custody of a friend or relative, placement in a nursing home, or referral to a community mental health clinic and home health aid services.

When a physician doubts a patient's capacity to consent, even though the patient has not been adjudged legally incompetent, the consent of the nearest relative should be obtained. In the *New York* case of *Collins v. Davis,* [44 Misc. 2d 622, 254 N.Y.S. 2d 666 (1964)], a hospital administrator sought a court order to permit a surgical operation upon an irrational adult patient whose life was in jeopardy. The consent of the patient's wife had been sought, but she refused to grant authorization for the procedure for reasons that she thought justifiable, although they were medically unsound. After the court had considered the entire situation, it pointed out that the physician and the hospital were faced with a choice: to perform the operation, contrary to the wishes of the spouse, or permit the patient to die. The court distinguished this situation from those where persons had refused medical attention or had forbidden a specific procedure for religious or other reasons. The court authorized the surgery for the reason that the patient had himself sought medical attention. The court ruled that the hospital was trying to provide the necessary medical treatment in conformity with sound medical judgment and that the spouse was interfering.

Where the patient is unable to consent, the spouse is the logical person from whom to seek consent first. But, if the patient is conscious and mentally capable of giving consent for treatment, the consent of the spouse without the consent of the competent patient would not protect the physician from liability in the event that the suit was instituted by the patient for nonconsensual touching.

## Emergency Situations

An emergency exists when immediate action is required to save a patient's life or to prevent permanent impairment of the patient's health. If it is impossible in an emergency to obtain the consent of the patient or someone legally authorized to give consent, the required procedure may be undertaken without any liability for failure to procure consent. This rule also applies when conditions discovered during an operation must be corrected immediately and the consent of the patient or someone authorized to give consent is not obtainable. This privilege to proceed in emergencies without consent is accorded physicians because inaction at such a time may cause greater injury to the patient and would be contrary to good medical practice.

In *Zoski v. Gaines,* [271 Mich. 1, 260 N.W. 99 (1935)], a case involving the removal of a minor child's infected tonsils without parental consent, the court stated that only in very extreme cases does a surgeon have the right to operate without consent. In this case there was no need to remove the tonsils before the parents could be consulted, although their removal at some later time would have been necessary.

Proof that a procedure will protect life or health of the patient in the face of an immediate threat can be provided by a notation on the patient's hospital record that a consultation occurred. In *Luka v. Lowrie,* [271 Mich. 122, 136 N.W.1166 (1912)], a case involving a 15-year-old boy whose left foot had been run over and crushed by a train, consultation was an important factor in determining the outcome of the case. When the boy arrived at the hospital, the defending physician and four house surgeons decided it was necessary to amputate the foot. The court said it was inconceivable that, if the parents had been present, they would have refused consent in the face of a determination by five physicians that amputation would save the boy's life. Thus, in spite of testimony at the trial that the amputation may not have been necessary, professional consultation prior to operation supported the assertion that a genuine emergency had existed and no consent was needed.

The hospital or physician should be able to establish that under the circumstances, obtaining the consent of the patient or someone legally authorized to give consent would mean a delay which would be likely to increase the hazards. If no consent is obtained after a reasonable attempt is made, the procedure may be undertaken.

## Refusal of a Patient to Consent

Adult patients who are conscious and mentally competent have the right to refuse to permit any medical or surgical procedure. This refusal must be honored whether it is grounded in doubt that the contemplated procedure will be successful, concern about the probable or possible results, lack of confidence in the surgeon or physician, religious belief, or mere whim. Every person has the legal right to refuse to permit a touching of his body; failure to respect this right will result in liability for assault and battery.

In *Erickson v. Dilgard,* [44 Misc. 2d 27, 252 N.Y.S. 2d 705 (1962)], the court held that a competent adult patient's wishes concerning his or her person may not be disregarded. The court was confronted with a request by the hospital to authorize a blood transfusion over the patient's objection. The court recognized that the patient's refusal might cause his death, but would not authorize the blood transfusion, holding that a competent individual has the right to make this decision even though it may seem unreasonable to medical experts.

Failure to consent to any treatment has the same legal effect as an express prohibition of a treatment or procedure, or an express prohibition of its extension. The physician would be liable for proceeding without the patient's consent. What is more, the responsibility of the hospital and its employees is clear when that hospital permits treatment of a patient despite the express refusal of consent. The hospital has a responsibility to use reasonable care to protect the patient from touching for which consent has been expressly refused.

If the patient refuses to sign a consent form for the contemplated procedures or orally communicates a refusal of consent to the hospital's nurses, the hospital will probably be held by the courts to have received notice of the patient's refusal to consent. The hospital then must prevent the procedure from taking place. Therefore, nurses who learn that a patient has refused contemplated treatment must communicate this knowledge to their supervisor so that the hospital can act to fulfill this duty.

## Release Form

When a patient refuses to consent to a procedure for any reason, religious or otherwise, a release form should be filled out to protect the hospital and its personnel from liability for failure to perform the procedure. The patient's medical record should note when treatment was refused. The completed release form provides proof of the patient's refusal to consent, and if the patient should refuse to sign the release form, this, too, should be noted.

When the patient is incompetent or unable to consent and the spouse or nearest relative refuses consent, it is essential that the person responsible for consent sign a release form. The release form, when properly signed by the patient's spouse or nearest relative, is evidence that the medical care furnished was in accordance with the patient's wishes. However, where the patient is conscious and mentally competent, a release form signed by the spouse or relative is not a substitute for the patient's own release form.

A conscious, mentally competent adult patient has the right to refuse medical treatment, even when the best medical opinion deems it essential to save the patient's life. In the *Illinois* case *In re Brook's Estate*, [32 Ill. 2d 3:61, 205 N.E. 2d 435 (1965)], the court held that a competent adult patient without minor children cannot be compelled to accept a blood transfusion which she has steadfastly refused because of her religious beliefs. In this case, the patient had made known her beliefs to her physician and the hospital before consenting to any medical treatment. She was aware at all times of the meaning of her decision and had signed a statement, releasing the hospital and her attending physician from liability for any consequences of her refusal to accept a blood transfusion.

Only a compelling state interest will justify interference with an individual's free exercise of religious beliefs. The Court of Appeals of the *District of Columbia* noted in *In re Osborne*, [294 A. 2d 372 (D.C. Ct. App. 1972)], that the state's concern for the welfare of the children of patients who refuse, for religious reasons, to consent to treatment is a possible overriding interest. However, the court found that this particular patient had made sufficient financial provision for the future well-being of his two young children, so, that if he were to die, they would not become wards of the state. Under the circumstances, the court held that there was no compelling state interest to justify overriding the patient's intelligent and knowing refusal to consent to a transfusion because of his religious beliefs.

In some cases, the courts *have* ordered medical or surgical treatment for patients who have refused consent. *Application of the President and Directors of Georgetown College, Inc.,* [331 F.2d 1000 (D.C. Cir., 1964)], involved a pregnant patient at the Georgetown Hospital. The hospital sought a court order authorizing blood transfusions because the patient's physicians considered them necessary to save her life. The patient and her husband had refused authorization because of their religious beliefs.

To learn whether the woman was in a mental condition to make a decision, the judge asked her what the effect would be in terms of her religious beliefs, of the authorization of the blood transfusions. Her response was that the transfusions would no longer be her responsibility. In its decision, the court stressed that since the woman had come to the hospital seeking medical attention, it was conceived she wanted to live. Furthermore, according to the woman's statement, if the court undertook to authorize the transfusions without her consent, she would not be acting contrary to her religious beliefs.

The *New Jersey* Supreme Court took the position in *John F. Kennedy Memorial Hospital v. Heston,* [58 N.J. 576, 279 A. 2d 670 (1971)], that the state's power to authorize a blood transfusion does not rest upon the patient's condition or competence; it rests upon the state's compelling interest in protecting the life of its citizen, which is sufficient to justify overriding the patient's determination to refuse vital aid. The opinion also highlighted the very difficult position in which the hospital and its staff are placed when treatment is refused.

In light of these decisions, hospitals, physicians, and nurses should seek legal advice and a court ruling when refusal of treatment poses a serious threat to the patient's health. A release form signed by the patient or the spouse or nearest relative if the patient is unable to sign, should be obtained, or the medical record should show any refusals to sign release forms.

## THE NURSE'S CONSENT

Nurses have two main duties with respect to a patient's consent to treatment. First, nurses generally assume responsibility for completing the consent form, delivering it to the patient, explaining the medical procedures in language comprehensible to the patient, and obtaining the patient's consent. Second, after an initial consent has been procured, nurses must notify the hospital administration of any changes in a patient's consent.

It is sometimes difficult to simultaneously explain a procedure clearly, to satisfy the legal requirement that the patient understand, and to avoid frightening the patient. Much discretion and care are required to avoid overemphasis or underemphasis of the risks.

Thus, it is preferable that the patient's consent be procured by the operating physician since the physician, who knows best what the diagnosis is and what the treatment or operative procedure involves, is best equipped to impart the necessary information for obtaining a valid consent and is best able to answer the patient's questions. And, if the consent is invalid, the physician will be liable, not the nurse, even if the nurse obtained the signature on the consent form. Furthermore, the discussion of the patient's condition and the recommended treatment also provides an excellent opportunity for establishing a more desirable physician-patient relationship. If the patient feels that the physician cares, the patient may be less inclined to sue, even if an error is made.

Since some state statutes, such as the one in Louisiana, may stipulate what is to be included in the consent form, nurses who are required to obtain consents should be familiar with the law and practice in the area and be certain that the consent conforms thereto. In addition, two witnesses should usually be asked to sign. In selecting witnesses, nurses should always select persons who can be located if a suit is brought at a later time.

Patients may withdraw consent at any time, and the withdrawal may be oral, even though the original consent was written. Therefore, after the initial consents have been obtained, nurses must continue to be alert to the patients' conditions and must relay to the hospital administration any changes in patients' consents. However, nurses must be careful to distinguish between nervousness and an actual retraction of consent. In any event, nurses should be alert to the possibility that a nonconsenting patient might be touched and a procedure completed that would later result in an assertion of liability.

Emergency rooms provide nurses with additional problems of patient consent. Because most patients who are treated in hospital emergency rooms need immediate care, it is generally unwise for nurses on duty in emergency rooms to withhold or delay treatment while consent forms are procured, filled out, and signed. The emergency room illustrates a situation in which presence and voluntary submission to treatment constitute implied consent. Unless it is clear that no harm can result from delay, treatment should be rendered immediately without the usual paperwork, including patient information and consent forms.

## CONSENT IMPLIED BY STATUTE

A battery is committed if a sample of a person's blood, urine, other bodily substances, or breath is taken without consent, even when the person is brought to the hospital by the police on suspicion of drunken driving. Both the nurse who withdraws the sample and the hospital may be liable for an unauthorized touching.

In some states, the motor vehicle laws provide that the acceptance of the privilege of driving upon the highways implies a person's consent to furnish a sample of blood or urine for chemical analysis when charged with driving while intoxicated. Generally, where statutes imply authorization of a test for intoxication, an action of assault and battery will not be upheld. It is not clear, however, whether an action for battery would apply if the test were conducted after the motor vehicle operator voiced objections. The *Kansas* statute, for example, assumes consent if a person accepts the privilege of driving, but it specifically acknowledges that such consent may be withdrawn and that the person may refuse to submit to the test. Several other states acknowledge that a person may withdraw consent and some states have also dealt with the issue of implied consent when the person is unconscious at the time a sample of blood, urine, or breath is taken. One state has specifically provided that an unconscious person is considered not to have withdrawn consent to any such test. Another has provided that, at least for the purposes of a criminal or civil case, it would be conclusively presumed that the person has refused to consent to and has objected to such tests. In states that have not specifically dealt with the issue of the unconscious person, the situation is not clear.

There are no reported decisions regarding the extent of hospital or personnel liability for obtaining a testing sample from a person who did not give consent when the sample was requested by a law enforcement officer. Some states have enacted statutes that imply that court action may be brought against the individual who obtains such a sample as well as against the hospital as the employer. However, some statutes protect physicians, hospitals, and their employees from any liability for obtaining a blood sample from a nonconsenting individual when a police officer requests the sample. Such a statute has been enacted in Louisiana. It provides:

> C. No person who administers any such test upon the request of a law enforcement officer as herein defined, no hospital in or with which such person is employed or otherwise associated or in which such test is administered, and no other person, firm or corporation by whom or which such person is employed or is in any way associated, shall be in any wise criminally liable for the administration of such test, or civilly liable in damages to the person tested.
>
> Added by Acts 1968, No. 273, § 14. Amended by Acts 1972, No. 534, § 1.

Such statutory protection would probably he held to exempt physicians, hospitals, and their employees from liability for performing a test in accordance with proper medical standards, but would not protect them from liability for negligent performance of a test resulting in injury or damages. In the absence of statutory protection, a procedure performed despite an individual's refusal to consent would constitute a battery. However, recovery would probably be limited to nominal damages unless physical harm resulted from negligent performance.

In *Rochin v. California*, [342 U.S. 165 (1952)], the United States Supreme Court held that removal of stomach contents without consent, which resulted in finding the defendant had swallowed narcotics was so shocking to the conscience that the evidence was not admissible. The exclusionary rule, which was judicially created, is intended to deter police officers from violating the constitutional right to freedom from unreasonable searches and seizures and from violation of one's right of privacy, which are guaranteed by the Fourth Amendment. Removal of stomach contents without consent is an unreasonable search of the person and violation of one's right of privacy, although a person can be compelled to give handwriting examples.

Most cases concerning blood, alcohol, urine, or breath tests have dealt with the issue of whether the test results were admissible as evidence in a prosecution against a defendant from whom a specimen was taken. In these cases, several constitutional questions arose from the lack of the defendant's consent. In *Schmerber v. California*, [384 U.S. 757 (1966)], the defendant was placed under arrest at the hospital, and blood was withdrawn by a physician for the test. The defendant had not consented to the procedure and, in fact, had objected on the advice of a lawyer. In a close decision, the United States Supreme Court held that when blood is withdrawn by a physician in a medically acceptable manner, the procedure does not offend the court's "sense of justice," nor does it deny the defendant the legal rights guaranteed by the Fourteenth Amendment. The majority of judges agreed that evidence derived from a blood test, although incriminating and obtained under duress, did not constitute testimony or some communicative act or writing. Thus, the results of such a test were admissible, and admitting them did not violate the defendant's right against self-incrimination.

The Court also considered the results of a blood test in terms of the Fourth Amendment, which prohibits unreasonable search and seizure. The evidence of the defendant's condition prior to the blood-sampling procedure was viewed, by the Court, as sufficient to establish probable cause for the police officer to arrest the defendant on a charge of driving while intoxicated. Once a valid arrest has been made, a search of a suspect is permitted if the search is reasonable. The Court held that the procedure used to withdraw the blood was performed according to accepted medical standards by a competent person and therefore met the test of reasonableness.

It must be recognized that, even though the admission of test results as evidence against a defendant in a criminal proceeding may not violate constitutional rights, the hospital employee who withdraws the blood might still be liable for an unauthorized touching. Furthermore, if the purpose for the withdrawal of blood is misrepresented, consent for the procedure may not be effective, thereby making the results of the test inadmissible and establishing a basis for imposing tort liability.

# Chapter 4

# Medical Records

The proper recording of the facts of a patient's illness, symptoms, diagnosis, and treatment is instrumental to the efficient and effective delivery of modern medical and hospital care. Nurses and physicians are primarily responsible for keeping accurate and up-to-date medical records. All hospital personnel who have access to medical records have both a legal and an ethical obligation to protect the confidentiality of the information in the records. For these and other reasons, it is important that the nurses know what the medical records are and what significance they have in the law.

## IMPORTANCE

Medical records are maintained primarily to provide accurate and complete information about the care and treatment of patients. They are the principal means of communication between physicians and nurses in matters relating to patient care, and they also serve as a basis for planning the course of treatment. The records show the extent and quality of care, both for statistical purposes and for research and education, and they may be used for later review, study, and evaluation of the care rendered to the patient. In addition, the records provide information for billing and reports. Finally, the records are a valuable aid in court proceedings.

The nurses' handling of medical records is particularly important because patients see nurses more than any other medical professional. Consequently, nurses are in a position to keep constant watch over the patients' illnesses, responses to medications, displays of pain and discomfort, and general conditions. The care rendered to the patients, as well as the nurses' observations, should be recorded fully, factually, and promptly. No nurse should attempt to make a diagnosis, even if the conclusions seem obvious. Also, nurses should promptly and accurately comply with the orders that physicians write in the records and should check, in case of doubt, to make certain that the orders are correct and that they have not already been completed.

## CONTENTS

A medical record is a complete, accurate, up-to-date report of the medical history, condition, and treatment of a patient and the result of the hospitalization.

A medical record is composed of at least two distinct parts, each of which may be made up of several types of itemizations and forms. The first part is usually compiled upon admission; it details the pertinent data of the patient's history such as name, age, and reason for admission. The second part is the clinical record, which is a continuing history of the treatment given to the patient while hospitalized. The information included in this part is prescribed by state licensing rules and regulations. Usually, it must contain the patient's physical history, complaint, temperature chart, admitting diagnosis, later diagnoses, consultations, medical notes, laboratory reports of tests, X-ray readings, surgical or delivery records (including anesthesia reports, operative procedures, and findings), nurses' notes, summaries, condition of the patient at the time of discharge, autopsy findings, and so forth. This record is maintained continually by the doctors and nurses who attend the patient. In most states, both doctors and nurses must sign or initial the record.

Legislation and regulations concerning medical records vary from state to state. Some states detail the information to be recorded, other states specify the broad areas of information concerning the patient's treatment which must be included, and some states simply declare that the medical record shall be adequate, accurate, or complete. State hospital licensure rules and regulations may also provide requirements and standards for the maintenance, handling, signing, filing, and retention of medical records.

In addition to specific requirements, all licensing regulations stipulate that all records must be accurate and complete. Furthermore, the Joint Commission on Accreditation of Hospitals and several licensing regulations require the prompt completion of records after the discharge of patients. Persistent failure to conform to a medical staff rule requiring the physician to complete records promptly was held, in *Board of Trustees of Memorial Hospital v. Pratt,* [72 Wyo. 120, 262 P.2d 682 (1953)], to provide a basis for suspending a staff member. Almost all regulations require that the practitioners sign the records. Some require that all orders be signed; others merely refer to the signing of the completed records.

## MEDICAL RECORDS IN LEGAL PROCEEDINGS

The increasing incidence of personal injury suits and the expanding acceptance of life, accident, and health insurance have made medical records important evidence in legal proceedings. These records aid police investigations, provide information for determining the cause of death, indicate the extent of injury in workmen's compensation or personal injury proceedings, and aid in determining mental competency in civil and criminal cases.

When nurses or physicians are called as witnesses in a proceeding, they are permitted to refresh their recollections of the facts and circumstances of a particular case by referring to the record. Courts recognize that it is impossible for a medical witness to remember the details of every patient's treatment, and the record may therefore be used as an aid in relating the facts. In this situation, the record stimulates the recall of the witness who testifies under oath and is subject to cross-examination.

A medical record itself may be admitted into evidence in legal proceedings. In this situation, the record is not under oath and is not subject to cross-examination. In order for medical record information to be allowed in evidence, the court must be assured that the information is accurate, that it was recorded at the time the event occurred, and that it was not recorded in anticipation of the particular legal proceeding. Thus, while it is recognized that witnesses may use records to refresh their memories and that records may be admitted into evidence, there is nevertheless a need for assurance that the information is trustworthy.

When a medical record is introduced, its custodian, usually the medical record librarian, must testify concerning the manner in which the record was created and the way in which it is protected from unauthorized handling and change. Whether such records and other documents are admitted or excluded is governed by the rules of evidence. Thus, whether the records are admissible depends on the facts and circumstances of the particular case.

Whatever the situation, it is clear that the record must be complete, accurate, and timely. If it can be shown that the record is inaccurate or incomplete or that it was made long after the event it purports to record, it will not be accepted.

The procedure by which records are obtained before trial for discovery purposes and at the time of trial for introduction into evidence is provided by state and federal statutes. The patient may consent to the medical records being provided to the party seeking them. If the patient refuses, the records may be obtained with an order of the court by filing a subpoena *duces tecum*. If the party continues to refuse to provide the records, a motion or rule to show cause why they shouldn't be provided may be filed and a hearing before the judge may be held. The judge determines if the records should be provided and will issue an order accordingly. The parties may stipulate that the records may be introduced into evidence. If there is a stipulation, the records will be offered for introduction and filing into the record. The judge determines their admissibility according to the rules of evidence. Usually, at trial, the original record is introduced into evidence, and on motion of one of the parties to the suit, the original record is returned to the health care provider after a copy is substituted for filing in the court record.

A medical record is the property of the health care provider, such as a hospital. Although the hospital has a property right to the record, the patient has a property right to the information in the record, to which access cannot be denied the patient. The procedure by which access to the record is obtained is controlled by statute in each state. The judge may hold the health care provider in contempt of court for failure to honor a subpoena of the medical record and the penalty may be a fine and/or imprisonment.

## CONFIDENTIAL COMMUNICATIONS

Under certain circumstances, a medical record may not be admitted into evidence in a court proceeding because the court considers it a confidential communication between the patient and the physician that is, therefore, protected from disclosure.

One party to a relationship based on trust and confidence may give information to the other party in a situation and under circumstances which legally imply that the information should remain undisclosed. The information given is called a confidential communication. In our legal system, the relationship between physician and patient is accorded the protection of confidential communications. Sometimes the privilege of confidential communications also extends to the nurse-patient relationship.

Medical information may be gathered by examination, treatment, observation, or conversation. A nurse, as well as a physician, has a clear moral obligation to keep secret any information relating to a patient's illness or treatment which is learned during the course of professional duties, unless the nurse is authorized by the patient to disclose the information or is ordered by a court to do so.

The confidentiality of communications in medical situations is a principal tenet of the nursing code of professional ethics. There are also state statutes that forbid physicians, dentists, and other health practitioners from disclosing, without the patient's consent, any information acquired during the course of caring for a patient. Some of the statutes expressly include disclosures made to professional, registered, or trained nurses, which means that nurses cannot be forced to testify in legal proceedings about information obtained while caring for a patient. However, according to most state statutes, nurses are not subject to the restrictions concerning revelation of confidential communications. The courts of a few states have held that, by implication, these statutes include nurses who are assisting or acting under the direction of a physician who treats the patient.

In civil cases, the federal courts follow the law relative to the physician-patient privilege of the state in which the federal court is located. However, there is no physician-patient privilege in criminal cases in federal courts. Volume 42 of the Federal Regulations, Sections 2.1 through 2.67-1 set forth what information may be disclosed, to whom it may be disclosed, and the procedure for disclosing information relative to patients receiving treatment for drug abuse in federally funded programs. In this regard, the regulations provide a civil penalty of $500.00 for the first wrongful disclosure and $5,000.00 for the second.

Although the statutory protection of information obtained in physician-patient relationships applies only to courtroom testimony, there is a general belief that some protection should be afforded the personal and private revelations of patients to physicians to prevent their general dissemination. Physicians do have an ethical duty not to disclose information received from patients. In most states, protection is limited to information furnished the physician that is necessary to enable treatment of the patient, and legislation often limits the physician-patient privilege to certain kinds of legal actions. Protection may cover information in hospital records as well as communications to physicians. To a lesser extent, these principles also apply to nurses working directly under physicians.

In the operation of a hospital and the delivery of patient care, staff physicians and hospital personnel may require the use of information from the records. Moreover, physicians, residents, interns, nurses, and other personnel may consult records for the purposes of research, statistical evaluation, and education. However, if the information so obtained is not kept confidential, the hospital may be held liable.

If the information from medical records is disclosed, without a court order or statutory authority to do so and without the patient's consent, the hospital or its employees may be held liable for damages if the patient's interests are harmed. Patients have alleged injury in these situations on the grounds of defamation or invasion of their right to privacy.

The restriction on disclosing information obtained in a confidential relationship usually does not apply to criminal matters, such as attempted suicide or the unlawful dispensing or taking of narcotic drugs. Likewise, a patient may waive the privilege by actions or words. For example, a patient who testifies about an illness can no longer claim protection for the information.

In addition, some statutes provide that by bringing an action for damages in a personal injury or workmen's compensation claim, the patient waives the claim to a privileged communication.

## NEGLIGENCE

Medical records must be both accurate and complete. Failure to comply with the minimum record maintenance standards set out in state statutes may cause the revocation of medical personnel licenses or hospital accreditation.

In addition, hospitals may be held liable for the breach of a duty to maintain accurate records. In *Hansch v. Hackett,* 190 Wash. 97, 66 P. 2d 1129 (1937), the *Washington* Supreme Court imposed liability on a hospital for an attending nurse's failure to observe and record the symptoms of eclampsia. The court attributed the patient's subsequent death to this omission because the physician might have ordered the prompt and necessary treatment if the information had been available. In a *Louisiana* case, *Favalora v. Aetna Casualty & Surety Co.,* 144 So. 2d 544 (La. Ct. App. 1962), the hospital and radiologist were held liable for injuries sustained by an elderly patient who fainted and fell while being X-rayed. The hospital was liable under *respondeat superior* for the failure of a nurse to complete the medical history portion of the X-ray requisition. The basis of the radiologist's liability was his failure to acquaint himself with the patient's history before he commenced the examination.

A nurse is also responsible for making the proper inquiry if there is uncertainty about the accuracy of an order in the record. In the *Louisiana* case of *Norton v. Argonaut Insurance Co.,* 144 So. 2d 249 (La. Ct. App. 1962), the court focused attention upon the responsibility of a nurse to obtain clarification of an apparently erroneous order from the patient's physician. The medication order of the attending physician, as entered in the chart, was incomplete and subject to misinterpretation. Believing the order to be incorrect because of the dosage, the nurse asked two physicians present in the ward whether the medication should be given as ordered. The two physicians did not interpret the order as the nurse did and, therefore, did not share the same concern. They told the nurse that the attending physician's instructions did not appear out of line. The nurse did not contact the attending physician but instead administered the misinterpreted dosage of medication. As a result, the patient died from a fatal overdose of the medication. The court upheld the jury's finding that the nurse had been negligent in failing to consult the attending physician before giving the medication. The nurse was held liable, as was the physician who wrote the ambiguous order that led to the fatal dose.

In discussing the standard of care expected of a nurse who encounters an apparently erroneous order, the court stated:

> Not only was [the nurse] unfamiliar with the medicine in question, but she also violated what has been shown to be the rule generally practiced by the members of the nursing profession in the community and which rule, we might add, strikes us as being most reasonable and prudent, namely, the practice of calling the prescribing physician when in doubt about an order for medication. True, [she] attempted to verify the order by inquiring of [two physicians] but evidently there was a complete lack of communication with these individuals. The record leaves no doubt but that neither [physician] was made aware of just what [the nurse] intended to administer.

The court noted further:

> For obvious reasons we believe it the duty of a nurse when in doubt about an order for medication to make absolutely certain what the doctor intended both as to dosage and route. In the case at bar the evidence leaves not the slightest doubt that whereas nurses in the locality do at times consult any available physician, it appears equally certain that all of the nurses who testified herein agree that the better practice (and the one which they follow) is to consult the prescribing physician when in doubt about an order for medication.

Thus, clarification was not sought from the physician who wrote the order, and this departure from the standard of competent nursing practice provided the basis for holding the nurse liable for negligence.

Failure to maintain an adequate medical record may cause great difficulty for the health care provider called upon to present a defense to allegations of malpractice. A good medical record will show what was done to arrive at the diagnosis, what treatment was rendered and what results were obtained. If an error occurs, care must be taken to document what happened, who was called to investigate, and what, if any, damage or injury was present. Nurses may find it advisable to maintain more extensive personal records for use in the event a law suit may be filed.

This personal record should contain all matters of significance including the names and addresses of people the nurse may have reason to locate. How much is placed in the hospital record must be determined by the facts and circumstances of each case, keeping in mind that such records are subject to subpoena and disclosure. Medical records should never be tampered with. If an attorney finds an attempted erasure or discovers that pages have been removed or recopied at a critical time this information can be used to cast doubt on the credibility of the health care provider. If an attorney presents a blown-up photograph, the fact finder may wonder why such effort was made to alter the records if there were nothing to hide. Also, to lie under oath about the contents of a medical record or what actually occurred is perjury, which is a criminal offense.

# Chapter 5

# Drugs and Medications

Nurses are required to handle and administer many drugs that are dispensed by a hospital pharmacy or prescribed by a physician. The medications may range from simple aspirin to the latest experimental drugs. Every nurse has a legal duty to handle these drugs in the manner prescribed by statute.

## PHARMACY ACTS

All states have promulgated statutes specifying that pharmacy may be practiced only by persons who are legally licensed. The individual statutes also define those activities which constitute the practice of pharmacy. Although the definitions vary from state to state, certain activities are common to all of the definitions.

Essentially, the practice of pharmacy includes preparing, compounding, dispensing, and retailing drugs, medicines, prescriptions, chemicals, and poisons. These activities may be carried out only by a pharamacist with a state license or by a person exempted from the provisions of the state's pharmacy statute. A physician is such an exempted person when he compounds, dispenses, or administers medicines or drugs to patients during his practice. A nurse is also exempt from the prohibitions of the various pharmacy statutes when administering a medicine or a drug to a patient upon an oral or written order of a physician. Any nurse who administered a drug without an order from a physician would be in violation of the state's pharmacy statute.

To abide by the provisions of t 1e state pharmacy acts, nurses should understand what specific activities constitute the compounding, dispensing, and retailing of pharmaceutical items. *Compounding* is the combining and mixing of drugs, chemicals, or poisons. For example, a pharmacist compounds a drug by filling a physician's prescription since this entails preparing and mixing the prescribed articles.

*Dispensing* is defined as delivering, distributing, disposing, or giving away a drug, medicine, prescription, chemical, or poison. Although some state statutes authorize nurses to dispense drugs in certain instances, most states do not provide such specific statutory authorization. Theoretically, nurses may not dispense drugs in states that do not provide specific authorization. However, in many hospitals it is the general practice and custom to allow nurses to enter the hospital pharmacy and obtain or remove drugs from the hospital's floor stock cabinet in order to carry out a physician's orders. Despite this generally accepted practice, the restrictions in the state pharmacy acts have been modified very little.

*Retailing* is simply the act of selling or trading a drug, medicine, prescription, chemical, or poison.

The articles that are compounded and dispensed by a pharmacist are drugs, medicines, prescriptions, chemicals, and poisons. The definition of *drug* in most state statutes is similar to the one found in the Federal Food, Drug, and Cosmetic Act, which states that drugs are articles recognized in the official United States Pharmacopoeia, official Homeopathic Pharmacopoeia of the United States, or official National Formulary, or their supplements, and articles (other than food) intended to affect the structure or function of the body of man or other animals.

Applying this definition, courts have decided that aspirin, laxatives, vitamin and mineral capsules, honey, and whole human blood can be drugs under certain circumstances. Therefore, when handling these drugs, nurses should be aware that they cannot be dispensed, compounded, or retailed.

## CONTROLLED SUBSTANCES

### Federal Regulation

The Comprehensive Drug Abuse Prevention and Control Act of 1970, commonly known as the Controlled Substances Act, was signed into law on October 27, 1970. Virtually all earlier federal laws dealing with narcotics, depressants, stimulants, and hallucinogens were replaced by this law. The Act also deals with hospital distribution systems, rehabilitation projects under community mental health programs, research in and medical treatment of drug abuse and addiction, and importation and exportation of controlled substances.

A number of definitions and concepts affecting the operative provisions of the law are especially important to nurses. Only practitioners are permitted to dispense or conduct research with controlled substances. Practitioners are defined in these words:

§ 802

\* \* \* \*

(20) The term "practitioner" means a physician, dentist, veterinarian, scientific investigator, pharmacy, hospital, or other person licensed, registered, or otherwise permitted, by the United States or the jurisdiction in which he practices or does research, to distribute, dispense . . . administer . . . a controlled substance in the course of professional practice or research.

\* \* \* \*

Thus, once properly licensed or registered, practitioners are authorized to dispense controlled substances. The term "dispense" is defined as follows:

§ 802

\* \* \* \*

(10) The term "dispense" means to deliver a controlled substance to an ultimate user or research subject by, or pursuant to the lawful order of, a practitioner, including the prescribing and administering of a controlled substance . . .

\* \* \* \*

Therefore, one registered to dispense may prescribe, administer, or dispense (in the traditional sense) under the Controlled Substances Act, if permitted to do so under state law. The term "administer" is defined thus:

§ 802

\* \* \* \*

(2) The term "administer" refers to the direct application of a controlled substance to the body of a patient or research subject by—

(A) a practitioner (or in his presence, by his authorized agent), or

(B) the patient or research subject at the direction and in the presence of the practitioner, whether such application be by injection, inhalation, ingestion, or any other means.

\* \* \* \*

These sections of the Controlled Substances Act indicate that a nurse is prohibited from prescribing controlled substances. However, a nurse is authorized to administer a controlled substance at the direction of a practitioner. Thus, a nurse may follow a physician's oral and written orders to administer or dispense a prescribed quantity of a drug at a specified time to the proper patient. The physician need not be present at the time the controlled substance is dispensed or administered by the nurse in accordance with the physician's orders.

Practitioners must register with the government in accordance with the provisions of the Act. Each registrant must take a physical inventory every two years and maintain inventory records, although a perpetual inventory is not required. However, a separate inventory is compulsory for each registered location and for each registered independent activity. In addition to inventory records, each registrant must maintain complete and accurate records of all controlled substances received and disposed of.

All registrants must provide effective controls and procedures to guard against theft and diversion of controlled substances. For example, a hospital's central storage should be under the direct control and supervision of the pharmacist and only authorized personnel should have access to the area. When controlled substances are stored in nursing units, they too should be kept securely locked, and only authorized personnel should have access to these drugs.

The controlled substances listed in Schedules I through IV of the Act include narcotics, depressants, stimulants, and hallucinogens. Drugs are placed in the schedules according to their potential for abuse, and whether there is a medical use for them. The severity of the criminal penalties for violation of the Controlled Substances Act depends upon which schedule the drug involved is in. When the drug is in Schedule I the penalty is a maximum of 15 years imprisonment and/or a $30,000.00 fine for the first offense. Imprisonment is followed by a mandatory three-year special parole. Less severe penalties are provided for offenses involving drugs in other schedules. For a multiple offender, the penalty is doubled.

It is often difficult for the prosecutor to prove that the medication was not prescribed or dispensed in the legitimate practice of medicine. Drug enforcement agents work undercover to obtain prescriptions and drugs from physicians prescribing and dispensing drugs illegally. Numerous cases have been made against physicians for illegally prescribing and dispensing diet pills and sedatives.

A nurse employed by a physician who is prescribing and dispensing drugs in violation of the Controlled Substances Act may be charged criminally as an aider and abettor, and will be subject to the same penalties as the physician, who is the principal. The nurse may also be charged with conspiracy to violate the Act. The elements of conspiracy are proof, which may be circumstantial, of an agreement between two or more persons to violate the Act and an act in furtherance of the conspiracy. Violation of this Act is a federal offense.

Nurses should use caution in administering drugs of abuse so that patients do not become addicted as the result of medical use. This is particularly a hazard to patients with long term illnesses and patients with orthopedic problems. Nurses should be observant of patients who ask frequently for narcotic drugs and should remind physicians when a patient's condition no longer appears to warrant a continued order for narcotics and/or sedatives.

## State Regulation

Before the enactment of the Controlled Substances Act, most states had adopted some version of the Uniform Narcotic Drug Act. Since Congress amended the federal law, the states have been steadily replacing their narcotic and depressant-stimulant laws with "mini" controlled substances acts.

The new state laws are based upon the Uniform Controlled Substances Act, which in turn is based upon the federal Controlled Substances Act. However, a number of states have modified the uniform act in various ways, and the law of each state must be examined before legal conclusions can be reached. The variations include prescription requirements and penalties for violations.

## DRUGS

## Federal Regulation

Since almost all the drugs handled and administered by nurses are rigidly regulated, every nurse who is authorized to deal with these drugs must understand the manner in which they are regulated.

*Drugs, Devices, and Cosmetics.* The Food, Drug, and Cosmetic Act applies to the purity, labeling, potency, safety, and effectiveness of various products in varying degree depending on how they are classified. Therefore, it is important to distinguish between them and the Federal Food, Drug, and Cosmetic Act and federal regulations promulgated under the Act should be consulted. There has been considerable litigation in this area, and these decisions must also be taken into account.

A number of items used by medical personnel that have been held to be drugs, although they may not seem to be drugs, include antibiotic sensitivity discs used in laboratory procedures to determine the inhibiting ability of various antibiotics on sample micro-organisms, diagnostic preparations listed in official compendia, and certain sutures used for tying off blood vessels during surgical procedures. Whole human blood and the plastic bags used for the storage of blood and other intravenous substances have also been held to be a drug within the context of the Food, Drug, and Cosmetic Act.

The Food and Drug Administration now has a special office to deal specifically with devices on the market, and special attention is being given to products affecting life itself, such as pacemakers. The Medical Device Amendments of 1976 were passed to protect the public from products not proven to be safe and effective for their alleged uses and to safeguard public health by enforcement of certain standards of purity and effectiveness. This Act, together with the Comprehensive Drug Abuse Prevention and Control Act of 1970, was passed by Congress with the intention of creating two complementary checks on production and marketing of new drugs. During the production and premarketing stage, the Food and Drug Administration has primary responsibility. Once a drug is cleared for marketing by way of a new drug application approval, when the drug is a controlled substance, permissible distribution is within the jurisdiction of the Justice Department.

*New and Investigational Drugs.* The definition of a "new drug" is crucial to analyzing the effect of the operative provision of the Food, Drug, and Cosmetic Act. The law and regulations establish an elaborate procedure for determining whether a new drug is safe and effective. As part of this procedure, the Food and Drug Administration may condition its approval to market a new drug upon specified stipulations.

Some of the conditions that have caused concern are indications for use or dosage levels which may be listed in the official labeling. Specifically, a problem may arise if a physician prescribes a new drug for a condition or in a dosage other than those listed in the approved labeling, and asks a pharmacist to dispense the drug and a nurse to administer it. As a general rule, physicians may prescribe and pharmacists may dispense new drugs for uses, in dosages, or in regimens different from those set forth in a drug's approved labeling without violation of the law.

The general law of negligence governs in cases involving the use of new drugs in ways other than those provided for in the official labeling. For example, in applying these principles to hospital practice, it appears prudent for a pharmacist to question a physician who prescribes a drug in a manner that deviates substantially from the package insert. In really questionable cases, an acknowledgment and assumption of liability form could be obtained from the physician to protect the pharmacist and hospital in the event of any subsequent liability suit.

*Labeling and Manufacturing.* Labeling specifications are set forth in the Food, Drug, and Cosmetic Act and in regulations pursuant to the Act. These labeling and prescription requirements are of major importance to the practice of hospital pharmacy.

When prescription drugs are ordered in writing there is no particular problem. The physician either fills out a prescription or writes an order on the patient's chart, which serves as the written prescription. However, if an oral order for the drug is given, the Act states that such prescriptions must be "... reduced promptly to writing and filed by the pharmacist. ..." Refills for such drugs must be treated likewise. Thus, the validity of hospital practices concerning drug orders telephoned to personnel other than pharmacists is questionable under the Act.

Every person who owns or operates any establishment engaged in the interstate or intrastate manufacture, preparation, propagation, compounding, or processing of drugs must register his name, place of business, and all such establishments with the Secretary of Health, Education and Welfare. The words "manufacture, preparation, propagation, compounding, or processing" include repackaging or otherwise changing the container, wrapper, or labeling of drugs for distribution to others who will make final sale or distribution to the ultimate consumer.

In addition to these registration requirements there are other manufacturing obligations under the Act, such as maintaining certain records, filing specified reports, and tolerating periodic plant inspections.

In 1972, Congress amended the Food, Drug, and Cosmetic Act to require all manufacturers to file, with the government, a list of all drugs they manufacture. The issue of importance to the current practice of pharmacy which arises under this amendment is whether the compounding of drugs and pharmaceuticals in large quantities or the unit dose packaging and relabeling of drugs constitutes manufacturing under the Act. For example, a hospital pharmacy that prepares large quantities of drugs for use by the institution's patients would appear to be exempt. On the other hand, a hospital pharmacy which was supplying these compounded or repackaged drugs to other institutions or pharmacies under circumstances other than emergencies, would not be exempt.

## State Regulation

Although certain provisions of the Federal Food, Drug, and Cosmetic Act specifically apply to intrastate commerce insofar as drugs are concerned, Congress has at various times specifically provided for the applicability of state law. Accordingly, most states now have food, drug, and cosmetic laws based primarily upon the Uniform State Food, Drug, and Cosmetic Bill. State laws vary in specific details and must be consulted to determine whether a specific course of conduct is in compliance with all applicable laws.

### LIABILITY

Violation of the pharmacy acts may be evidence of negligence, but there has been no court decision holding a nurse negligent because the action which resulted in harm was also in violation of the state pharmacy act.

Although state pharmacy acts define the minimum qualifications for dispensing drugs, nurse licensing laws may also provide standards of practice relevant to drug dispensing. For example, in Louisiana licensed practical nurses are not permitted to give intravenous injections, because of the greater risk in giving such medications. Only graduate, professional nurses are permitted to give intravenous injections.

In *Barber v. Reinking,* 68 Wash. 2d 122, 411 P. 2d 861 (1966), the court found that a practical nurse's violation of the state Nurse Practice Act, which provided that only a licensed professional nurse could administer an inoculation, was relevant evidence of negligence. The nurse, who was concerned over the large number of patients waiting in the physician's office, administered a polio booster shot to a two-year-child. The needle broke in the child's buttock and was not removed until nine months later. The practical nurse was found negligent by the court.

Violation of a licensing statute can produce liability only when it can be proved that the violation was the cause of the harm. If it is foreseeable that harm may result if an unlicensed person performs acts that are restricted to licensed persons with professional training and experience, and if an unlicensed person performs such an act and in fact causes harm, liability will be imposed. However, when no harm results from the violation of a licensing statute, the appropriate state licensing board must decide whether to prosecute for violation of the statute.

# Chapter 6

# Intentional Wrongs

Although most incidents raising the issue of a nurse's liability concern harm which allegedly results from negligence, a nurse may also be liable for intentional wrongs. Intentional tortious conduct (that is, conduct implying a civil wrong) that may arise in the context of patient care includes assault, battery, false imprisonment, invasion of privacy, libel, and slander.

There are two major differences between intentional and negligent wrongs. One is the element of intent to wrong, which is present in intentional but not in negligent wrongs. The second difference is less obvious. An intentional wrong always involves a willful act which violates another's rights; a negligent wrong may not involve an act at all. In a situation involving negligence, a person may be held liable for not acting in the way that a reasonably prudent person would have acted. Thus, negligence can be a failure to act as well as a careless act.

## ASSAULT AND BATTERY

An assault is an intentional act designed to place another person in apprehension of a battery. A battery is an intentional, unconsented touching of another's person. Liability for these wrongs is based on an individual's right to be free from invasion of his person. When an assault and/or a battery occurs, a right has been invaded, and the law provides the injured person with a remedy for the interference. Thus, an injured person can sue a wrongdoer for the damages suffered. Even where benefits are incurred or no actual harm results, the law presumes a compensable injury to the person by virtue of the fact that the assault and/or battery occurred.

In the health context, the principles of law which relate to assault and/or battery and the requirement of consent to medical and surgical procedures are of critical importance. Liability of hospitals, physicians, and nurses for acts of assault and/or battery is most common in situations involving patient consent to medical and surgical procedures. It is inevitable that a patient in a hospital will be touched by many persons for many reasons. Procedures ranging from surgery to taking X-rays involve some touching of a patient. Even the administration of some medications may entail touching. Therefore, medical and surgical procedures must be authorized by the patient. If they are not authorized, the person performing the procedure will be subject to an action for battery.

It is of no legal significance that a procedure constituting a battery has improved the patient's health. If there was no patient consent to the touching, the patient may be entitled to damages. In *Mohr v. Williams,* 104 N.W. 12 (1905), the patient consented to surgery on her right ear. When the patient was anesthetized and the physician could examine her better he discovered that the left ear was in a more serious condition than the right ear. However, the patient had consented to surgery on the right ear but not on the left. The physician operated on the left ear, and a judgment of $39.00 was awarded after a second trial. There was no assault since the patient was asleep and could not have been placed in apprehension of an unwanted touching. There was a battery since surgery was performed on the left ear, an unwanted touching to which there had been no consent.

Nurses may be sued for battery as a result of restraining disoriented patients and children. A nurse who forces an uncooperative patient to take a bath or do some other activity under protest could be sued for assault and battery.

Defenses to these allegations may be consent, self-defense, defense of others, prevention of self-inflicted harm by the patient, defense of property, and discipline, as of a child or mentally deficient person to maintain necessary order and safety in the facility. The amount of force that can legally be used is that which is reasonably necessary under the circumstances.

## FALSE IMPRISONMENT

False imprisonment is the unlawful restraint of an individual's personal liberty or the unlawful detention of an individual. The actual use of physical force is not necessary to constitute a false imprisonment. A reasonable fear that force, which may be implied by words, threats, or gestures, will be used to detain the individual is sufficient.

Refusing to allow a patient to leave a hospital until all bills have been paid, may constitute false imprisonment. However, hospitals or nurses are not liable for false imprisonment if they compel a patient with a contagious disease to stay in the hospital. Mentally ill patients may also be kept in the hospital if there is a danger that they will take their own lives or jeopardize the lives and property of others. But mental illness alone is not sufficient reason to detain a patient. Those who are mentally ill or insane can be restrained only if they present a danger to themselves or to others.

How much force can be used to restrain a patient? Only as much as is reasonable under the circumstances. The use of excessive force may produce liability for a battery for the hospital and the nurse. If a mentally ill patient must remain in the hospital, procedures should begin immediately to provide commitment to a mental institution.

A patient of sound mind, who needs further medical attention but wants to go home, should not be detained merely because the medical staff believes the patient would benefit from further hospitalization. The nature of the patient's condition and the probable consequences of a premature departure should be explained. The patient's insistence on leaving should be noted on the medical record, and the patient should be asked to sign a form releasing the hospital from liability for harm resulting from premature departure. It is important to note that in this situation the patient does not actually have to be constrained to be falsely imprisoned. A threat of restraint which the patient may reasonably expect to be carried out might be enough to constitute false imprisonment.

## INVASION OF PRIVACY

The right of privacy, as recognized by the law, is the right to be left alone—the right to be free from unwarranted publicity and exposure to public view, as well as the right to live one's life without having one's name, photograph, or private affairs made public against one's will. Hospitals, physicians, and nurses may become liable for invasion of privacy if they divulge information from a patient's medical record to improper sources or if they commit unwarranted intrusions into the patient's personal affairs.

Hospitals could be held liable under this principle if they were responsible for the unwarranted intrusion into the private affairs of a patient. For example, a hospital was sued for allowing photographs to be taken of a malformed dead child. In another case, a doctor who photographed a patient's disfigured face while she was in extreme pain and semiconscious was legally restrained from developing or making prints of the negatives.

The information on a patient's chart is confidential and cannot be disclosed without the patient's permission. Nurses, who come into possession of the most intimate and personal information about patients, have both a legal and an ethical duty not to reveal confidential communications. The legal duty arises because the law recognizes a right to privacy, and to protect this right there is a corresponding duty to obey. The ethical duty is broader and applies at all times.

There *are* occasions when a nurse has a legal obligation or duty to disclose information. The reporting of communicable diseases, gunshot wounds, child abuse, and other matters is required by law.

There are also certain exceptions to the right of privacy. Virtually all the activities of a person who is a public figure are of legitimate interest to the public. Relatively obscure people may voluntarily take certain actions to bring themselves before the public or may be involved in newsworthy occurrences. A patient may also waive the right to privacy by actions or words.

The liberty extended to the publication of personal matters, names, or photographs varies. Public figures probably will not be heard to complain if their lives are given publicity and ordinary citizens who voluntarily adopt a course of conduct which is newsworthy have no grounds for complaint if the activity is reported along with their names and photographs. Generally, the subject of a newsworthy occurrence cannot complain if the occurrence is reported in a newspaper along with photographs, but the identity of the subject loses importance as time passes and cannot be exploited by unwarranted publication.

Nurses should not allow photographs to be taken without the patient's consent. Furthermore, every hospital should implement rules and policies outlining the freedom permitted visitors in the hospital. If any visitor tries to explore, peeking into rooms or reading charts, nurses should try to prevent these invasions lest the hospital be held liable.

## DEFAMATION

Defamation is defined as the written or oral communication, to someone other than the person defamed, of matters concerning a living person which tend to injure that person's reputation. By tradition, libel is the written form and slander the oral form of defamation. To be an actionable wrong, defamation must be communicated to a third person.

Defamatory statements communicated only to the injured party are not grounds for an action.

No proof of actual damage is needed in order for libel to be actionable. In the case of slander, on the other hand, actual damage must be proved by the person bringing suit. There are four generally recognized exceptions which require no proof of any actual harm to reputation in order to recover damages for slander: accusing someone of a crime; accusing someone of having a loathsome disease; using words which affect a person's profession or business; and calling a woman unchaste.

The *Georgia* case of *Barry v. Baugh,* [111 Ga. App. 813, 143 S.E. 2d 489 (1965)], considered the exception of slandering a person professionally. In this case a nurse brought a defamation action, charging that a physician had slandered her in the course of a consultation concerning the commitment of her husband to a mental institution. During a telephone conversation with a county official, the physician referred to the nurse as "crazy." As a result of this statement, the nurse requested damages for mental pain, shock, fright, humiliation, and embarrassment. The nurse alleged that, if the physician's statements were made known to the public, her job and reputation would be adversely affected. The court held that the physician's statement concerning the nurse did not constitute slander because the physician was not referring to the nurse in a professional capacity.

When any allegedly defamatory words are used to refer to a person in a professional capacity, the professional need not show that the words caused damage. It is presumed that any slanderous reference to someone's professional capacity is damaging, and the plaintiff, therefore, has no need to prove damage. In this case, however, since the court held that the physician's statement did not refer to the nurse in her professional capacity, the plaintiff was required to demonstrate damage in order to recover. The plaintiff was unable to show damage of this kind and therefore lost the case.

Nurses are legally protected against libel when complying with a law requiring a report of venereal or other diseases which might be considered "loathsome."

Essentially, there are two defenses to a defamation action: truth and privilege. When a person has said something that is damaging to another person's reputation, the person making the statement will not be liable for defamation if it can be shown that the statement was true. A privileged communication is a disclosure that might be defamatory under different circumstances, but is not because of a higher duty that the person making the communication must honor. The person making the communication must also do so in good faith, on the proper occasion, in the proper manner, and to a person who has a legitimate reason to receive the information.

The defense of privilege is illustrated in the case of *Judge v. Rockford Memorial Hospital,* 17 Ill. App. 2d 365, 150 N.E. 2d 202 (1958). A nurse brought an action for libel based on a letter written to a nurse's professional registry by the director of nurses at the hospital where the nurse had done private duty work. In the letter the director of nurses stated that the hospital did not wish to have the nurse's services available to them as a result of certain losses of narcotics during times when this particular nurse was on duty. The court refused the nurse recovery. Since the director of nurses had a legal duty to make the communication in the interests of society, the director's letter constituted a privileged communication. Therefore, the court held, because the letter was privileged it did not constitute libel.

The current trend is to hold the hospital liable for malpractice of attending, independent physicians where the hospital should know of the physician's incompetence. Examples are *Darling v. Charleston Community Memorial Hospital,* 33 Ill. 2d 326 (1965) and *Gonzales v. Nork,* 60 L.A. 3d 728, 131 Cal. Rpt. 717 (1976). Therefore, hospitals have a responsibility to screen the staff and deny or limit hospital privileges to those considered incompetent. The nursing staff must be selected with the same care and caution. Hospitals and persons involved in staff selection and disciplinary action may find themselves sued for defamation and, thus, there may be reluctance for members of the medical and nursing professions to police their members. To insure against a possible defamation action, any allegations made should be supported with evidence.

## MALICIOUS PROSECUTION AND ABUSE OF PROCESS

Protection from unjustifiable litigation is afforded by actions for malicious prosecution and abuse of process. The person alleging malicious prosecution by the defendant and suing for damages bears the burden of proving the perversion of legal process to improper ends. Such proof requires showing that (1) the defendant brought an action against the plaintiff; (2) the proceeding was terminated in favor of the party sued; (3) probable cause for the proceeding was absent; and (4) the defendant brought action because of malice.

Some physicians who were sued for malpractice and who have been successful in defending themselves have sued the patient who sued them and the patient's attorney for malicious prosecution. An attorney lost a malpractice case brought by him and his client against a physician and the physician then sued the attorney, alleging he had no medical expert evidence of malpractice. The attorney filed an exception of no cause of action as the physician did not allege malice. The attorney's exception was maintained and the physician was granted 15 days to amend her pleadings. The physician did not amend her pleadings, and her appeal on that judgment was dismissed, as the district court judgment was held *not* a final judgment by the appellate court in *Spencer v. Burglass,* 288 So. 2d 68 (La. App. 1974). Subsequently, the case was dismissed by the district court and Dr. Spencer appealed. In *Spencer v. Burglass,* 337 So. 2d 596 (La. App. 1976), the court found no malice. The court noted that generally, public policy requires that all persons shall fully resort to the courts for redress of wrongs and the law protects them when they act in good faith upon reasonable grounds in commencing either a civil or criminal proceeding. Consideration must be given to the "chilling effect" on the basic right of a citizen to redress in court that may result from a suit filed against a plaintiff's attorney by a defendant vindicated in a contested case. The appellate court affirmed the judgment dismissing her suit. The attorney then sued Dr. Spencer and her attorneys for malicious prosecution. The district court dismissed the case for failure to state a cause of action. An appeal was taken from that decision.

# Part II

# Nurses and Their Employers

# Chapter 7

# Licensing Laws and Scope of Practice

Nurses may discover that the procedures permitted by the licensing authority and those required by an employer are different. These potential conflicts arise from differing interpretations of a nurse's "scope of practice," the range of tasks which a nurse is permitted to perform.

For the nurse, the consequences of exceeding the scope of practice can be severe. The nurse may be accused of a violation of licensure provisions or of performing tasks that are statutorily reserved for a physician. However, because of the increasing complexity of medical procedures and hospital organization, and the advent of the new health professionals, nurse practitioners and physician assistants, it has become more difficult to distinguish the tasks that are clearly reserved for physicians from those that may be performed by professional nurses. These developments have been a stimulus to changes in legislation which defines the role of nurses.

## NURSE LICENSING LAWS

Licensure can be defined, in general terms, as the process by which a competent authority grants permission to a qualified individual or entity to perform certain specified activities which would be illegal without a license. In the context of health care delivery, licensure refers to the process by which licensing boards, agencies, or departments of the various states grant, to individuals who meet certain predetermined standards, the legal right to practice a health profession and/or to use a specified health practitioner's title.

The commonly stated objectives of licensing laws are to limit and control admission into the various health occupations and to protect the public from unqualified practitioners by promulgating and enforcing standards of practice within the professions.

The authority of states to license health care practitioners derives from the police or regulating power of the states which permits them to regulate occupations affecting the public health, morals, and welfare. However, this state regulating power does not extend to occupations which do not involve the public interest. The power to license implies the authority to collect license fees, establish standards of practice, require certain qualifications of applicants, and impose on applicants such other requirements as may be necessary to protect the general welfare. This authority, which is vested in the legislature, may be delegated to political subdivisions or state boards, agencies, and departments. In some instances the scope of the delegated power is made quite specific in the legislation, whereas, in other cases, the licensing authority may have wide discretion in performing its functions. In either situation, however, the authority granted by the legislature may not be exceeded.

## Licensing Boards

A separate board, organized and operated within the guidelines of specific legislation, is established in each state to license all professional and practical nurses. Each board is in turn responsible for the determination of eligibility for initial licensing and for relicensing; for the enforcement of licensing statutes, including suspension, revocation, and restoration of licenses; and for the approval and supervision of training institutions.

The state's governor generally appoints the members of the nurse licensing board. These selections are made from a list of names submitted by professional associations that represent nurses. Many licensing acts require this advisory input from the associations. But most governors solicit recommendations from the associations before making their selections, even when they are not statutorily required to do so.

The number of members on nurse licensing boards ranges from 3 to 20, although the great majority of boards have no more than 10 members. Usually the members have a direct interest in the areas of nursing which they regulate, and often the statutes stipulate that board members must have practiced in the state for a minimum number of years.

Recently there has been a trend toward placing members of the general public on licensing boards to give some representation to nonprofessional interests; however, this trend has been slight and is generally perceived to represent token gestures.

## Requirements for Licensure

Formal vocational training is necessary for nurse licensure in all states. The course requirements vary, but all courses must be completed at board-approved schools or institutions. Although many state nurse licensing boards still adhere to their own standards for accreditation, an increasing number of boards now accept standards established by professional nursing associations and national accrediting agencies. This trend toward the application of a national standard has tended to standardize the program of instruction at nursing schools.

Many nurse licensing acts permit the substitution of actual work experience for certain educational requirements. This provision manifests a recognition of the value of experience as an alternative to formal education and facilitates the licensing of greater numbers of qualified personnel.

Each state requires that the applicant pass an examination for nurse licensure. The examinations are usually written, although they may be oral, practical, or a combination, and are usually administered twice a year. The nurse licensing board may formulate the examination completely or they may use material prepared by professional examination services or national examining boards. For about 25 years, the national, standardized licensing examination has been used by state nursing licensing boards. Some states will waive their written examination for applicants who present a certificate from a national nursing examining board.

The nurse licensing statutes also specify certain personal qualifications: the applicant must have attained a minimum age, most often 21, must demonstrate good moral character, and must be a United States citizen or have filed a declaration of intent to become a citizen.

## Special Licensing Procedures

Because each state has its own nurse licensing statutes, boards have been confronted with the problem of licensing nurses who have qualified in other states. Generally, there are four methods by which boards license out-of-state licensees: reciprocity, endorsement, examination, and waiver.

*Reciprocity* is a formal or informal agreement between two states whereby a nurse licensing board in one state agrees to recognize licensees of the other state if the board of that state will extend reciprocal recognition to licensees from the first state. Reciprocity requires that the initial licensing requirements of the two states be essentially equivalent.

Although some nurse licensing boards use the term "endorsement" interchangeably with "reciprocity," the two words actually have different meanings. In licensing by *endorsement,* boards will license an out-of-state licensee if the out-of-state nurse's qualifications were equivalent to their own state requirements at the time of initial licensure. As a condition for endorsement many states require that the qualifying examination taken in the other state be comparable to their own. As with reciprocity, endorsement becomes much easier where uniform qualification standards are applied by the different states. The trend toward national nursing examinations and national standards for schools of nursing has simplified both endorsement and reciprocity licensure. As the trend continues, the mobility of nurses will increase.

Licensing out-of-state nurses by *waiver* and *examination* is much less common than licensing by reciprocity and endorsement. Where applicants do not meet all the requirements for licensure, but have equivalent qualifications, the specific educational, experience, or examination prerequisites may be waived. Some states will not recognize out-of-state licensees and require all applicants to pass the regular examination as well as fulfill the other requirements for initial licensure.

Most states grant temporary licenses for nurses. These licenses may be granted pending a decision by the board on permanent licensure or may be issued to out-of-state nurses who intend to be in a jurisdiction for only a limited time.

Generally, nurse licensing boards are quite cautious in licensing persons educated in foreign countries. Canadian-trained professionals are treated the same as graduates of U.S. schools, because the quality of education in Canada can be quickly ascertained. Graduates of schools in most other foreign countries are more carefully scrutinized and are required to meet the same qualifications as U.S. trained nurses. Many state boards have established special training, citizenship, and experience requirements for students educated abroad, and others insist upon additional training in the United States. A few states have reciprocity or endorsement agreements with some foreign countries.

## Suspension and Revocation

All nurse licensing boards have the authority to suspend or revoke the license of a nurse found in violation of specified norms of conduct. Such violations may include procurement of a license by fraud; unprofessional, dishonorable, immoral, or illegal conduct; performance of specific actions prohibited by the act; and malpractice.

Suspension and revocation procedures are usually provided in the licensing act; however, in some jurisdictions the procedure is left to the discretion of the board or is contained in general administrative procedure acts. Generally, suspension and revocation proceedings are administrative rather than judicial and do not carry criminal sanctions. However, minimum due process standards must be maintained. These include: (1) notifying the nurse of the charges, with enough certainty and definiteness so the nurse is able to prepare a defense, and (2) holding a hearing at which the nurse is permitted to present evidence. The hearing need not conform with full judicial hearings, but the final order must spell out the grounds for any action taken.

Several states have a great number and variety of grounds for revoking a nurse's license to practice. For example, revocation of license has been warranted when a nurse removed drugs from the employer's supply without authorization or for an unauthorized use and when a nurse interfered in matters concerning the treatment of patients which tended to promote friction between physicians and their patients.

Some licensing acts specifically authorize judicial review of board proceedings. This right may be limited to a review of the fairness and legality of the board action or it may permit a complete new trial, depending on the jurisdiction. Usually, the legislation designates which state court will hear the matter. The right to a judicial review of board proceedings is presumed in states in which nurse licensing acts do not provide specifically for it. The appropriate court is usually the lowest court of general jurisdiction. However, the general rule is that all administrative appeals must be exhausted before resorting to the courts.

## Liability for Practicing Without a License

Failure to obtain a license to practice nursing does not in itself imply a presumption or inference of negligence, nor does it constitute negligence per se. A plaintiff must allege and prove injury resulting from the unlicensed practitioner's negligence or lack of skill. The standard of care and skill against which the unlicensed nurse's actions are measured is the one prevailing among properly licensed nurses. However, a patient may delay proper treatment, and be harmed by the delay, because of reliance upon the diagnosis and treatment of an unlicensed nurse. To establish proximate cause for the injury, it may be sufficient to show that the delay of proper treatment resulted in the injury, even though the unlicensed nurse's treatment itself may not have caused the injury.

Insofar as a hospital's secondary liability is concerned, the general considerations of the doctrine of *respondeat superior* seem to apply. The mere fact that an unlicensed practitioner was hired and utilized by a hospital would not itself impose additional liability. Rather, an injured patient would be required to prove that the person allegedly responsible for the harm, whether a licensed or an unlicensed practitioner, had in fact been negligent. Most nurse practice acts provide for the imposition of a penalty for practicing nursing without a license. Penalties imposed are a fine and/or a term of imprisonment. Nursing care rendered without a license by a family member, neighbors and domestic help is generally exempt from the penalties for practicing nursing without a license.

## DEFINITION OF NURSING PRACTICE

State nursing practice laws differ in their definitions of nursing practice. Whether a particular procedure in patient care falls within nursing practice or within medical practice is often a difficult question to answer, especially where licensing laws contain only a general definition of nursing practice. Physicians, hospitals, and other employers of nurses need authoritative and reliable guidelines. Nurses, as well as their employers, often need to know whether a contemplated activity or procedure is within the scope of nursing practice. The entry of physician assistants and nurse practitioners into health manpower, advances in nursing education, and the changing role of the nurse in performing functions previously considered the practice of medicine have stimulated revision of nurse and medical practice acts. Additional changes granting legislative authority to the new health professionals to perform functions previously restricted to licensed, professional nurses or physicians will probably be forthcoming. Yet, there may be no way to obtain an authoritative answer that eliminates the risk of suit against nurses for infringing upon the practice of physicians.

### Compulsory and Voluntary Acts

The trend in health occupation licensing has been toward compulsory licensing acts which permit only licensed personnel to practice the regulated occupation, and prohibit unlicensed persons from such practice. In contrast to this form of mandatory licensing, the system of voluntary licensing permits only licensees to use a particular title or designation, but does not prohibit unlicensed persons from practicing the regulated occupation. Under voluntary licensing, the only restriction on unlicensed persons is the prohibition to use the protected title. Often health fields are initially controlled by voluntary licensing requirements which eventually become compulsory.

In the context of nursing laws, mandatory licensing statutes forbid unlicensed persons to practice nursing and require that a person must have met all the requirements relating to education, experience, and examination to be licensed.

Voluntary nursing acts simply forbid an unlicensed person to use the protected professional title or to claim to be licensed. The nursing statute of the *District of Columbia* is an example of voluntary licensing:

§2-401 REGISTRATION REQUIRED.

No person shall in the District of Columbia in any manner whatsoever represent herself to be a registered, certified graduate, or trained nurse, or allow herself to be so represented, unless she has been and is registered or is registered by the Nurses' Examining Board in accordance with the provisions of this subchapter. . . .

§2-410 NONREGISTERED NURSES MAY PRACTICE AS SUCH.

Nothing in this subchapter shall be construed to prevent any person from nursing any other person in the District of Columbia, either gratuitously or for hire; *Provided,* That such person so nursing shall not represent herself as being a registered, certified, graduate, or trained nurse.

It is interesting to note that the pronouns "her" and "herself" are used in this statute. The pronoun "his" is generally used in statutes and may refer to a person of either sex as is stated in the definition of "his" in *Black's Law Dictionary* and the cases cited therein, *Danforth v. Emmons,* 124 Me. 156, 126A. 821, 823 and *Wilmette v. Brachle,* 110 Ill. App. 356. "Her" and "herself" are not defined in *Black's Law Dictionary.* This is evidence that in the past women primarily have entered the nursing profession. With more men becoming nurses, and the changing role of women in society, the terms in future legislative enactments will probably reflect less of a sexist connotation.

Not all health professionals are licensed in the same manner. State licensing regulations of such fields as medical practice, dentistry, chiropractic, pharmacy, optometry, podiatry, and osteopathy are always compulsory. In contrast, practitioners such as sanitarians, physical therapists, and social workers may be licensed under either compulsory or voluntary acts, depending on the jurisdiction. Professional associations which represent the practitioners in a particular field often actively seek the enactment of compulsory licensing legislation for their professions in order to improve the quality of care rendered by members of the profession and to upgrade their professional status.

## Professional Nursing Defined by State Law

The role of the nurse has expanded so that duties formerly performed only by physicians are now being performed by professional nurses. This is particularly true of nurses employed in emergency rooms, operating rooms, and intensive care units, and nurse anesthetists, nurse practitioners and nurse midwives.

There has been an effort by the nursing and medical associations to clearly define the practice of professional nursing in the nurse practice acts in order to grant legal authority for nurses to perform the functions now delegated to them that formerly could be performed only by those licensed to practice medicine or under the supervision and at the direction of those licensed to practice medicine. These functions are diagnosis, treatment, performance of operations and prescription of medication and treatment.

The American Nurses' Association adopted the following definition of professional nursing:

> The term "practice of professional nursing" means the performance, for compensation, of any acts in the observation, care, and counsel of the ill, injured, or infirm or in the maintenance of health or prevention of illness of others, or in the supervision and teaching of other personnel, or the administration of medications and treatments as prescribed by a licensed physician or a licensed dentist; requiring substantial specialized judgment and skill and based on knowledge and application of the principles of biological, physical, and social science. The foregoing shall not be deemed to include acts of diagnosis or prescription of therapeutic or corrective measures.

The United States Department of Health, Education and Welfare has published a "Review and Analysis of State Legislation and Reimbursement Practices of Physician Assistants and Nurse Practitioners" in which a comparison of state regulations is made. It was observed that nurse practitioners are regulated by nurse practice acts in each state. Some states have no additional legislation or regulations covering the additional roles of nurse practitioners.

The nurse practitioner's role is merely an expansion of the role played for many years by nurses under nurse practice acts. For physician assistants to practice, new legislation has been required. Twenty-nine states have either the definition of the American Nurses' Association or a similar definition of "the practice of professional nursing" or of "registered nurse." Many of these similar statutes and statutes of a few states with new definitions of "nursing" include specifically that nurses are prohibited from performing acts of medical diagnosis, treatment, and/or prescription of therapeutic measures, and practicing medicine. The traditional nursing statutes do not permit nurses, even with advanced nurse practitioner training, to perform medical acts.

There is no clear distinction between nursing and medical diagnosis and treatment. Therefore, many states have amended their statutes to expressly permit nurses to perform "medical acts" or "additional acts," which are recognized as proper by the medical and nursing professions. These amendments generally grant authority to the state board of nursing to promulgate regulations as to education and experience for nurse practitioners and the tasks they may perform. In some states approval of the regulations by the board of medicine is also required, but the regulations are usually administered by the board of nursing.

A few states have enacted a "delegatory amendment" to the medical practice act authorizing physicians to delegate medical tasks to nurses provided the tasks are performed under the supervision of a physician.

Several states that have adopted a new definition of the practice of professional nursing have incorporated the New York statute, which reads as follows:

New York Education Law, Article 139, §§6901, 6902

The "practice of the profession of nursing as a registered professional nurse" is defined as diagnosing and treating human responses to actual or potential health problems through such services as case finding, health teaching, health counseling and provision of care supportive to or restorative of life and well-being, and executing medical regimens prescribed by a licensed or otherwise legally authorized physician or dentist. A nursing regimen shall be consistent with and shall not vary any existing medical regimen.

"Diagnosing" in the context of nursing practice means that identification of and discrimination between physical and psychosocial signs and symptoms essential to effective execution

and management of the nursing regimen. Such diagnostic privilege is distinct from a medical diagnosis.

"Treating" means selection and performance of those
therapeutic measures essential to the effective execution and
management of the nursing regimen, and execution of any
prescribed medical regimen.

"Human responses" means those signs, symptoms and processes which denote the individual's interaction with an actual
or potential health problem.

These statutes distinguish between medical and nursing regimens and in-
fer that nurses may not perform the same tasks as physicians and make
independent judgments as to problems and needs of patients.

The California statute provides legal authorization for nurses to perform medical tasks. The statute speaks in terms of collaboration between
physicians and nurses and not delegation by physicians to nurses. The
nurse practitioner who works in collaboration with the physician can
provide nursing diagnosis and treatment services, and there may be no
formal distinction between nursing and medical services. The California
statute defines nursing as follows:

In amending this section at the 1973-74 session, the Legislature
recognizes that nursing is a dynamic field, the practice of which
is continually evolving to include more sophisticated patient
care activities. It is the intent of the Legislature in amending
this section at the 1973-74 session to provide clear legal
authority for functions and procedures which have common acceptance and usage. It is the legislative intent also to recognize
the existence of overlapping functions between physicians and
registered nurses and to permit additional sharing of functions
within organized health care systems which provide for collaboration between physicians and registered nurses.

Such organized health care systems include, but are not limited
to, health facilities licensed pursuant to Chapter 2 (commencing
with Section 1250) of Division 2 of the Health and Safety Code,
clinics, home health agencies, physicians' offices, and public or
community health services.

The practice of nursing within the meaning of this chapter
means those functions helping people cope with difficulties in
daily living which are associated with their actual or potential

health or illness problems or the treatment thereof which require a substantial amount of scientific knowledge or technical skill, and includes all of the following:

(a) Direct and indirect patient care services that insure the safety, comfort, personal hygiene, and protection of patients; and the performance of disease prevention and restorative measures.

(b) Direct and indirect patient care services including, but not limited to, the administration of medications and therapeutic agents, necessary to implement a treatment, disease prevention, or rehabilitative regimen prescribed by a physician, dentist, or podiatrist.

(c) The performance, according to standardized procedures, of basic health care, testing, and prevention procedures, including, but not limited to, skin tests, immunization techniques, and the withdrawal of human blood from veins and arteries.

(d) Observation of signs and symptoms of illness, reactions to treatment, general behavior, or general physical condition, and (1) determination of whether such signs, symptoms, reactions, behavior, or general appearance exhibit abnormal characteristics; and (2) implementation based on observed abnormalities, of appropriate reporting, or referral, or standardized procedures, or changes in treatment regimen in accordance with standardized procedures, or the initiation of emergency procedures.

"Standardized procedures," as used in this section, means either of the following:

(California Nursing Practice Act, Chapter 6, §2725)

(1) Policies and protocols developed by a health facility licensed pursuant to Chapter 2 (commencing with Section 1250) of Division 2 of the Health and Safety Code through collaboration among administrators and health professionals including physicians and nurses;

(2) Policies and protocols developed through collaboration among administrators and health professionals, including physicians and nurses, by an organized health care system which is not a health facility licensed pursuant to Chapter 2

(commencing with Section 1250) of Division 2 of the Health and Safety Code. Such policies and protocols shall be subject to any guidelines for standardized procedures which the Board of Medical Examiners and the Board of Nursing Education and Nurse Registration may jointly promulgate; and if promulgated shall be administered by the Board of Nursing Education and Nurse Registration.

Nothing in this section shall be construed to require approval of standardized procedures by the Board of Medical Examiners or the Board of Nursing Education and Nurse Registration.

Except as otherwise provided herein, this chapter confers no authority to practice medicine or surgery.

The California definition is the only one of the new definitions which does not perpetuate traditional concepts of the nurse's medical role and considers that not only do the functions of nurses and physicians overlap to some extent, but the two professions work in collaboration. The preamble of the statute expresses the legislative intent to recognize this overlapping of functions and to permit additional sharing of functions within organized health care systems. For further information see V.C. Hall, "The Legal Scope of Nurse Practitioners under Nurse Practice and Medical Practices Acts," *The New Health Professionals,* Chapter 7, pages 106-115 (1977) and Department of Health, Education and Welfare Report, Review and Analysis of State Legislation and Reimbursement Practices of Physician's Assistants and Nurse Practitioners, January 1978.

## Practical Nursing Defined by State Law

States provide certain standards of performance, knowledge, functions, and results in their legislative definitions of practical nursing. The American Nurses' Association provides the following model definition of practical nursing:

The term "practical nursing" means the performance, for compensation, of selected acts in the care of the ill, injured, or infirm under the direction of a licensed professional nurse or a licensed physician or a licensed dentist; and not requiring the substantial specialized skill, judgment, and knowledge required in professional nursing.

Although the definition provides for a lesser degree of specialized skill, judgment and knowledge than is required of a professional nurse, the practical nurse often must assume the duties and responsibilities of the professional nurse. This practice is particularly prevalent in medically underserved geographical areas and in homes for the aged and mentally ill.

The ANA definition is similar to those in certain states and provides reasonable guidelines for nurses in those states which do not make a clear distinction between professional and practical nursing.

## Medical Practice Defined by State Law

Despite the fact that state laws vary in their definitions of what constitutes nursing practice, every state does clearly define the components of medical practice. Each state has enacted a medical practice act that permits only those individuals who meet the necessary qualifications to use the Medical Doctor (M.D.) title and to practice medicine.

Essentially, the practice of medicine includes three functions: diagnosis, treatment, and prescription. A physician's license demonstrates that the state, as the representative of the public, has confidence that the physician has sufficient training, experience, and ability to make diagnostic judgments, indicate courses of treatment, and specify medications, instruments, or procedures which will alleviate or cure a patient's ailment. Although medical personnel other than a physician may actually carry out medical techniques and procedures at the direction or under the supervision of the physician, the physician's authority to make the necessary medical judgments is in no way impaired. Indeed, one primary judgment a physician must undertake is to determine what duties are to be carried out by either professional or practical nurses.

For example, a duly licensed and trained nurse who administers anesthetics under the personal direction and supervision of a licensed physician and surgeon is not engaging in the practice of medicine within the meaning of a licensing statute, even though such service is usually performed by a physician. The close relationship between the two professions is obvious in this example.

Although physicians may perform all medical acts and are granted unlimited medical authority by virtue of state medical practice acts, hospitals may limit the medical procedures that physicians may actually perform. A hospital may require that before being permitted to perform certain medical procedures and before being certified by a specialty board a physician must pass certain tests or engage in extra study and practice. For example, a physician may not be recognized as a psychiatrist until several years of special training are completed. However, the state medical practice acts authorize a licensed physician to perform any act in the entire range of health services. No other health professional has that authorization.

# Chapter 8

# New Nursing Professionals

Nurses have traditionally served in a dependent capacity to physicians. During the 1960's greater emphasis was placed on collegiate education for nurses and the number of diploma programs has decreased. Opposition by nurses to the AMA's proposal of an extended role for nurses resulted in the establishment of the non-nurse physician assistant. Because of the uneven availability of medical services and the increasing escalation of medical care costs, the new health professionals (NHPs), physician assistants (PAs), MEDEX, and nurse practitioners (NPs) have emerged since 1970. The Manpower Supply and Utilization Branch, Division of Medicine, Bureau of Health Manpower predicts that PAs and MEDEX will increase in numbers almost seven-fold, from 2,540 in 1975 to 18,520 in 1990, while certificate and Master's degree NPs will increase four-fold from 5,100 in 1975 to 23,030 in 1990. The predictions are based on the assumption that federal funding will be maintained at the current level.

## REPORT OF THE PHYSICIAN EXTENDER WORK GROUP

A Physician Extender Work Group was established in 1975 by the Deputy Administrator of the Health Resources Administration of the United States Department of Health, Education and Welfare. In 1977, the work group published a report of its study of issues involving nurse practitioners and physician assistants.

### Nurse Practitioner/Physician Assistant Training

The work group concluded that training programs which focus on educating practitioners to deliver primary care should be supported and programs preparing candidates for highly specialized non-primary care should not be encouraged. According to the work group's report, "primary health care includes services for the promotion and maintenance of health, prevention of illness and disability, basic care during acute and chronic phases of illness, guidance and counseling of individuals and families, and referral to other health care providers and community resources when appropriate. Primary health care is the entrance into the health care system and may be initiated by the client and/or provider in a variety of settings."

Such factors as the type of applicants, the geographical location, and local or regional educational health care objectives were considered to make programs unique. The diversity of structure and the cost of programs will be affected by new health initiatives such as national health insurance and changes in the organizational structure of health care delivery.

The work group concluded that pluralistic approaches to the curriculum and structure of physician assistant and nurse practitioner programs are needed because of variations in the entry level characteristics of students and the potential, though undefined, role differentiation. The programs have been supported by the Health Manpower Training Act of 1971 and the Nurse Training Acts of 1971 and 1975. A 1976 study differentiated the categories as master's nurse practitioners, certificate nurse practitioners (pediatric, family, adult), physician assistants, and MEDEX.

The majority of program directors viewed the role of the nurse practitioner and physician assistants as interdependent providers. The nurse practitioner master's programs ranged from 44 to 72 weeks with an average of 60 weeks. The certificate nurse practitioner programs were 16 to 68 weeks in length with a median of 36 weeks. The physician assistants programs extended 104 weeks and MEDEX programs ranged from 61 to 72 weeks.

The curricula of physician assistants and MEDEX programs placed greater emphasis on basic sciences than the nurse practitioner programs did, and included surgery and emergency care skills rarely emphasized in nurse practitioner programs. The differences in the curricula arise in part from differences in the backgrounds of the students. Nurse practitioner students were expected to already have a strong background in the basic sciences and be familiar with surgery and emergency care skills since most of these students were graduates of nursing programs. All programs included training in provider-patient communications and counseling and role development, but there was greater emphasis on these skills in the nurse practitioner programs. Research methodology was emphasized in the master's curricula in all programs, particularly in the nurse practitioner programs.

The work group found that the predominant age group in all categories was 25-29. The nurse practitioner certificate programs, however, attracted some students over 40. The median age of students in all programs was approximately 30. There were few minority students. Educational entry levels varied. The nurse practitioner master's students had BSN degrees or the equivalent. The nurse practitioner certificate students were RN's from either diploma, AD, BSN or Master's preparation. Approximately 45% of the physician assistants had a BA/BS degree and most of the MEDEX had some college.

In the GMENAC Staff Papers, Supply and Distribution of Physicians and Physician Extenders, prepared by the staff of the Manpower Supply and Utilization Branch, Division of Medicine, Bureau of Health Manpower, it is stated that programs are available for nurse practitioners specializing in pediatrics, midwifery, maternity care, family health, adult care and psychiatry. All formally trained nurse practitioners must have an R.N. The length of training for certificate programs was 3 to 15 months, with most programs lasting 12 months. Master's degree programs ranged from 9 to 26 months in length, with most programs lasting 24 months. Between 1970 and 1975 the programs graduated 3,800 certified nurse practitioners and 1,300 master's degree nurse practitioners. Approximately 60% of the graduates of these programs are providers of primary care. Of the graduates providing primary care, 35% are pediatric nurse practitioners, 26% are family nurse practitioners, 22% are adult nurse practitioners and the remainder are nurse midwives, maternity nurses and psychiatric nurses. Sixty-three percent of the nurse practitioners providing primary care are in ambulatory practice settings. Other large groups are employed in non-hospital, institutional and community settings, 16 and 10% respectively. Nearly all students, 98%, are female, and 90% are white. About half are between 25 and 34 years of age.

## Patient Satisfaction

Factors found to most affect acceptance by the consumer or patient of the nurse practitioners and physician assistants were: (1) their personal qualifications and characteristics, (2) their acceptance and endorsement by the physician; and (3) the manner in which their qualifications and benefits of services were explained to the patient. No difference was found in patient satisfaction with care provided by nurse practitioners and physician assistants. These studies involved clinics and prepaid group practices which may be atypical of settings in which the majority of health services are provided. Studies since 1970 have consistently shown parent satisfaction with pediatric nurse practitioners. Two studies reflected that the patient's acceptance and satisfaction with the nurse practitioner was equal to or greater than acceptance and satisfaction with the physician. When patients were given the option to see a pediatric nurse practitioner at half the pediatrician's fee, the pediatric nurse practitioner's practice increased 38%.

## Physician/Employer Acceptance

Whether physicians or other employers such as institutions will employ physician assistants and nurse practitioners will be based on the balance of benefits to be derived, such as increased revenue and practice productivity, and costs, such as salary, overhead, supervision and consultation, tuition or on-the-job training. Non-monetary benefits include increasing the physician's time for leisure, research, etc. The employer may also believe that joint or team care would result in improved quality of care.

Studies have shown that physicians are more likely to employ nurse practitioners because of their associated prior roles as nurses, but more likely to delegate tasks to physician assistants. Solo practitioners prefer to train their own physician extenders. This is significant since nurse practitioners from baccalaureate programs have the required basic knowledge but do not pose a threat to the physician.

Reasons given for physicians' unwillingness to employ nurse practitioners and physician assistants are: unwillingness to relinquish functions related to the total management of the patient, including routine care; possible threat to financial status; and dislike of supervisory responsibilities.

## Quality of Care

The work group evaluated the performance of nurse practitioners and physician assistants and compared their performance with that of physicians. The group found it difficult to measure the quality of care. Two approaches were used. An evaluation was made of the degree of concurrence in history taking, diagnostic assessments, or recommended therapeutic measures between the nurse practitioners, physician assistants and physicians for the same group of patients. Comparisons were also made of patient outcome in randomized, controlled experiments where one group was seen by a nurse practitioner or physician assistant and another by a physician. Performance of nurse practitioners and physician assistants compared favorably with that of the physician with respect to both process and outcome, and the quality of their care was at least as high as that of the physician's with whom they were compared.

## THIRD PARTY PAYMENT

The fate of the nurse practitioner and physician assistant programs depends largely on the establishment of reimbursement policies by third parties for payment of services rendered. Most of the new health professionals are employed and work on a salary basis. Few work independently. Few are reimbursed on a fee-for-service basis. Salaries of new health professionals averaged between $14,000 and $19,000 in 1976, which was approximately one-third the income received by physicians. [See J. G. Fox and S. R. Zatkin, "Third Party Payment for Non-Physician Health Practitioners: Realities and Recommendations," *Family and Community Health,* vol. 1, no. 1, (April 1978): 69-80.]

Who is to be reimbursed will depend upon whether the nurse practitioners and physician assistants are permitted to practice independently or dependently, under supervision and direction of a physician, or semi-independently in collaboration with a physician. If they are permitted to practice independently and/or semi-independently in geographically underserved areas, this should be advantageous in overcoming the lack of availability of medical care and desirable if reimbursement reflects their costs and savings. Standards for reimbursement must be determined as well as who should set the standards. If federal policy is set for reimbursement, a choice must be made between state or national standards or a combination of both.

The level of reimbursement must be determined. Arguments for payment at the same level as physicians are that payment is for the same service and to pay less would possibly imply the service was of a lower quality. Argument for a lesser amount is that cost of education was less and salary demand is less. It has been proposed that if supervision is required there should be a proportionment of the fee between the physician and the nurse practitioner or physician assistant. This would not reduce costs of medical care which is one of the prime objectives in use of nurse practitioners and physician assistants.

The Rural Health Clinic Bill favors reimbursement for services based on billings for actual cost for providing services. Another approach is reimbursement under a different schedule than physicians because the new health professionals are trained with a different orientation than physicians. It has been suggested that if reimbursement were at a single rate for services of nurse practitioners, physician assistants and physicians, and if the level were between the new health professionals' real cost and the usual physician rates, this would cover salary cost, physician supervision and overhead and provide inducement to employ the new health professionals or to otherwise increase efficiency of care. This would result in a reduction of costs of medical care.

## EFFECT ON MEDICAL MALPRACTICE

Whether risks of suits for malpractice will be increased or decreased by the use of nurse practitioners and physician assistants remains to be determined. It is possible that malpractice suits will decrease because the time of physicians will be conserved to permit them to exercise greater care in their functions. A better relationship may be developed with the patients with greater patient satisfaction.

There are significant differences among the states in education, regulation and reimbursement of nurse practitioners and physician assistants. The increase in the number of nurse practitioners and physician assistants has brought to light the need for legislation and regulation. Proliferation of training programs, availability of professional opportunities and method of third-party reimbursement will determine the future for nurse practitioners and physician assistants. As opportunities expand and roles change so will legislation and regulation change.

The required degree of supervision by a physician varies among the states, and is not clearly defined. Nurse practitioners and physician assistants practicing in rural areas are not required to have as great a degree of supervision as when employed by a hospital or a physician. The report of the study of the United States Department of Health, Education and Welfare, Review and Analysis of State Legislation and Reimbursement Practices of Physician's Assistants and Nurse Practitioners published in January of 1978 reflects a lack of clarity in the legislation of many states, a lack of uniformity among the states, and a lack of conceptual ties between inter-state regulations and reimbursement practices. The study points out the necessity of further defining the guidelines for practices of nurse practitioners and physician assistants and for more extensive investigation of practice patterns such as physician supervision, drug dispensing, regulation of practices and education and reimbursement.

Among the primary causes of the medical malpractice crisis are poor quality of medical care; high cost of care; and a poor personal relationship between the patient and the physician. Use of nurse practitioners and physician assistants may reduce the medical malpractice actions by obtaining a greater degree of patient satisfaction. Performance of tasks formerly limited to physicians should serve to provide additional time to the physician; the physician should be able to function more competently by taking advantage of continuing education and by having more time to devote to the management of the patient's care and treatment. More personalized attention can be devoted by the physician as well as the nurse practitioner and physician assistant. This should establish a better personal relationship with the patient. If a patient likes the health care provider the patient may hesitate to sue. As a result of more time spent with the patients than the physician could devote, the nurse practitioner and physician assistant may observe signs, symptoms and problems more readily than the physician, and proper care and treatment timely instituted may reduce the probability of injury from failure to diagnose and treat. The quality of care can be improved with reduction in malpractice actions. On the other hand, if nurse practitioners and physician assistants programs do not properly prepare the students for the responsibilities placed upon them, and if physicians use them to increase their practice, then the quality of care may be poor and the medical malpractice crisis may become more severe.

Regulation of education and licensing to assure competence is essential. The degree of physician supervision needed will depend upon the education and competency of nurse practitioners and physician assistants. When the health care provider is competent and the quality of care is high, the likelihood of injury due to negligence is less and it follows that the number of suits for malpractice will decrease.

The medical profession may be reluctant to relinquish control over what has traditionally been considered the practice of medicine. Certainly, safety of the consumer must be considered in determining the extent of permitted performance, particularly unsupervised care by nurse practitioners and physician assistants. Perhaps a guide for this determination will come from observation of care rendered in rural areas under less supervision and from comparison of performance of nurse practitioners and physician assistants with that of physicians.

The legal standards for determining liability of nurse practitioners and physician assistants will be the same as previously discussed. The community standard and what the reasonable nurse practitioner and physician assistant should do under the circumstances will be determined by the jury based on evidence of what the nursing and medical professions consider proper practice for these new health professionals and on legislation regulating their practice. If they practice under supervision and control of their employer, a hospital and/or a physician, then the employer will be liable under the doctrine of *respondeat superior*. Under the Good Samaritan Act of some states, immunity from liability has been granted to paramedics in emergency situations, unless they are grossly negligent.

Patterns of regulation and reimbursement by third parties to nurse practitioners and physician assistants will probably continue to change as will the extent of their practice. With increase in responsibilities there is a greater probability of being sued. The future of these new midlevel professionals depends upon educational and employment opportunities and third party reimbursement. The need for future analyses and an update on a regular basis has been recommended to the United States Department of Health, Education and Welfare.

Chapter 9

# The Nurse as an Employee

When a hospital employs a nurse the hospital assumes reponsibility for the nurse's work because the nurse is acting for the hospital in providing health care. The nurse can be considered a representative of the hospital. Moreover, the hospital assumes responsibility for a nurse's negligent actions, and will be held liable along with the nurse in a malpractice suit.

Occasionally, a physician assumes responsibility for a nurse's actions, and if a nurse is negligent while acting under a physician's direct supervision, the physician will also be held negligent.

## HOSPITAL LIABILITY—RESPONDEAT SUPERIOR

*Respondeat superior* is the term for a form of vicarious liability wherein an employer is held liable for the wrongful acts of an employee even though the employer's conduct may be without fault. Liability predicated on *respondeat superior* may be imposed upon an employer only if a master-servant relationship exists between the employer and employee and if the wrongful act of the employee occurs within the scope of employment. If the employer has the right to control the physical conduct of the employee's performance of duties, then a master-servant relationship sufficient to invoke the doctrine of *respondeat superior* exists. An act is "within the scope of employment" when it is so closely related to what the employee has been hired to do, or so fairly and reasonably incidental to employment, that it may be regarded as a method of carrying out the orders of the employer. Furthermore, the propriety or impropriety of that method has no bearing whatsoever on the determination of whether the act is within the scope of employment.

The doctrine of *respondeat superior* does not absolve the employee of liability for wrongful acts. Not only may the injured party sue the

101

employee directly, but the employer may also seek compensation from the employee for the financial loss occasioned by the employee's wrongful act.

The doctrine of *respondeat superior* does not apply to the wrongful conduct of an independent contractor. An independent contractor is usually an agent of a principal, over whom the principal has no right of control concerning the manner in which the work is to be performed. Thus, a master-servant relationship does not exist and, therefore, the doctrine of *respondeat superior* does not apply.

The doctrine of *respondeat superior* may impose liability upon a hospital for a nurse's acts or omissions that result in injury to a hospital patient. Whether such liability attaches depends upon whether the conduct of the nurse was wrongful and whether the nurse was subject to the control of the hospital at the time the act in question was performed. To determine whether the nurse's acts were wrongful in a given situation, the nurse's conduct is measured against the standard of conduct to which the nurse is expected to adhere. For liability purposes, the nurse who is subject to the control of the hospital at the time of the negligent conduct is considered an employee of the hospital, not the "borrowed servant" of a staff physician or surgeon.

It is impossible to list all the acts and omissions which may constitute negligence on the part of a nurse and may render a hospital liable under the doctrine of *respondeat superior,* but a few examples will illustrate the circumstances under which the doctrine will apply. Cases of neglience on the part of a nurse have involved the application of overheated hot water bottles, the administration of an enema that was too hot, the injection of incorrect medication, the failure to catheterize a patient at the intervals requested by the patient's physician, and the failure to warn a patient of the danger inherent in lowering a bed.

A hospital will also be held liable if a nurse continues to inject a solution after noticing its ill effects. For example, in the *Florida* case of *Parrish v. Clark,* 107 Fla. 598, 145 So. 848 (1933), the court deemed a nurse negligent for continuing to inject saline solution into an unconscious patient's breast after noticing its ill effects. Thus, once the undesirable results of the administration of the solution were observed, the nurse had the duty to stop injecting the solution.

The failure of nursing personnel to take action when a patient's personal physician is clearly unwilling or unable to cope with a situation that threatens the life or health of the patient also results in liability for the hospital. In a *California* case, *Goff v. Doctors General Hospital,* 166 Cal. App. 2d 314, 333 P. 2d 29 (1958), two hospital nurses believed that a patient was bleeding to death after childbirth because the physician had failed to suture her properly. The nurses testified that they were aware of the patient's dangerous condition and that the physician was not present in the hospital. Both nurses knew that the patient would die if nothing was done, but neither nurse contacted anyone except the physician. The court held the hospital liable for the nurses' negligence in failing to notify the supervisors of the patient's serious condition, which resulted in the patient's death.

When a nurse deviates from the orders of the attending physician and the patient thereby suffers injury, the hospital may incur liability under the doctrine of *respondeat superior.* If the physician's therapeutic regimen for a patient is medically sound, liability may be incurred although the deviation from orders may be considered acceptable practice by other physicians or institutions. If the physician's therapeutic regimen is not medically sound and the nurse should have been aware of this, liability may be incurred for carrying out the orders where injury is sustained.

## PHYSICIAN LIABILITY—"BORROWED SERVANT"

The "borrowed servant" doctrine is a special application of the doctrine of *respondeat superior* that applies when one employer lends an employee to another for a particular employment. Although the employee remains the servant of the regular employer, under the borrowed servant doctrine the regular employer is not liable for injury negligently caused by the servant while in the special service of another employer.

The borrowed servant rule provides that in certain situations, a nurse employed by a hospital may be considered the employee of a physician. In these situations, the physician is the special or temporary employer and is thus liable for the negligence of the nurse. Whether the physician is liable under the doctrine of *respondeat superior* depends upon whether the physician had the right to control and direct the nurse at the time of the negligent act. If it is proved that the physician was in exclusive control, and if the nurse is deemed to have been the physician's temporary special employee, the physician, not the hospital, is liable for the nurse's negligent acts.

The borrowed servant doctrine usually arises in a hospital case within the context of the operating room. The application of this doctrine to the operating room situation is based on acceptance of the "captain of the ship" concept, which considers the surgeon to be in total command of the operating room. In the *Minnesota* case of *St. Paul-Mercury Indemnity Co. v. St. Joseph Hospital,* 212 Minn. 558, 4 N.W. 2d 637 (1942), the court provided the rationale for this concept:

The desirability of the rule is obvious. The patient is completely at the mercy of the surgeon and relies upon him to see that all the acts relative to the operation are performed in a careful manner.

It is the surgeon's duty to guard against any and all avoidable acts that may result in injury to his patient.

The rule is plain that when the general employer assigns his servant to duty for another and surrenders to the other direction and control in relation to the work to be done, the servant becomes the servant of the other insofar as his services relate to the work so controlled and directed. His general employer is no longer liable for the servant's torts committed in the directed and controlled work. In the operating room the surgeon must be master. He cannot tolerate any other voice in the control of his assistants. In the case at bar the evidence is clear that the doctor had exclusive control over the acts in question, and therefore the hospital cannot be said to have been a "joint master" or "comaster," even though the nurses were in its general employ and paid by it.

## Nurse Anesthetists

An anesthesiologist is a specialist and is considered a consultant to the surgeon and a member of the team of physicians performing the surgical procedure. Generally, the surgeon is not responsible for the administration of the anesthesia unless a technician performs this procedure under the surgeon's direction. The anesthesiologist who administers an anesthetic is responsible for the choice of the anesthetic and the care of the patient.

When a nurse anesthetist, rather than a physician anesthesiologist, administers the anesthetic, the nurse anesthetist may be found by the court to be an independent contractor, not under the control of the surgeon and not the surgeon's borrowed servant. The surgeon would then not be liable under the doctrine of *respondeat superior*. A nurse who is qualified in accordance with the American Association of Nurse Anesthetists may be far more knowledgeable than the surgeon in the administration of anesthetics and would thus be considered an independent contractor, not the surgeon's borrowed servant, since the surgeon's control over the nurse anesthetist would be lacking. If the physician has no control, then the physician is not "captain of the ship." If the nurse anesthetist is an employee of a hospital and/or an anesthesiologist and under their control, then a master-servant relationship exists and the doctrine of *respondeat superior* may be applicable.

In *Hillyer v. St. Bartholomew's Hospital,* 2 K.B. 820 (C.A. 1909), the court considered it impossible that the administrator of anesthetics or a surgeon could be servants as they are professional "men," employed by the defendant hospital to exercise their profession to the best of their abilities according to their own discretion, but in exercising it they were considered in no way under orders or bound to obey the direction of the defendant hospital. The American cases generally do not follow this reasoning and have held physicians and nurses performing professional as well as administrative acts to be borrowed servants of the hospital.

A nurse anesthetist is considered to be a nurse practitioner. The requisite degree of supervision by a physician varies among the states. Arizona, New Hampshire, North Dakota and West Virginia require nurse anesthetists to work only in the physical presence of their supervising physician.

## The Nature of a Nurse's Acts

Several courts have developed a distinction between a nurse's clerical or administrative acts and those involving professional skill and judgment, which are considered medical acts. The courts use this distinction to determine the liability of the surgeon and the hospital for the acts of a nurse. If an act is characterized as administrative or clerical, it is the hospital's responsibility; if the act is considered medical, it is the surgeon's responsibility. This rule was enunciated in the *Minnesota* case of *Swigerd v. City of Ortonville,* 246 Minn. 339, 75 N.W. 2d 217 (1956), when the court stated:

> A hospital is liable for the negligence of its nurses in performing mere administrative or clerical acts, which acts, *though constituting a part of patient's prescribed medical treatment,* do not require the application of the specialized technique or the understanding of a skilled physician or surgeon. This rule, in recognizing that the right of control remains with the hospital as the general employer, is consistent with the nature of such acts and is in accord with the custom which in everyday practice governs the relationship between the hospital staff and the attending physicians. It is generally recognized that the nature of the acts performed, and the custom as to the control ordinarily exercised in the performance of similar acts, are factors indicative of where the right to control exists.

In considering which acts may be properly labeled administrative, the *Swigerd* court noted further:

> No all-embracing definition of what acts are administrative will be attempted but a few illustrations from actual cases will suffice to disclose their nature. It has been held that the order of an attending physician that sideboards be placed on a bed for the patient's protection is a medical determination for which the hospital is not responsible. In contrast, however, the physical or manual act of attaching the sideboards, in compliance with that order, is merely an administrative act since it can be performed by anyone in the hospital's employ and its performance requires no professional knowledge, skill, or experience. Similarly, where a doctor ordered that his patient be served tea, the negligent serving of the tea, whereby the patient was painfully burned, was an administrative act for which the hospital was liable in damages.

Although courts occasionally consider the distinction between administrative and other acts to assist in determining whether the hospital or the physician is liable for a nurse's negligent acts, in *New York* where this distinction was first advanced and in many other jurisdictions it is regarded as an unsound basis for judgment.

## SPECIAL DUTY NURSE

Hospitals have generally not been held liable for the negligence of a special duty nurse, a nurse hired by the patient or the patient's family to perform nursing services. Generally, a master-servant relationship does not exist between the hospital and the special duty nurse.

The relationships of special duty nurses and staff physicians to hospitals are, in some respects, similar. Thus, a hospital may exclude a special duty nurse from practicing within the institution. As with staff physicians, special duty nurses may be required to observe the rules as a precondition to working in the hospital. The nurse's observance of hospital rules is insufficient, however, to constitute the existence of a master-servant relationship between the hospital and the special nurse. Since a special nurse is generally employed by the patient, the hospital has no authority to hire or fire or to control the nurse's conduct on the case. However, the hospital does retain a responsibility to protect patients from incompetent and unqualified special nurses.

Even though a special duty nurse is employed by the patient, the hospital may be held liable if the nurse is negligent in performing administrative duties required by the hospital. Moreover, the use of the designation "special duty nurse" does not preclude consideration of the nurse as an employee or agent of the hospital. If the master-servant relationship does in fact exist between the hospital and the special nurse, the doctrine of *respondeat superior* may be applied to impose liability upon the hospital for the nurse's wrongful conduct. Thus, in *Emory University v. Shadburn*, 47 Ga. App. 643, 171 S.E. 192 (1933), the court, emphasizing that the nurse was procured and paid through the hospital, stated:

> Where an application in behalf of the patient is made to the hospital to furnish to the patient a special nurse, and a special nurse is selected and procured by the hospital and placed in charge of the patient, notwithstanding the services of the nurse may be specifically charged for by the hospital and paid for by the patient, but where the hospital itself is paid for the services of the nurse and the hospital afterwards settles with the nurse, the inference is authorized that the special nurse is the agent of the hospital to care for and look after the patient; and where the injuries received by the patient in jumping out of the window of the hospital under the conditions referred to are caused from any negligence of the nurse leaving the patient alone, such negligence is imputable to the hospital.

Thus, even though a patient pays the special duty nurse, the existence of an employer-employee relationship, which determines the applicability of *respondeat superior,* is a matter of fact to be determined by the jury under proper instructions.

In the landmark case of *Darling v. Charleston Community Memorial Hospital,* 33 Ill. 2d 326 (Sup. Ct. 1965), a young man sued for the amputation of his leg, which resulted from the development of gangrene and allegedly negligent orthopedic treatment of his broken leg. The court held that the hospital was liable to the plaintiff. In discussing the responsibility of the hospital, the court stated:

> The conception that the hospital does not undertake to treat the patient, does not undertake to act through its doctors and nurses, but undertakes instead simply to procure them to act upon their own responsibility, no longer reflects the fact. Present-day hospitals, as their manner of operation plainly demon-

strates, do far more than furnish facilities for treatment. They regularly employ on a salary basis a large staff of physicians, nurses and interns, as well as administrative and manual workers, and they charge patients for medical care and treatment, collecting for such services, if necessary, by legal action. Certainly, the person who avails himself of 'hospital facilities' expects that the hospital will attempt to cure him, not that its nurses or other employees will act on their own responsibility, (Fuld, J., in *Bing v. Thunig* (1957), 2 N.Y.2d 656, 143 N.E.2d 3,8.). The Standards for Hospital Accreditation, the state licensing regulations and the defendant's bylaws demonstrate that the medical profession and other responsible authorities regard it as both desirable and feasible that a hospital assume certain responsibilities for the care of the patient.

For additional information on the subject of hospital liability, see Walkup, *Hospital Liability: Changing Patterns of Responsibility* 8 U.S.F.L. Rev. 247 (1973).

## SUPERVISING NURSE

Supervising nurses are not liable under *respondeat superior* for the negligent acts of the nurses being supervised. A supervising nurse has the right to direct the nurses who are being supervised but the hospital is the employer, and supervisory powers are delegated to the supervisory nurse directly from the hospital's right of control. However, the supervisory nurse is liable for personal negligent behavior, and the hospital may be liable for the negligent acts of all its employees, including supervisors.

For example, in the case of *Bowers v. Olch,* 120 Cal. 2d 108, 260 P. 2d 997 (1953) a supervising nurse assigned two nurses to an operating room. One of the nurses left a needle in a patient's abdomen after an operation. The patient charged that the supervising nurse was liable under the doctrine of *respondeat superior* because she assigned the nurse to the operating room. The court dismissed the case against the supervising nurse and stated that the doctrine of *respondeat superior* did not apply because the supervising nurse could not exercise control over the conduct of the nurses.

# Chapter 10

# Labor

Many federal and state laws regulate the relationship between employers and employees. Some of these laws pertain to the relationship between hospitals and nurses. Such laws concern union activity and employment practices, including wages, hours, child labor, and workmen's compensation.

## UNIONS AND HOSPITALS

Nurses employed by hospitals are likely to be more concerned with labor relations than nurses who are privately employed. Furthermore, nurses in general are much more concerned with labor relations today than they were fifteen years ago. Unions have only recently become an important factor in hospital-employee relations. Until the mid-1930s, union organizational activity in hospitals was minimal, and until the late 1950s it increased relatively slowly. However, since 1960, unions have begun to play a considerably greater part in hospital-employee relations.

A number of different labor organizations are now heavily involved in attempts to become the recognized collective bargaining representatives of employees in the hospital field. There are craft unions whose primary organizing efforts are devoted to skilled employees, such as carpenters and electricians; industrial unions and unions of governmental employees, which seek to represent large groups of unskilled or semiskilled employees; and professional and occupational associations, which are interested in representing their members. To the extent that the professional organizations seek goals directly concerned with wages, hours, and other employment conditions and engage in bargaining on behalf of employees, they perform the functions of labor unions.

Union activity in the hospital field has generally been successful in the geographical areas where unions have been successful in other industries. It is not unreasonable to assume that this pattern will continue.

## FEDERAL LABOR ACTS

### Labor-Management Relations Act

The Labor-Management Relations Act (LMRA) defines certain conduct of employers and employees as unfair labor practices and provides for hearings upon complaints that such practices have occurred. This Act consists of the National Labor Relations Act of 1935, the Taft-Hartley amendments of 1947, and certain amendments contained in the Labor-Management Reporting and Disclosure Act of 1959.

*Jurisdiction.* Nearly all proprietary hospitals have, for some time, been subject to the provisions of the Labor-Management Relations Act. The National Labor Relations Board (NLRB), which is entrusted with enforcing and administering the act, has jurisdiction over matters involving proprietary hospitals with gross revenues of at least $250,000 per year.

Governmental hospitals were exempted in the 1935 enactment of the National Labor Relations Act, and charitable hospitals were exempted in 1947 by judicial decision. However, a July 1974 amendment to the National Labor Relations Act extended coverage to employees of nonprofit health care institutions that had previously been exempted from its provisions. In the words of the amendment, a health care facility is "any hospital, convalescent hospital, health maintenance organization, health clinic, nursing home, extended care facility, or other institution devoted to the care of the sick, infirm or aged persons."

The amendment also enacted unique special provisions for employees of health care facilities who oppose unionization on legitimate religious grounds. These provisions allow a member of such an institution to make periodic contributions to one of three nonreligious charitable funds selected jointly by the labor organization and the employing institution, rather than pay periodic union dues and initiation fees. If the collective bargaining agreement does not specify an acceptable fund, the employee may select a tax-exempt charity.

In 1975, the NLRB rejected guidelines establishing a dichotomy between direct and indirect patient care for determining appropriate bargaining units in health care institutions, and adopted instead a five-unit structure consisting of: registered nurses and nurse practitioners; all other professionals; technical personnel, including licensed practical nurses; business office clerical personnel; and service and maintenance employees, excluding guards. Head nurses with authority to recommend wage increases, settle grievances, and assign work have been considered supervisory personnel. Charge nurses and team leader nurses engaged primarily in patient care have been classified as employees and placed in the registered nurses' units. The NLRB has not disturbed units already established under state labor relations statutes where a secret-ballot election was conducted within the preceding 12 months where the parties voluntarily participated and where there was no substantial deviation from due process requirements. Effect has been given to units, though they are not in conformity with the bargaining units adopted by the Board, when the union and the health care provider agree and stipulate to such units. The Board has not followed strictly the units adopted by the Board but has accepted units based on facts and circumstances of each case, as is reflected in the reported decisions.

*Elections.* The LMRA sets out the procedures by which employees may select a labor organization as their collective bargaining representative to negotiate with the hospital over employment and contract matters. A hospital may choose to recognize and negotiate with the union without resorting to the formal LMRA procedure. If the formal process is followed, the employees vote on union representation in an election held under NLRB supervision. If a union wins the employees' approval, it is certified by the NLRB as the employees' bargaining representative.

The LMRA provides that the representative selected by a majority of employees in a bargaining unit is the exclusive bargaining agent for *all* employees in the unit. The scope of the bargaining unit is often the subject of dispute, for these boundaries may determine the outcome of the election, the extent of the employee representative's bargaining power, and the level of labor relations stability.

When the parties cannot agree on the appropriate unit for bargaining, the NLRB has broad discretion to decide the issue. However, the NLRB's discretion is limited to determining appropriate units only for those employees who are classified as professional, supervisory, clerical, technical, or service and maintenance employees and who are to be included in units outside of their particular category. This is the case unless there has been a self-determination election, in which the members of a certain group vote, as a class, to be included within the larger bargaining unit. For example, nurses and other professional employees of a hospital can be excluded from a bargaining unit composed of service and maintenance employees, unless the professionals are first given the opportunity to choose separate representation and reject it. Supervisory nurses are also entitled to a bargaining unit separate from the unit composed of general duty nurses.

Although the LMRA does not require that the employee representatives be selected by any particular procedure, the act does provide for the NLRB to conduct representation elections by secret ballot. The NLRB may only conduct such an election when a petition for certification has been filed by an employee, a group of employees, an individual, a labor union acting on the employees' behalf, or an employer. When the petition is filed the NLRB must investigate and must direct an election if it has reasonable cause to believe a question of representation exists. After an election, if any party to the election believes that it was accompanied by conduct which created an atmosphere that interfered with employee free choice, that party may file objections with the NLRB.


*Unfair Labor Practice.* The Labor-Management Relations Act prohibits hospitals from engaging in certain conduct classified as employer unfair labor practices. For example, firing an employee for holding union membership is not permitted. The LMRA stipulates that the employer must bargain in good faith with representatives of the employee. Failure to do so constitutes an unfair labor practice, and the NLRB may order the employer to fulfill the duty to bargain.

If the employer dominates or controls the employees' union, or interferes by supporting one of two competing unions, the employer is committing an unfair labor practice. For example, when two unions are competing for members in a hospital, and for recognition as the organization to bargain on behalf of the employees, if the hospital permits one of the unions to use hospital facilities for its organizational activities, but denies the use of the facilities to the other union, the hospital has committed an unfair labor practice by supporting one of the unions. Financial assistance from the employer to one of the competing unions also constitutes an unfair labor practice.

The LMRA also places certain responsibilities on labor organizations and prohibits certain employee activities that are classified as employee unfair labor practices. The coercion of employees by the union constitutes a union unfair labor practice. Activities such as mass picketing, assaults on nonstrikers, and following groups of nonstrikers away from the immediate area of the hospital plainly constitute coercion and the NLRB will order that they be stopped. Breach of a collective bargaining contract by the labor union is another example of a union unfair labor practice.

*Labor Disputes.* Congress enacted the Norris-LaGuardia Act to limit the power of the federal courts to issue injunctions in cases involving or growing out of labor disputes. The act requires that strict standards be met before such injunctions can be issued. Essentially, a federal court may apply restraints in a labor dispute only when the case has been heard in open court and the open court has concluded that unlawful acts will be committed unless restrained and that substantial and irreparable injury to the complainant's property will follow.

The Norris-LaGuardia Act is aimed at reducing the number of injunctions issued to restrain strikes and picketing. However, the 1974 amendment to the National Labor Relations Act sets out procedures which limit strikes in health institutions.

This amendment sets out special procedures for handling labor disputes which develop out of collective bargaining at the termination of an existing agreement or arise during negotiations for an initial contract between a health institution and its employees. The procedures were designed to ensure that the needs of patients would be met during any work stoppage (strike) or labor dispute in such an institution.

In consideration of both the community's need for continuous health services and the good-faith intentions of labor organizations to avoid a work stoppage whenever possible and accept arbitration when negotiations reach an impasse, the amendment provides for the creation of a board of inquiry if a dispute threatens to interrupt health care in a particular community. The board members are appointed by the director of the Federal Mediation and Conciliation Service (FMCS) within 30 days after notification of either party's intention to terminate a labor contract. The board then has 15 days in which to investigate and report its findings and recommendations. The board's findings are intended to provide a framework for arbitrators' decisions. Once the report is filed with the FMCS, both parties in the dispute are expected to maintain the status quo for an additional 15 days.

The amendment also mandates certain notice requirements for labor groups in health care institutions. First, the institution must be given 90-days' notice of the expiration of a collective bargaining agreement and the Federal Mediation and Conciliation Service must be given 60-days' notice. Previously, only 60-days' notice to the employer and 30-days' notice to the FMCS were required. However, if the bargaining agreement is the initial contract between the parties, only 30-days' notice need be given to the FMCS.

During the period of notification, the FMCS must contact the parties and attempt to reach a settlement by mediation and conciliation. The

FMCS can invoke a 30-day "cooling off" period if it determines that a strike or lockout would "substantially interrupt" the continuity of health care in the community. The FMCS must establish a board of inquiry to investigate the issues and make a public report within 30 days of notification of the expiration of a contract or, in the case of an initial contract, within 10 days of notification of a bargaining impasse.

More significantly, 10-days' notice is required in advance of any strike, picketing, or other concerted refusal to work, regardless of the source of the dispute. Furthermore, this notification requirement applies even if the strike follows a 30-day cooling off period. This allows the NLRB to determine the legality of a strike before it occurs and also gives health care institutions ample time to ensure the continuity of patient treatment. However, any attempt to utilize this period to undermine the bargaining relationship is implicitly forbidden.

The 10 days of the strike notice may be concurrent with the final 10 days of the expiration notice. Any employee violation of these provisions amounts to an unfair labor practice and may automatically result in the discharge of the employee. In addition, injunctive relief may be available from the courts if the circumstances warrant such relief.

In summary, the amendment's provisions are designed to ensure that every possible approach to a peaceful settlement is fully explored before a strike is called in a hospital or other health care facility and to provide sufficient time for the health care provider to be prepared when a strike is imminent.

The two most important strike issues have been wages and length of the contract. (Contracts in the health care industry are usually for two years.) Other issues have been proper patient care, opportunities for continuing education and attendance of professional meetings, union security, vacations, holidays, hours of work, overtime, insurance, management prerogatives, and working conditions. Searce and Tanner provide a review of the experience of the FMCS during the first year following passage of the 1974 amendments in "Health Care Bargaining: The FMCS Experience" [*Labor Law Journal* 27, no. 7 (July 1976): 387-398].

The United States Department of Labor is funding projects to study the effects of the 1974 Amendments to the National Labor Relations Act. Results of one such study by Miller, Becker and Krinsky, discussed in their article, "Union Effects in Hospital Administration: Preliminary Results from a Three-State Study" [*Labor Law Journal* 28, no. 8 (August 1977): 515-519] show that as a general rule the rate of unionization tends to be positively correlated with hospital size, community size and nonreligious ownership. The only states included in this study were

Minnesota, Illinois and Wisconsin. The 1974 NLRA amendments had not markedly affected the level of unionization. Once the unions became established in the hospitals, there were few strikes and the parties continued to agree contractually to resolve their contract disputes by arbitration.

Reasons given for the low level of conflict are: (1) there has been only one dominant union in the area; (2) the mutual desire of unions and management to avoid conflict; (3) fear of public repercussions of hospital strikes; and (4) difficulty in organizing and maintaining strong hospital unions because of the nature of the work. Grievance procedures and arbitration were probably seldom used because hospital administrators endeavored to resolve employee problems quickly. Nonunion hospitals have attempted to resolve problems to avoid unionization. Unionized hospitals have endeavored to avoid discontented employees and their turning to more militant unions.

The study revealed that unionized hospitals experienced a 2% to 4% rise in the cost of operation due to unionization. The results of this study are based on information from three states and therefore do not represent nationwide trends; however, they do indicate that unions will probably not be a major factor in causing inflation of hospital costs. The discretion of hospital administrators in the operation of facilities was not significantly affected by unionization.

## Labor-Management Reporting and Disclosure Act

The Labor-Management Reporting and Disclosure Act of 1959 places controls upon labor unions and the relationships between unions and their members. In addition, it requires that employers report payments and loans to officials or other representatives of labor organizations or any promises to make such payments or loans. Payments to employees for the purpose of influencing the way they exercise their rights to organize and bargain collectively are illegal unless the employer discloses such payments at the time they are made. Expenditures with the object of interfering with employee rights to organize and bargain collectively as well as agreements with labor relations consultants under which such persons undertake to interfere with certain employee rights must also be disclosed.

Reports required under this law must be filed with the Secretary of Labor and are then made public. Both charitable and proprietary hospitals that make such payments or enter into such agreements must file the reports, but governmental hospitals are not subject to these provisions.

Penalties for failure to make the required reports, or for making false reports, include fines of as much as $10,000 and imprisonment for one year.

## Fair Labor Standards Act

The Fair Labor Standards Act establishes minimum wages and maximum hours of employment. The employees of all governmental, charitable, and proprietary hospitals are covered by this act, and hospitals must conform to the minimum wage and overtime pay provisions. However, bona fide executive, administrative, and professional employees are exempted from the wage and hour provisions.

For enforcement purposes, the Wage and Hour Division of the Department of Labor does not include, as employees, students in training at a hospital to become registered nurses, licensed practical nurses, radiologists, medical technologists, or other paramedical personnel, where on-the-job training is combined with classroom lectures and laboratory instruction to comprise an extensive program of education generally leading to licensing, registration or certification by a board or society. A scholarship or stipend granted a student as a subsistence allowance does not create an employment relationship. However, an employer-employee relationship may exist in the training of nurses' aides and ward attendants.

A hospital staff nurse who works as a private duty nurse outside her regular working hours, under contract with her patient as to compensation and conditions of employment, is not an employee of the hospital while working as a private nurse. There is an employer-employee relationship between the hospital and sitters where the hospital maintains a roster of persons available as sitters, provides the space for sitting, determines the rate which shall be charged, and determines which sitter shall be assigned to a specific patient and when the assignment shall be performed.

A patient worker is an ill, aged, mentally ill or mentally or physically handicapped individual who receives treatment or care by a hospital or residential care establishment, either as an in-patient or out-patient, and is employed by the health care facility in some capacity other than as a participant in a sheltered workshop program. In *Souder v. Brennan*, 367 F. Supp. 808 (D.D.C. 1973), the court stated that the test of employment is economic reality. If the institution derives any consequential economic benefits, the economic reality test indicates that an employment relationship, rather than a mere therapeutic exercise exists. A patient does not become an employee merely by performing personal housekeeping chores such as maintaining personal living quarters or by making crafts which, if sold, result in proceeds belonging to the patient, shared with those participating in the program or used to buy new materials. In *Weidenfeller v. Kiderlis*, 380 F. Supp. 445 (E.D. Wis. 1974), requiring a patient to work for the economic benefit of the health care facility without paying compensation for such services was held to be a violation of the Thirteenth Amendment's prohibition of slavery.

The reasonable cost or fair value of meals, lodging or other facilities customarily provided for the benefit of the employee may be considered wages unless excepted by a collective bargaining agreement. If the facilities are provided primarily for the employer's, rather than for the worker's benefit, their cost may not be included in computing wages.

Learners, apprentices, patient or resident workers, other handicapped workers and full-time students in retail or service establishments may be paid less than the minimum wage under certain conditions if special certificates are first obtained from the Administrator of the Wage and Hour Division of the United States Department of Labor. However, regular full-time employees must be paid the minimum wage.

The law permits hospitals to enter into agreements with employees, establishing an alternative work period of 14 consecutive days, rather than the usual seven-day week. If the alternative period is chosen, the hospital is required to pay the overtime rate only for any hours worked in excess of 80 hours during the 14-day period. However, the alternate 14-day work period does not relieve the hospital of its obligation to pay overtime for hours worked in excess of 8 in any one day, even if no more than 80 hours are worked during the period.

Under the equal pay provisions of the Fair Labor Standards Act, employers are prohibited from discriminating against any employee on the basis of sex. Work performed by female nurses' aides and male orderlies has been found equal within the meaning of the statute. Wage differential is permitted when it is based on such factors as seniority, merit, and quality or quantity of production. Labor organizations are prohibited from causing or attempting to cause an employer to discriminate against an employee in violation of equal pay provisions.

The Fair Labor Standards Act promotes the employment of older workers based on ability. Arbitrary age discrimination is prohibited. Persons between the ages of 40 and 65 are protected from age discrimination in employment. After January 1, 1979, the upper limit is age 70.

The employer is required to display a poster which displays an outline of the act's basic requirements. Records of required information must be preserved for three years and supplementary items, such as time cards, must be kept for two years.

## Equal Employment Opportunity

Title VII of the Civil Rights Act of 1964, as amended by the Equal Employment Opportunity Act of 1972, prohibits private employers and state and local governments from discriminating on the basis of race, color, religion, sex, or national origin. An exception to these prohibited employment practices may be permitted when religion, sex, or national origin is a bona fide occupational qualification necessary to the operation of a particular business or enterprise.

The act also exempts hospitals operated by religious corporations or societies, but only with respect to employees directly concerned with religious activities. However, practically all employment in hospitals operated by religious bodies is unrelated to religious activity.

Many states have enacted "protective" laws with respect to the employment of females. The EEOC guidelines on sex discrimination make it clear that state laws limiting the employment of females in certain occupations are superseded by Title VII and are no defense against a charge of sex discrimination.

## Age Discrimination in Employment Act

The Age Discrimination in Employment Act of 1967 prohibited discrimination on the basis of age against persons between the ages of 40 and 65 and legislation effective January 1, 1979 increases the upper age limit to 70. There are some exceptions to the prohibitions of this act, such as when age is a bona fide occupational qualification. Employment policies which grant salary increases less frequently to older workers have been considered a form of age discrimination.

## Child Labor

Under the provisions of the Fair Labor Standards Act, a minor 16 years of age may be employed in a hospital or residential care facility in any occupation except those declared hazardous by the Secretary of Labor which require a minimum age of 18. A minimum age of 18 is required for the driver of a motor vehicle and ambulance and for the helper. Minors 16 and 17 are permitted to drive motor vehicles on public highways if such driving is occasional and incidental to their regular jobs and all criteria are met. They may be helpers on motor vehicles if they ride in the cab with the driver. They may ride in the front of ambulances but not in the rear with the patient. A minimum age of 18 is required for occupations involving exposure to radioactive substances and for operation of nonautomatic elevators. Workers 16 and 17 may operate automatic and automatic signal type elevators; minors 14 and 15 may be employed in a variety of nonmanufacturing and nonhazardous occupations. Such employment must be outside of school hours between 7:00 A.M. and 7:00 P.M. except between June 1st through Labor Day when minors may work until 9:00 P.M. They may not work longer than 3 hours on a school day and 18 hours in a school week. They may work 8 hours on a nonschool day and 40 hours in a nonschool week. They may be employed as nurses' aides, maids, office and clerical help, and kitchen and cleaning personnel. Most laundry work requires a minimum age of 16.

Employers must obtain proof of age in accordance with regulations of the Secretary of Labor. The Act provides for enforcement by civil and criminal proceedings and the civil penalty is a maximum fine of $1,000 for each violation. If there is also a state law, the most stringent must be observed.

## Federal Agencies Administering Statutes and Orders Prohibiting Discrimination

The statutes and orders which prohibit discrimination are administered and enforced by the following federal agencies:

- The Equal Employment Opportunity Commission (EEOC), established by the Civil Rights Act of 1964, enforces the statutory prohibition against discrimination in employment based on race, color, religion, sex or national origin.

- The Department of Justice represents the Secretary of Labor in enforcing Executive Order 11246 prohibiting discrimination by government contractors and discrimination in federal grant programs, and it is responsible for litigation against state and local governments under Title VII of the Civil Rights Act.

- The Civil Service Commission (CSC) enforces the prohibition of discrimination in federal service and requires that each federal agency have an affirmative action plan in accordance with Section 717 of Title VII of the Civil Rights Act and Executive Order 11478 of August 12, 1969. The Commission also enforces the Age Discrimination in Employment Act and the Equal Pay Act in federal employment.

- The Office of Federal Contract Compliance Programs (OFCCP) in the Department of Labor administers and enforces Executive Orders 11246 and 11375 which prohibit discrimination in employment by government contractors on the basis of race, religion, national origin and sex and require affirmative action.

- The Wage and Hour Division of the Employment Standards Administration of the Department of Labor enforces the Equal Pay Act of 1963 (EPA), which provides the minimum wage an employer can pay and the Age Discrimination in Employment Act of 1967 (ADEA), which prohibits discrimination on the basis of age between the ages of 40 and 65, and after January 1, 1979, the upper limit of age 70.

## STATE LAWS

### State Labor-Management Relations Act

Since hospitals operated by the state or its political subdivisions are excluded from coverage in the LMRA the regulation of labor-management relations in these hospitals is left to state law. State laws vary considerably in their coverage, and often employees of state and local governmental hospitals are covered by separate public employee legislation. Some of these statutes cover both state and local employees, whereas others cover only state or only local employees.

Most states have no labor relations statutes. In these states, unless the state constitution guarantees the right of employees to organize and imposes the duty of collective bargaining on the employer, most hospitals would not be required to bargain collectively with their employees. In states that do have labor relations acts, the obligation of a hospital to bargain collectively with its employees is determined by the applicable statute.

A number of states have statutes similar to the Norris-LaGuardia Act, which restrict the granting of injunctions in labor disputes. There are anti-injunction acts in several other states which are different from this type, and decisions under them do not fall into an easily recognized pattern.

Of the states which have labor relations acts granting the employees of hospitals the right to organize, join unions, and bargain collectively, some states have specifically prohibited strikes and lockouts and have provided for compulsory arbitration whenever a collective bargaining contract cannot otherwise be executed amicably. Anti-injunction statutes would not forbid injunctions to restrain violations of these statutory provisions.

The courts have almost uniformly held that labor strife involving a charitable hospital does not constitute a labor dispute within the meaning of the anti-injunction acts. Where a proprietary hospital is involved, the courts may also decide that the anti-injunction act is inapplicable and may therefore grant an injunction. However, the determination would be based on the particular situation, rather than on any theory that all hospitals should be excluded.

The doctrine of federal preemption, as applied to labor relations, displaces the states' jurisdiction to regulate an activity that is arguably an unfair labor practice within the meaning of the LMRA. Despite the broad sweep of the doctrine of federal preemption, the U.S. Supreme Court has ruled that states can still regulate labor relations activity that also falls within the jurisdiction of the NLRB where deeply rooted local feelings and responsibility are affected. Thus, violence, threats of violence, mass picketing, and the obstruction of streets may be regulated by the states.

## Union Security Contracts and Right-to-Work Laws

Labor organizations frequently seek to enter into union security contracts with employers. There are two types of such contracts: the closed shop contract, which provides that only members of a particular union may be hired; and the union shop contract, which makes continued employment dependent upon membership in the union, although an employee need not have been a union member to apply for the job or to be hired.

More than one-third of all the states have made such contracts unlawful. Statutes for forbidding such agreements are generally called right-to-work laws on the theory that they protect everyone's right to work, regardless of union membership status. Several other state statutes or decisions purport to restrict union security contracts, or to require the completion of certain procedures before such agreements may be made.

## Anti-Discrimination Acts

State acts which prohibit discriminatory practices in employment are of little importance in light of the broad coverage of the federal equal employment opportunities provisions. All hospitals, except governmental hospitals, are employers under this federal statute and are therefore subject to its provisions. A few state statutes specifically prohibit discrimination because of age.

## Wage and Hour Laws

State legislation establishing minimum wage rates is also of minor importance considering the 1966 amendment to the federal Fair Labor Standards Act which provides that hospital personnel be covered by the act. Where state minimum wage standards are higher than federal standards, the state's standards are applicable to hospital employees.

## Child Labor Acts

Many states prohibit the employment of minors below a certain age and restrict the employment of other minors. Child labor legislation commonly requires that working papers be secured before a child may be hired, forbids the employment of minors at night, and provides that minors may not operate certain types of dangerous machinery.

This kind of legislation rarely exempts charitable hospitals, although some exceptions may be made with respect to the hours when student nurses may work.

## Regulation of Employee Occupational Health and Safety

Congress enacted the Occupational Safety and Health Act of 1970 to establish administrative machinery for the development and enforcement of standards for occupational health and safety. Standards developed for various industries (including hospitals) are mandatory for employers covered.

Information regarding hospital administration and regulation is available from the Joint Commission on Accreditation of Hospitals, the American Hospital Association, American Medical Association, National Safety Council, National Institutes of Health, and the Center for Disease Control. The OSHA requirements are in the General Industry Standards, Code of Federal Regulations, Title 29, Part 1910—Occupational Safety and Health Standards.

Under the laws of some states, employers are charged with the duty of furnishing employees with a safe place to work. Of course, even in the absence of such statutes, a hospital would be liable if employees were injured because of negligence in the care of the premises or the upkeep of equipment, unless the doctrine of charitable or governmental immunity were applicable, or unless the employees were covered by workmen's compensation.

In addition to provisions relating to safety, other state statutes require that certain facilities be provided for the employees. An example of such required facilities is lavatories. The city and county in which a hospital is located may also prescribe rules regarding the health and safety of employees. Many communities for example, have enacted sanitary health codes that require certain facilities or standards. In most instances, convenience and safety laws do not exempt charitable institutions.

## Workmen's Compensation

An employee who is injured while performing job-related duties may sue the employer for injuries suffered. State legislatures have recognized that it is difficult and expensive for employees to recover from their employers and have therefore enacted workmen's compensation laws.

Workmen's compensation laws provide a legal way for employees to obtain compensation for injuries on the job. The acts do not require the employee to prove that the injury was the result of the employer's negligence. Workmen's compensation laws are based on the employer-employee relationship and not on the theory of negligence.

The scope of workmen's compensation varies widely. Some states limit an employee's compensation to the amount recoverable as stipulated in the workmen's compensation law, and further lawsuits against the employer are barred. Other states permit the employee to choose whether to accept the compensation provided by law or institute a lawsuit against the employer. Some acts go further and provide a system of insurance which may be under the supervision of state or private insurers.

Recovery by an employee begins with a hearing on the claim before a board of commissioners. Following the hearing, the commissioners decide whether there was an employer-employee relationship, whether the injury is covered by the act, and whether there is a connection between the employment and the injury. The commissioners then award compensation according to a predetermined schedule based on the nature of the injury. Though the amount of compensation is generally not as high as might be recovered in a lawsuit for negligence, the employee is more likely to receive some compensation. Generally, workmen's compensation boards tend to be liberal in interpreting the law to provide compensation for employees.

# Chapter 11

# Insurance

Today, almost everyone has some form of insurance. People insure their automobiles against collision and theft, and maintain fire insurance on their homes. They insure their personal property, themselves, and the members of their family. Professional personnel also buy insurance to protect themselves from suit in the event that others are injured as a result of their professional services. Individual needs determine what kinds of insurance are purchased.

## DEFINITION

Insurance is a contract in which the insurer agrees to assume certain risks of the insured, in exchange for a premium. In the terms of the contract, also known as the insurance policy, the insurer promises to pay a specific amount of money if a specified event takes place. An insurance policy contains three necessary elements: (1) identification of the risk involved; (2) the specific amount payable; and (3) the specified occurrence.

A risk is the possibility that a loss will occur. The major function of insurance is to provide security against this loss. Insurance does not prevent or hinder the occurrence of the loss, but it does compensate for the damages.

There are three categories of risks to which an insured individual may be exposed: (1) risks of property loss or damage; (2) personal risks or loss of life; and (3) legal liability. Property risk is the possibility that an insured's property may be damaged or destroyed by fire, flood, tornado, hurricane, or other catastrophe. Personal risk is the possibility that the insured may be injured in an accident or may become ill or die. The typical life insurance plan insures against the possibility of death. Legal liability risk is the possibility that the insured may become legally liable to pay money damages to another. Accident and professional liability insurance cover legal liability risks.

## NURSING RISKS

A nurse who provides professional services to another person for pay may be legally responsible for any harm that the person suffers as a result of the nurse's negligence; furthermore, the nurse may be subject to a loss of money in the form of legally awarded damages. Many nurses protect themselves from the risk of a legal loss by acquiring a professional liability insurance policy. A student nurse may also be legally liable for any harm that stems from nursing negligence. For this reason some student nurses obtain professional liability insurance, similar in coverage to policies for registered nurses, in order to be protected in the event of legal losses.

## PROFESSIONAL LIABILITY INSURANCE POLICIES

A nurse who is covered by a professional liability insurance policy must recognize the rights and duties inherent in the policy. The nurse should be able to identify the risks that are covered, the amount of coverage, and the conditions of the contract.

Although coverage may vary in the policies of different insurance companies, the standard policy usually states that the insurance company will "pay on behalf of the insured all sums which the insured shall become legally obligated to pay as damages because of injury arising out of malpractice, error, or mistake in rendering or failing to render nursing services."

A standard liability insurance policy has five distinct parts: (1) the insurance agreement; (2) defense and settlement; (3) policy period; (4) amount payable; and (5) conditions. [For a sample policy and the ANA's Professional Liability Plan, see Appendix C.]

### Insurance Agreement

An insurance policy usually states that the insurer will pay, on behalf of the insured, all sums of money which the insured becomes legally liable to pay. The insurer, under the terms of the policy, has no obligation to pay any sum over and above the legal liability and will not pay a sum of money merely because the insured feels a moral obligation toward an injured party.

Under a professional liability policy, a nurse is protected from damages arising from rendering or failing to render nursing services. Thus, a nurse who performs a negligent act resulting in legal liability is personally protected from paying an injured party. The actual payment of the legal monetary damages to the injured party is accomplished by the insurer.

## Defense and Settlement

In the defense and settlement portion of the professional liability insurance policy, the nurse and the insurance company agree that the company will defend any lawsuit against the nurse arising from performance or nonperformance of nursing services, and that the company is delegated the power to effect a settlement of any claims as it deems necessary. A policy stating that the insurer will provide a defense of all lawsuits guarantees such a defense in any suit including those that are groundless, false, or fraudulent. In the case of a professional liability policy, the duty of the insurer under this clause is limited to the defense of lawsuits against the nurse which are a consequence of nursing services.

If an insurance company has established the right to obtain a settlement of any claim before trial, the company's only obligation is to act reasonably and not to the detriment of the insured.

## Policy Period

The period of coverage of the policy is always stated in the insurance contract. The contract provides protection only for risks that occur during the time when the policy is stated to be effective. Thus, any accident that occurred before or after the policy period would not be covered under the insuring agreement.

## Amount Payable

The amount to be paid by the insurer is determined by the amount of damage suffered by the injured party. This determination may be made by a jury or by the insurance company, and the injured party may obtain a settlement before a lawsuit comes to trial or before the jury has determined the amount of damages. In any event, the insurance company will pay to the injured party no more than the maximum coverage stated in the insurance policy.

For example, if a jury determines that a nurse is liable to an injured person for $45,000, and the maximum coverage in the nurse's insurance policy is $40,000, the insurance company will pay only $40,000 to the injured party. The remaining $5,000 must be provided by the nurse from other resources.

Another example is the policy whose maximum coverage is $40,000 for each claim and $120,000 for aggregate claims. Under this policy, the aggregate claims figure is the total amount payable to all injured parties. Thus, the insured is protected on each individual claim up to $40,000; when there is more than one claim, the insured is protected up to $40,000 on each of three claims. If there were more than three claims, the aggregate $120,000 would be spread across all claims, but payment would not exceed $40,000 on any one claim.

## Conditions of the Policy

Each insurance policy contains a number of important conditions, and failure to comply with these conditions may result in forfeiture of the policy and nonpayment of claims against it. Generally, insurance policies contain the following conditions:

1. *Notice of occurrence.* When the insured becomes aware that an injury has occurred as a result of acts covered under the contract, the insured must promptly notify the insurance company. The form of notice may be either oral or written, as specified in the policy.

2. *Notice of claim.* Whenever the insured receives notice that a claim or suit is being instituted, notice must be sent promptly by the insured to the insurance company. The policy will specify what papers are to be forwarded to the company.

3. *Assistance of the insured.* The insured must cooperate with the insurance company and render any assistance necessary to reach a settlement.

4. *Other insurance.* If the insured has pertinent insurance policies with other insurance companies, the insured must notify the insurance company so that each company may pay the appropriate amount of the claim.

5. *Assignment.* The protections contracted for by the insured may not be transferred unless permission is granted by the insurance company. The insurance company will endeavor to avoid protecting persons other than the policyholder since the risks of other persons were not taken into account when the policy was issued.

6. *Subrogation.* Subrogation is the right of a person who pays another's debt to be substituted for all rights of the other person in relation to the debt. When an insurance company makes a payment for the insured under the terms of the policy the company becomes the beneficiary of all the rights of recovery which the insured has against any other persons who may also have been negligent. For example, if several nurses were found liable for negligence arising out of the same occurrence, and the insurance company for one nurse pays the entire claim, the company will be substituted for the rights of that nurse and may collect a proportionate share of the claim from the other nurses.

7. *Changes.* The insured cannot make changes in the policy without the written consent of the insurance company. Thus, an agent of the insurance company usually cannot modify or remove any condition of the liability contract. Only the insurance company, by written authorization, may permit a condition to be altered or removed.

8. *Cancellation.* A cancellation clause spells out the conditions and procedures necessary for the insured or the insurer to cancel the liability policy. Written notice is usually required. The insured person's failure to comply with any of the conditions may result in nonpayment of a claim by the insurance company. An insurance policy is a contract, and failure to meet the terms and conditions of the contract may result in the penalties associated with breach of contract, such as nonpayment of claims.

## MEDICAL PROFESSIONAL LIABILITY INSURANCE

The fundamental tenets of insurance law and its application to the typical liability insurance policy are pertinent to the provisions of medical professional liability insurance as applied to individuals and institutions.

Professional liability policies vary in the broadness of the insuring clauses, the exclusions from coverage, and the interpretations a company places on language of the contract.

There are three medical professional liability classes:

1. Individuals, including (but not limited to) physicians, surgeons, dentists, nurses, osteopaths, chiropodists, chiropractors, opticians, physiotherapists, optometrists, and various types of medical technicians. This category may also include medical laboratories, blood banks, and optical establishments.

2. Hospitals and related institutions, such as extended care facilities, homes for the aged, institutions for the mentally ill, sanitariums, and

other health institutions where bed and board are provided for patients or residents.

3. Clinics, dispensaries, and infirmaries where there are no regular bed or board facilities. These institutions may be related to industrial or commercial enterprises. However, this class does not include facilities operated by dentists or physicians, which are usually covered under individual professional liability contracts.

The insuring clause will usually provide for payment on behalf of the insured if an injury arises from:

1. Malpractice, error, or mistake in rendering or failing to render professional services in the practice of the insured's profession during the policy period.

2. Acts or omissions during the policy period on the part of the insured as a member of a formal accreditation or similar professional board or committee of a hospital or a professional society.

The "injury" is not limited to bodily injury or property damage. However, the injury must result from malpractice, error, mistake, or the failure to perform acts that should have been performed.

The most common risks covered by medical professional liability insurance are negligence, assault and battery from failing to obtain consent to a medical or surgical procedure, libel and slander, and invasion of privacy for betrayal of professional confidences. Coverage varies from company to company because of differences in the interpretation of the same or similar language. The premium rates for each state are generally established by the state legislature, and the rates differ for individuals, hospitals, and clinics.

Many states have passed recent legislation in an effort to alleviate the malpractice crisis. Such statutes provide for agreements to arbitrate before bringing legal actions into the courts. Some provide for malpractice insurance through the state and set forth the conditions of coverage, and the procedure for processing claims. These statutes may also provide for the establishment of medical review panels and a risk management authority.

The institution of a medical review panel and the prohibition of *ad damnum* clauses were held to be constitutional in *Everett v. Goldman,* 359 So.2d 1256 (La. Sup. Ct., 1978). An *ad damnum* clause is a statement in the pleading of a case of the money loss or damages claimed. (See Appendix C for the Louisiana medical malpractice statute, a typical state malpractice statute.)

# Part III

# The Nurse and Society

# Chapter 12

# Civil Rights

Civil rights are rights assured by the Constitution of the United States and by acts of Congress and state legislatures. Generally, the term includes all the rights of each individual in a free society. Nurses will be specifically interested in three major areas of law which deal with civil rights. First, the Civil Rights Act of 1964 contains provisions relating to hospitals. Second, the Hill-Burton Act stipulates certain requirements for hospitals receiving aid under its program. And third, some state laws deal with discriminatory admission policies in hospitals and other health facilities, which often directly involve nurses.

Nurses share a hospital's legal responsibility in the enforcement of civil rights. In dealing with patients, visitors, and fellow employees, nurses are prohibited from making discriminatory distinctions based on race, color, religion, sex, or national origin.

## DISCRIMINATION

### Federal Regulations

Discriminatory practices in hospitals and other health facilities have been dealt with by Congress and the federal courts. Discrimination in the admission of patients and the segregation of patients on racial grounds is, for all practical purposes, proscribed in any hospital receiving federal financial assistance. Pursuant to Title VI of the Civil Rights Act of 1964, the guidelines of the Department of Health, Education and Welfare (HEW) require that there be no racial discrimination practiced by any hospital or agency receiving money under any program supported by HEW. This includes all hospitals which are "providers of service" receiving federal funds under Medicare legislation.

133

According to the Fourteenth Amendment to the Constitution, a state cannot act so as to deny to any person equal protection under the laws. If a state or a political subdivision of a state, whether through its executive, judicial, or legislative branch, acts in any way which unfairly denies to one person the rights accorded to another, the amendment has been violated. The acts of the executive, judicial, and legislative branches of government encompass the acts of government agencies as well, and "state action" has been extended to include activities of nongovernmental entities under certain circumstances. For example, if the state supports or authorizes an activity for the benefit of the public, it is possible that a nongovernmental institution engaging in such activity may be considered to be engaged in state action and subject to the Fourteenth Amendment.

Considering the constitutional requirements together with the HEW guidelines and Title II of the Civil Rights Act of 1964, which prohibits discrimination in restaurants and other places of public accommodation and thus, may include restaurants in hospitals, it is apparent that racial discrimination is prohibited in practically all hospitals.

The Civil Rights Act of 1964 is particularly important to nurses because it provides that a hospital must treat nurses, along with patients, physicians, and other employees, in a nondiscriminatory manner. Title VII makes it illegal to deny equal job opportunities on the basis of race, color, religion, sex, or national origin; it also prohibits a nurse, as an employee of the hospital, from discriminating against patients, physicians, or fellow employees.

## State Regulations

Most states have enacted laws to protect the civil rights of their citizens. Some of these statutes declare that life, liberty, and the pursuit of happiness should not be denied; others adhere closely to the language of federal civil rights legislation.

For example, the *Massachusetts* Civil Rights Act forbids discrimination in places of "public accommodation, resort or amusement" against persons who belong to any religious sect, creed, class, race, color, sex, denomination, or nationality. The statute defines the phrase "place of public accommodation, resort or amusement" to include hospitals, dispensaries, and clinics operating for profit. However, it excludes places owned or operated by any religious, racial, or denominational institution or organization, as well as any organization operated for charitable or educational purposes.

The *Pennsylvania* Human Relations Act is somewhat similar to the *Massachusetts* act in that it specifically includes dispensaries, clinics, and hospitals with its definition of public accommodation, resort or amusement. But the *Pennsylvania* Act does not apply to distinctly private institutions.

*Missouri's* act is not as specific as either the *Pennsylvania* or *Massachusetts* acts. It does not specifically mention hospitals with its coverage. However, the phrase "places of public accommodation" would seem to include hospitals, since the definition includes all places or businesses offering services, facilities, and accommodations for the peace, comfort, health, welfare, and safety of the general public.

Some state laws still require separation of the races or other discriminatory practices in governmental and private institutions, including hospitals. The methods and manner of discrimination vary. Although these laws remain on the books, they are not valid. If they were attacked in the courts, they would undoubtedly be ruled unconstitutional.

## THE HILL-BURTON ACT

The Hospital Survey and Construction Act, popularly known as the Hill-Burton Act, provides that any hospital receiving funds from this program must make a reasonable number of services available to persons unable to pay. Regulations promulgated by the Department of Health, Education and Welfare in July 1972 established numerical guidelines for what the Hill-Burton Act refers to as a "reasonable volume of services." While these guidelines do not require that any particular person who is unable to pay be admitted, they do require that at least some amount of services be provided to this group by every hospital that has received Hill-Burton funds. See *Saine v. Hospital Authority of Hall County*, 502 F.2d 1033 (5th Cir. 1974). In addition, the act authorizes federal assistance for the construction of public and nonprofit hospitals and public health centers in conjunction with state-approved construction programs, provided that state and local resources help to build and maintain the new facilities.

The provisions of the act and its corresponding regulations have been interpreted by the courts to require a policy of nondiscrimination in the administration and use of the facilities constructed, renovated, or maintained under authorized state-approved construction programs. Thus, hospitals receiving Hill-Burton funds are subject to the Fifth and Fourteenth Amendments.

In *Simkins v. Moses H. Cone Memorial Hopsital*, 323 F.2d 959 (4th Cir. 1963), a federal court held that two hospitals were prohibited from denying appointments to physicians on the basis of race. The court also prohibited the hospitals from refusing to admit patients or segregating patients on the basis of race.

In *Smith v. Hampton Training School for Nurses,* 360 F.2d 577 (4th Cir. 1966), a federal court reviewed a case involving the dismissal of Negro nurses for eating in the all-white cafeteria of a hospital receiving federal assistance under the Hill-Burton Act. The court relied heavily on the *Simkins* case in deciding that the dismissal constituted unlawful discrimination on the part of the hospital.

The *Smith* case clearly illustrates that the prohibition against discrimination in employment is not satisfied by merely hiring members of a minority group. Once a member of a minority group has been hired, the employer has a continuing duty to treat that person fairly and on an equal basis with all other employees. In the *Smith* case, this duty was clearly neglected when Negro nurses were not allowed to eat in the cafeteria where other nurses ate.

## HOSPITAL ADMISSION

Although nurses are not directly concerned with the legal aspects of the admission of hospital patients, in certain situations nurses have been found liable for discrimination in admission practices.

Usually no legal problems arise when a hospital accepts a person through formal arrangements made beforehand by the person's physician. On the other hand, there may be legal difficulties when a hospital does not want to treat an individual who presents himself to the emergency service of the hospital or a patient recommended for admission by a physician with admitting privileges.

The courts have been reluctant to depart from the traditional view that no person has a positive right to be admitted to a hospital. Generally, this reluctance has been displayed with respect to charitable and governmental as well as proprietary hospitals. Discrimination in admission practices on the basis of race, color, creed, sex, or national origin may constitute a violation of laws forbidding discrimination. Yet such provisions merely forbid the use of these criteria; they do not establish a positive right to be admitted. In judicial decisions, the courts have displayed a marked tendency to adhere to the traditional view but have found other bases for imposing a duty upon hospitals to admit persons for care under various circumstances.

Statutes and hospital regulations which require a period of residency within a state as a basis for eligibility for admission to a public hospital have been held unconstitutional since such requirements deny the equal protection guaranteed by the Fourth Amendment.

## Governmental Hospitals

Whether a person is entitled to admission to a particular governmental hospital depends on the statute establishing that hospital. Governmental hospitals are, by definition, the creatures of some unit of government, and their primary concern is service to the population within the jurisdiction of that unit. In all cases a person must have some connection with the unit operating the hospital to be entitled to use the hospital facilities. Some of the statutes cover all inhabitants of the geographic area and, in addition, are broad enough to apply to any person within the area who falls ill or suffers traumatic injury and requires hospital care. However, many of the statutes purport to limit the use of hospital facilities to residents of the governmental unit operating the hospital.

The statutes which create governmental hospitals sometimes describe the facilities as existing for the benefit of the indigent sick residents of the area. Indigency usually refers to the inability of a patient, or the persons legally responsible for the patient's support, to pay for hospital care. Admission procedures thus encompass the determination of the patient's financial status. This may vary from an affidavit, or a certification by the patient or physician, to a general investigation by an agency of the hospital or a separate social welfare agency.

Not all governmental hospitals are limited to indigent patients. Many are specifically authorized to admit both paying and nonpaying patients. In order to be admitted, a patient must meet the legal requirements for admission, and the patient's physical condition must warrant hospital care. Governmental hospitals that are operated as general hospitals may limit their facilities, in the same way that charitable and proprietary hospitals do, by excluding certain persons on the basis of the ailment or the care required. Contagious diseases, such as tuberculosis and certain venereal diseases, are commonly excluded because it has been found to be more efficient to treat them in special hospitals or special units. The admission of mental patients is usually restricted to hospitals with special facilities for such patients. Some statutes provide that where there is a clear need for immediate hospital care to preserve life or to prevent permanent injury, the hospital need not comply with specified preadmission procedural requirements, such as proof of indigency, before admitting a patient. Once a governmental hospital has rendered assistance to a person seeking emergency treatment, it must continue treatment in accordance with the applicable standard of care.

Patients admitted to governmental hospitals may be permitted to remain in the hospital for a longer period of time than patients in private facilities where costs are considered in determining the length of hospitalization. A paraplegic patient admitted to a United States Public Health Service hospital because of a spinal cord injury was permitted to remain in the hospital for three and a half years as a kindness to the patient. The patient eventually received an award of $500,000 from the party who caused his injury. At the government's request the patient's attorney agreed to and did recover from the tortfeasor, that is the one who caused the injury, money for medical treatment to which the government was entitled under the Medical Care Recovery Act. After recovering the money, the patient and his attorney refused to pay the government, and the government filed suit. The patient then sued the government for malpractice alleging, as one basis for his action, that he was wrongfully kept at the hospital as a patient for three and a half years. He alleged that the amount of the charges for medical treatment was unreasonable because he should have been sent to a spinal cord injury center and discharged within six months after his initial injury. The case was settled at a loss to the government.

Although persons who are not within the statutory classes have no right of admission, hospitals and their employees have a duty to extend reasonable care to those who present themselves for assistance and are in need of immediate attention. With respect to such persons, governmental hospitals are subject to the same rules that apply to nongovernmental hospitals.

## Nongovernmental Hospitals

According to common law, an individual has no right to aid from another individual or from a hospital. Thus, the law imposes no affirmative duty on an uninvolved stranger to go to the aid of another person, even when that person is in obvious distress. In *Le Jeune Road Hospital, Inc. v. Watson,* 171 So.2d 202 (Fla. 1965), the *Florida* Supreme Court recognized the following common law principle: "Harsh as this rule may sound, it is permissible for a private hospital to reject for whatever reason, or no reason at all, any applicant for medical and hospital services ...."

However, once control over the person is exercised, merely stating that there was no duty to act does not relieve an individual or a hospital of liability if the person is harmed as the result of unreasonable conduct. The exercise of control subjects a hospital and its employees to a duty which can be discharged only by acting in accordance with the appropriate standard of care. Most of the litigation defining when the duty to act arises has revolved around charitable hospitals, but there have been no decisions to suggest that private, for-profit hospitals will be judged according to a different standard.

Also, if an individual's conduct, although not negligent, is responsible for an injury, then a duty exists either to make a reasonable effort to render assistance or to desist from aggravating the original injury. If the original injury is aggravated, liability will be imposed only for the aggravation, rather than for both the original injury and its aggravation.

## Responsibility to Emergency Patients

The original Hill-Burton legislation required that each state submit a plan which would provide adequate hospitals and other facilities for all persons residing within its boundaries. The 1970 amendments to the act place a special emphasis on emergency service. Each hospital's emergency department would be considered in the development of the state plan for providing emergency care for its citizens. Consequently, state legislation imposing upon hospitals a duty to provide emergency care is increasing. These statutes implicitly, and sometimes explicitly, require that hospitals provide some degree of emergency service. However, the courts have established a clear mandate that hospitals must admit all patients seeking emergency care.

For example, in *Hill v. Ohio County,* 468 S.W.2d 306 (Ky. 1971), a pregnant woman approached a nurse working at her desk in the Ohio County Hospital in *Kentucky* and stated that she was afraid she would not be able to get back to her physician in Illinois before she delivered her baby. Two of the four members of the hospital's medical staff were called to authorize admission, but both refused to do so. That night, after the woman left the hospital, her baby was born at home, unattended. An ambulance rushed her to Owensboro Hospital about 25 miles from the defendant hospital, but she was dead on arrival. The Court held:

> In the instant case, the decedent was not admitted to the hospital nor was the element of critical emergency apparent. The hospital nurse acted in accordance with valid rules for admission to the facility. The uncontradicted facts demonstrate that no breach of duty by the hospital occurred.

Therefore, the hospital and the nurse were entitled to dismissal of the suit as a matter of law.

The rationale of the *Delaware* Supreme Court's decision in *Wilmington General Hospital v. Manlove*, 54 Del. 15, 174 A.2d 135 (1961), was based upon a finding of an invitation to the patient to seek emergency care from the hospital. The case concerned the refusal of a nurse on emergency duty in Wilmington General Hospital, a charitable hospital, to examine or treat an infant who had been suffering from diarrhea and a high temperature. The nurse tried to reach the child's physician but failed and then instructed the parents to bring the child back the next day when the pediatric clinic was open. The child died several hours later. The court held that where a private hospital maintains an emergency unit, refusal to render service to a person in an "unmistakable emergency" may give rise to liability when such refusal causes injury. What constitutes an unmistakable emergency is itself a difficult question.

The distinction between the *Wilmington General Hospital* case and similar cases is the judicial recognition that a hospital, even a charitable hospital, which maintains an emergency service may not refuse to give treatment without any valid reason to one who appears to, and in fact does, require emergency attention. The underlying theory of this position is that during the time when a person is making a fruitless attempt to obtain aid at the hospital, his condition may be deteriorating. Thus, the court applied the principle that the hospital's operation of an emergency service constitutes an invitation to those in need of aid.

In *Stanturf v. Sipes*, 447 S.W.2d 558 (Mo. 1969), the *Missouri* Supreme Court reversed a judgment in favor of the defendant, a hospital administrator who had refused to allow a patient to be admitted because of inability to pay a $25 admission charge. The patient had suffered frostbite of both feet. The court held that the hospital "was the only hospital in the immediate area, it maintained an emergency service, and . . . plaintiff applied for emergency treatment and was refused . . ."

> The members of the public . . . had reason to rely on the [hospital], and in this case it could be found that plaintiff's condition was caused to be worsened by the delay resulting from the futile efforts to obtain treatment from the . . . [h]ospital.

In *Thomas v. Corso*, 265 Md. 84, 288 A.2d 379 (1972), the *Maryland* court sustained a verdict against the hospital and a physician. The patient was brought to the hospital emergency room after being struck by a car. However, he was not personally attended by a physician although he was in shock, as indicated by dangerously low blood pressure. There was some telephone contact between the nurse in the emergency department and the physician, who was providing on-call coverage, but the physician did not come to the hospital until the patient was close to death.

The court reasoned that expert testimony was not even necessary to establish what common sense made evident: that a patient who had been struck by a car may have suffered internal injuries and should have been evaluated and treated by a physician. Lack of attention in such cases is not reasonable care by any standard. The concurrent negligence of the nurse, who failed to contact the on-call physician after the patient's condition had worsened, did not relieve the physician of liability for his failure to come to the emergency department at once. Rather, under the doctrine of *respondeat superior,* the nurse's negligence was a basis for holding the hospital liable as well.

The doctrine of *respondeat superior* imposes liability upon the hospital, as an employer, for the legal wrongs of its employees which occur during the furtherance of the employer's enterprise. Imposing liability in this way is justified because the burden of recompensing the person injured is more easily borne by the employer and also because in theory the employer's liability is motivation to supervise employees closely.

Another automobile accident emergency case, *Citizens Hospital Association v. Schoulin,* 48 Ala. 101, 262 So.2d 303 (1972), reached a conclusion similar to that of the *Thomas* case. This accident victim sued the hospital and the attending physician for their negligence in failing to discover and properly treat his injuries. The court held the hospital liable because its employee failed to communicate properly to the on-call physician and failed to discover, within a reasonable time after admission, that the patient had a broken back.

## A Patient's Bill of Rights

Following a three-year study by the American Hospital Association's board of trustees and four consumer representatives, the AHA Bill of Rights was approved as a national policy statement and most hospitals adopted the statement. The rights are:

1. The patient has the right to considerate and respectful care.
2. The patient has the right to obtain from his physician complete current information concerning his diagnosis, treatment, and prognosis in terms the patient can be reasonably expected to understand. When it is not medically advisable

to give such information to the patient, the information should be made available to an appropriate person in his behalf. He has the right to know, by name, the physician responsible for his care.

3. The patient has the right to receive from his physician information necessary to give informed consent prior to the start of any procedure and/or treatment. Except in emergencies, such information for informed consent should include but not necessarily be limited to the specific procedure and/or treatment, the medically significant risks involved, and the probable duration of incapacitation. Where medically significant alternatives for care or treatment exist, or when the patient requests information concerning medical alternatives, the patient has the right to such information. The patient also has the right to know the name of the person responsible for the procedures and/or treatment.

4. The patient has the right to refuse treatment to the extent permitted by law and to be informed of the medical consequences of his action.

5. The patient has the right to every consideration of his privacy concerning his own medical care program. Case discussion, consultation, examination, and treatment are confidential and should be conducted discretely. Those not directly involved in his care must have the permission of the patient to be present.

6. The patient has the right to expect that all communications and records pertaining to his care should be treated as confidential.

7. The patient has the right to expect that within its capacity a hospital must make reasonable response to the request of a patient for services. The hospital must provide evaluation, service, and/or referral as indicated by the urgency of the case. When medically permissible, a patient may be transferred to another facility only after he has received complete information and explanation concerning the needs for and alternatives to such a transfer. The institution to which the patient is to be transferred must first have accepted the patient for transfer.

8. The patient has the right to obtain information as to any relationship of his hospital to other health care and educational institutions insofar as his care is concerned. The pa-

tient has the right to obtain information as to the existence of any professional relationships among individuals, by name, who are treating him.

9. The patient has the right to be advised if the hospital proposes to engage in or perform human experimentation affecting his care or treatment. The patient has the right to refuse to participate in such research projects.

10. The patient has the right to expect reasonable continuity of care. He has the right to know in advance what appointment times and physicians are available and where. The patient has the right to expect that the hospital will provide a mechanism whereby he is informed by his physician of the patient's continuing health care requirements following discharge.

11. The patient has the right to examine and receive an explanation of his bill regardless of source of payment.

12. The patient has the right to know what hospital rules and regulations apply to his conduct as a patient.

## Rights of the Mentally Ill

In *Wyatt v. Adehold,* 503 F. 2d 1305 (5th Cir. 1974), and in *O'Connor v. Donaldson,* 493 F.2d 507 (5th Cir., 1974) remanded 95 S. Ct. 2486 (1975), the Fifth Circuit Court of Appeals held that civilly committed mental patients have a constitutional right to such individual treatment as will help each to be cured or improve his or her mental condition. The only permissible justification for civil commitments and abridgment of constitutionally protected liberties entailed thereby are danger of the individual to himself or to others or the individual's need for treatment and care. Where justification for involuntary commitment is treatment, fundamental rights of due process are offended if treatment is not provided. Where justification for involuntary commitment is danger of the patient to himself or herself or to others, treatment must be provided as the quid pro quo, or mutual consideration, and society must pay for the extra safety it derives from the denial of the individual's liberty.

## Rights of Drug Abusers to Medical Treatment

Persons who are mentally ill as a result of the abuse of drugs often have difficulty in obtaining treatment of their illness. They may too often seek commitment without success. Since the passage of the Harrison Narcotic Act in 1914, narcotic addicts have been classified as criminals and the medical profession has, for the most part, abdicated its role in the treatment of drug abuse. In many cities in the United States, no facilities are available for the treatment of drug abuse. Although methadone maintenance is recognized as a treatment modality, opposition to this method of treatment has resulted in a failure to provide facilities in areas having a high incidence of addiction. Many communities refuse to admit that a drug abuse problem exists and therefore refuse to establish proper treatment programs. Federal grant funds have been given to poorly operated treatment programs resulting in a bad investment of the taxpayers' dollars and disenchantment with any hope of successful treatment of drug abusers.

The Community Mental Health Centers Act was amended to add that if an application for a grant under this part for a community mental health center is made for any fiscal year beginning after June 30, 1972, the Secretary of Health, Education and Welfare is to determine whether it is feasible for the center to provide a treatment and rehabilitation program for addicts and other drug abusers residing in the area served by the center and whether the need in that area is of such magnitude as to warrant conduction of such a program by the center. The application is not to be approved unless there is assurance that the center may be used to the maximum extent practicable in treatment and rehabilitation programs.

No private or public general hospital which receives support in any form from any program financed in whole or in part by funds appropriated to any federal department or agency, may refuse to admit any patient suffering with an emergency medical condition solely because of suspected drug abuse. If, after a hearing, a hospital continues to violate this provision, all or part of the support received from any program administered by the Secretary of Health, Education and Welfare may be suspended or revoked. However, whether these statutes are being enforced is questionable.

# Chapter 13

# Legal Reporting Obligations

Every society wishes the best possible environment for its members. Government acts as an agent of society in protecting its people through health regulations and statutes. Only through reliable observations and reports can proper measures be instituted to safeguard the environment of the society. Therefore, the role of nurses or any other medical professionals is very important. Because medical professionals are in a position to observe and gather information about diseases, parental neglect, mistreatment of individuals, and criminal acts, every professional has an obligation to relay this information to the appropriate authority so that corrective measures can be taken.

Health statutes requiring that certain information be transmitted to governmental officials are of prime importance to nurses. Although most statutory reporting requirements do not contain an express immunity from suit for unauthorized disclosure, the person making the report under statutory command will, as a general rule, be protected by the doctrine of privilege. Reporting statutes are the legal means by which the states regulate the health, welfare, and safety of their citizens through the exercise of the state's general police power.

## ABUSED CHILDREN

The physically abused or neglected child is a medical, social, and legal problem. Determining whether a child has been abused is difficult because it is often impossible to ascertain whether the child was injured intentionally or accidentally. Even the legal definition of a child varies. In one state a 12-year-old is an adult in the eyes of the law; in another state an 18-year-old is legally still a child. To compound the confusion, some state laws apply to minors but do not define "a minor," and others use the word "child" without further definition.

There was a time when health practitioners had good reason to avoid reporting their suspicions about injured children. Anyone who made a report of child abuse to the proper authorities could have been sued by the child's parents on the basis that the report was a defamation of the parents' character or an invasion of their privacy. Health practitioners could also have been liable for money damages if their suspicions were proved wrong.

Today, however, all of the states and the *District of Columbia* have enacted laws to protect abused children. Furthermore, almost all states protect the persons required to report cases of child abuse. [For a summary of child abuse laws, see Appendix E.]

The various laws differ in their definition of an abused child. Generally, an abused child is one who has had serious physical injury inflicted by other than accidental means. The injuries may have been inflicted by a parent or any other person responsible for the child's care. Some states extend the definition to include a child suffering from starvation. Other states include moral neglect in the definition of abuse. For example, *Arizona* mentions immoral associations; *Idaho* includes endangering the child's morals; and *Mississippi* describes being found in a disreputable place or associating with vagrant, vicious, or immoral persons as a form of moral neglect. Sexual abuse is also enumerated as an element of neglect in the statutes of a few states.

Most state laws require certain people to report suspected cases of abuse. In a few states, although they are not required to report instances of child abuse, certain identified individuals who do so are protected. The child abuse laws may or may not provide penalties for failure to report. The classification of individuals covered by the various statutes ranges from physicians to "any person." Many of the statutes specifically include nurses.

Any report of child abuse must be made with a good faith belief that the facts reported are true. What "good faith" means is ultimately up to a court when deciding a law suit which involves child abuse statutes. But, when a health practitioner's medical evaluation establishes reasonable cause to believe a child's injuries were not accidental, making the report will not result in liability.

All abused child statutes provide protection from civil suit for anyone making or participating in a good faith report. Most states also provide immunity from criminal liabilty, and, in states that do not, it is extremely unlikely that anyone making a good faith report of suspected child abuse would be subject to criminal liability.

Reporting laws specify the nature and content of the report of child abuse. Almost all the statutes require that when a person covered by statute is attending a child as a staff member of a hospital or similar institution, and child abuse is suspected, the staff member must notify the person in charge of the institution, who in turn makes the necessary report. Typical statutes provide that an oral report be made immediately, followed as soon as possible by a written report. Most states require that the report contain the following information: the name and address of the child, the persons responsible for the child's care, the child's age, the nature and extent of the child's injuries (including any evidence of previous injuries), and any other information that might be helpful in establishing the cause of the injuries and the identity of the perpetrator.

## DISEASES IN NEWBORNS

Many states require anyone in attendance at birth to report, either to the physician in charge or to an appropriate health officer, all instances of diarrhea, staphylococcal disease, or other infections. Most states provide for penalizing any violator of these laws.

In particular, health personnel must report inflammation, swelling, redness, or unnatural discharge from an infant's eyes. The *Rhode Island* statute is typical:

§23-13-6 REPORTS OF OPHTHALMIA NEONATORUM
It shall be the duty of any physician, midwife, nurse, parent or other person or persons assisting any woman in childbirth or assisting in the care of any infant to report within twelve (12) hours after noting the same, any such case of ophthalmia neonatorum coming to his or her attention, to the department of health.

Statutory reporting requirements are made under each state's police power. A state requires treatment of ophthalmia neonatorum because public funds might have to be used to train or care for blind children, as well as because the state is interested in maintaining the health of its citizens.

## PHENYLKETONURIA IN NEWBORNS

Phenylketonuria (PKU) is one of the most recent additions to the list of reportable conditions. Actually, the chief purpose of the reporting requirements is to encourage the testing and treatment of infants for PKU. Some statutes, such as *Louisiana's,* require a report to an appropriate health agency if tests reveal PKU in an infant. Louisiana also has a similar requirement concerning sickle cell anemia:

> Part XV. Phenylketonuria: Meniscocytosis
> §1299.1   Tests
>
> A.  The physician attending a newborn child, or the person attending a newborn child that was not attended by a physician, shall cause said child to be subjected to a phenylketonuria test that has been approved by the State Department of Public Health; provided, however, no such test shall be given to any child whose parents object thereto. If the test is positive the attending physician or person shall notify the State Department of Public Health. The State Department of Public Health shall follow up all positive tests with the attending physician who notified the department thereof and with the parents of the newborn child when such notification was made by a person other than a physician, and, when confirmed, the services and facilities of the said State Department of Public Health, and those of other state boards, departments and agencies cooperating with the Department of Public Health in carrying out the program shall be made available to the extent needed by the family and physician. The State Department of Public Health and the other state departments and agencies cooperating with it shall, in cooperation with the attending physician, provide for the continued medical care, dietary and other related needs of such children, where necessary or desirable.
>
> B.  In addition to the test prescribed by Subsection A hereof, there shall be administered to a newborn child a test for meniscocytosis, commonly known as sickle cell anemia; provided, however, that no test shall be given to any child whose parents object thereto. The attending physician, or the person attending a newborn child who was not attended by a physician, shall cause said child to be subject to such test. If the test is positive the attending physician or person shall notify the State Department of Public Health. The department shall follow up

all positive tests with the attending physician who notified the department thereof and with the parents of the newborn child when such notification was made by a person other than a physician, and, when confirmed, shall inform the physician and/or parents of the services and facilities of the State Department of Public Health and those of other state boards, departments and agencies cooperating with the Department of Public Health in carrying out the program and in cooperation with the attending physician shall be made available to the extent needed by the family and physician to provide for the continued medical care, dietary and other related needs of such children where necessary or desirable which are now, or may hereafter become, available for the care and treatment of meniscocytosis. Amended by Acts 1972, No. 28, §1.

Many statutes provide that only parents may object to testing for PKU, and only on religious grounds.

The PKU statutes, as well as the statutes related to ophthalmia neonatorum and the Louisiana statute concerning sickle cell anemia illustrate the state's power to regulate preventive as well as corrective medicine.

Statutes providing for testing for genetic disorders before and after birth have been the subject of controversy. Dr James E. Bowman, Professor of Pathology and Director of the Comprehensive Sickle Cell Center of the University of Chicago, has stated in his article, "Ethical, Legal and Humanistic Implications of Sickle Cell Programs, La Dreparocytose, Sickle-Cell Anemia," JNSERM, 1975, Vol. 44, pp. 353-378, that too often in the effort to resolve genetic problems, there have been premature proposals and precipitous action in the name of progress, resulting in regression, not progress, and the result has been psychological, social and economic disaster. In his opinion, this has been particularly true of some sickle cell haemoglobin ventures.

Mandatory sickle cell screening laws have been passed in Massachusetts, the District of Columbia, Virginia, Maryland, New York, Illinois, Mississippi, Indiana, Kentucky, Georgia, Arizona and Louisiana. Questionable laws have been approved in some other states. Through a concerted effort of those opposed to such statutes, legislation has been passed repealing mandatory screening laws in New York, Illinois, Massachusetts, Maryland, the District of Columbia, Georgia, and Virginia.

Sickle haemoglobin is found in many groups in the United States and some persons classified as white are descendants of African ancestors. In Dr. Bowman's opinion, there is currently no public health jurisdiction for mandatory screening for prevention of genetic disease. Since genetic screening programs are in the realm of human experimentation, they should be conducted in accordance with guidelines of the Department of Health, Education and Welfare and the National Sickle Cell Anemia Control Act to protect research subjects.

## COMMUNICABLE DISEASES

Many states have enacted laws which require that actual or suspected cases of communicable disease be reported to the proper authorities. Although other persons are affected, the responsibility for reporting generally falls upon public health nurses. For example, a *New York* regulation provides:

> SANITARY CODE, Ch. 1, Sec. 2.12 (1973). Reporting by others than physicians of cases of diseases presumably communicable.
> When no physician is in attendance it shall be the duty of the head of a private household or the person in charge of any institution, school, motel, boarding house, camp or vessel or any public health nurse or any other person having actual knowledge of an individual affected with any disease presumably communicable, to report immediately the name and address of such person to the local health officer. Until official action on such case has been taken, strict isolation shall be maintained.

Statutes requiring the reporting of communicable diseases emphasize the need for such statutes. If the state is to protect its citizens' health through its power to quarantine, the state must have developed procedures insuring the prompt reporting of infection or disease.

## BIRTHS OUT OF WEDLOCK

The responsibility for reporting births out of wedlock does not fall primarily upon nurses. However, there are situations where a nurse may be the appropriate person to make the report. For example, *North Dakota* provides:

§50-20-03 RESPONSIBILITY FOR REPORTING
Births out of wedlock or with congential deformities which occur in a licensed maternity home or hospital shall be reported by the licensee of such home or hospital. All such births occurring outside of maternity homes or hospitals shall be reported by the legally qualified physician in attendance, or in the event of absence of a physician, by the registered nurse or other attendant.

A statute requiring the reporting of births enables a state to keep its records of births and deaths accurate.

## GUNSHOT WOUNDS

Gunshot wound laws require reports where injuries are inflicted by lethal weapons or, in some cases, by unlawful acts. Some statutes even include automobile accidents within their definition of lethal weapons. The *New York* statute is typical:

§265.25 CERTAIN WOUNDS TO BE REPORTED (Penal Law)
Every case of a bullet wound, gunshot wound, powder burn or any other injury arising from or caused by the discharge of a gun or firearm, and every case of a wound which is likely to or may result in death and is actually or apparently inflicted by a knife, icepick or other sharp or pointed instrument, shall be reported at once to the police authorities of the city, town or village where the person reporting is located by: (a) the physician attending or treating the case; or (b) the manager, superintendent or other person in charge, whenever such case is treated in a hospital, sanitarium or other institution . . . .

The connection of guns with crime makes this law a valid exercise of police power. Information provided by these reports is also useful for making statistical studies of crime.

## CRIMINAL ACTS

In addition to those subjects specified by statute as reportable, nurses may have a moral or legal duty to report to the police such acts as attempted suicide, assault, rape, or the unlawful dispensing or taking of narcotic drugs. Much of this information may be learned while caring for patients and would ordinarily be privileged communication. Therefore, care must be taken that only the police are given such information.

# Chapter 14

# Good Samaritan Laws

Most states have enacted good samaritan laws which relieve physicians, nurses, and in some instances laymen from liability in certain emergency situations. Good samaritan legislation encourages health professionals to render assistance at the scene of emergencies. By offering immunity, the laws attempt to overcome the widespread notion that physicians, nurses, and others who render assistance in an emergency are likely to be held liable for negligence.

## PURPOSE

State legislatures have enacted good samaritan statutes for a variety of legal, ethical, and moral reasons. It is a generally accepted legal principle that there is no *legal* duty to assist a stranger in a time of distress. However, if one person caused distress to another, the person causing distress does have a legal obligation to assist the person in distress. This principle extends to physicians, who are not legally bound to answer the call of strangers who are dying and might be saved. However, in our society it is a generally recognized *moral* duty to help a person in distress. Thus, physicians have a moral and ethical duty to respond to requests for assistance in medical emergencies. The statement of medical ethics of the American Medical Association includes a provision that recognizes this duty.

Regardless of the limits on legal duty to assist, the law does require that anyone who volunteers to aid another in distress assumes a legal responsibility to exercise reasonable care and skill in rendering such aid. Thus, the fact that a good samaritan acts in good faith and for no payment is immaterial. It is the act of giving aid that creates a duty and subjects the good samaritan to liability if there is a lack of due care. However, one who is confronted with a medical emergency is not held to the same standard of care normally applied in a nonemergency situation.

The first good samaritan law was passed in 1959 in *California* to encourage on-the-spot emergency care and treatment by persons with the proper knowledge and skill. Since 1959, 48 states and the *District of Columbia* have enacted good samaritan statutes. The statutes vary markedly with regard to the persons protected, the standard of care required, and the circumstances provided protection.

## CONTENTS

### Persons Immune From Civil Liability

Of the 49 jurisdictions which have enacted good samaritan statutes, 22 restrict immunity to licensed physicians and registered nurses, and 4 others grant immunity to physicians only. Of the states that grant immunity to physicians, 18 also extend immunity to physicians licensed in any state, and 15 of the states that extend immunity to nurses include nurses licensed in any state. In 23 states, *any* person who renders aid or treatment at the scene of an emergency falls within the coverage of the statute. [For an analysis of good samaritan statutes, see Appendix F.]

### Scope of Immunity

Each good samaritan statute provides a standard of care that delineates the scope of immunity for those persons eligible under the law. The standards vary widely from state to state and are often ambiguous. In most states, the scope of immunity is generally qualified by the statement that the person giving aid must act in good faith. Some statutes require that the physician or the person rendering the care must act with "due care," without "gross negligence," or without "willful or wanton" misconduct.

No cases have been found which interpret the language of these statutes or which have imposed liability on a physician or nurse for negligence in rendering assistance at the scene of an emergency. Likewise, there are no cases holding a physician or nurse blameless in rendering care at an emergency.

Despite problems of interpretation, it is clear that the purpose of the statutes is to encourage volunteer medical assistance in emergency situations. The language which grants immunity also supports the conclusion that the doctor, nurse, or layman who is covered by the act will be protected from liability for ordinary negligence in rendering assistance in an emergency.

## CIRCUMSTANCES COVERED

Under most statutes, immunity is granted only in an emergency or for rendering emergency care. The concept of emergency usually refers to a combination of unforeseen circumstances requiring spontaneous action to avoid impending danger. Some states have tried to be more precise as to what constitutes an emergency or accident. According to the *Alaska* statute, the emergency circumstances must suggest that the giving of aid is the only alternative to death or serious bodily injury. The *Pennsylvania* statute defines an emergency as an unexpected occurrence involving injury or illness in public or private places.

Some statutes are so broadly worded that they could include emergencies that occur in an institution. However, because the purpose of the legislation is to encourage assistance where none is usually available, the more extreme definitions will probably not apply.

Most statutes require that emergency services be rendered without payment or an expectation of payment. Apparently this provision was inserted to emphasize that the actions of a good samaritan must be voluntary. Even so, the courts have recognized a physician's right to compensation in some emergencies. For example, physicians have the right to compensation for assisting in rescue operations. In order to be legally immune under the good samaritan laws, however, a physician or nurse must render help voluntarily and without expectation of later pay.

## EFFECT ON NURSES

Nurses are covered in the good samaritan statutes of 45 jurisdictions. Although the legislation is designed to encourage voluntary emergency care, the laws do provide a nurse with a legal choice: to stop at the scene of an emergency, render assistance, and feel some assurance of protection from liability for negligence; or to pass the scene without suffering legal consequences. However, if the nurse chooses to stop and render care, the quality of care provided must be adequate in light of the circumstances of the emergency.

# Chapter 15

# Abortion

The law regarding abortion procedures has undergone substantial change in recent years. Medically, an abortion may be defined as "the premature expulsion from the uterus of the products of conception— of the embryo, or of a nonviable fetus." [*Dorland's Illustrated Medical Dictionary* (24th ed. 1965)]

An abortion may further be classified as spontaneous or induced. It may occur as the incidental result of a medical procedure which is not intended to abort an embryo or nonviable fetus.

The term has been defined legally as:

> The expulsion of the foetus at a period of utero-gestation so early that it has not acquired the power of sustaining an independent life. The unlawful destruction, or the bringing forth prematurely, of the human foetus before the natural time of birth, . . . [s]ometimes loosely used for the offense of procuring a premature delivery; but strictly, the early delivering is the abortion; causing or procuring abortion is the full name of the offense. [*Black's Law Dictionary* (4th rev. ed. 1968)]

The concern here is the deliberately, directly and voluntarily induced abortion, and the focus is therefore on the legal issues involved in such a procedure.

## LEGAL STATUS

As a result of court decisions, women may now elect to have an abortion although there may be no medical reason for performing the abortion. Where there is a conflict between state and federal law, the federal law controls. Thus, state statutes imposing criminal liability for performing abortions prior to viability of the fetus unless there is a medical reason are in conflict with the federal law and are no longer valid.

## Analysis of Supreme Court Decisions

In *Roe v. Wade,* 410 U.S. 113 (1973), the U.S. Supreme Court held the *Texas* penal abortion law unconstitutional:

> A state criminal abortion statute ... that excepts from criminality only a *life-saving* procedure on behalf of the mother, without regard to pregnancy stage and without recognition of the other interests involved, is violate of the Due Process Clause of the Fourteenth Amendment.

The Court then went on to delineate what regulatory measures a state may lawfully enact during the three stages of pregnancy. In the companion decision, *Doe v. Bolton,* 410 U.S. 179 (1973), in which the Court considered a constitutional attack on the *Georgia* abortion statute, further restrictions were placed on state regulation of the procedure. The provision of the *Georgia* statute establishing residency requirements for women seeking abortions and the provision requiring that the procedure be performed in a hospital accredited by the Joint Commission on Accreditation of Hospitals were declared constitutionally invalid. In considering legislative provisions establishing medical staff approval as a prerequisite to the abortion procedure, the Court decided:

> Interposition of the hospital abortion committee is unduly restrictive of the patient's rights and needs that ... have already been medically delineated and substantiated by her personal physician. To ask more serves neither the hospital nor the State.

The Court was unable to find any constitutionally justifiable pertinence in a statutory requirement of advance approval by the abortion committee of the hospital's medical staff. Insofar as statutory consultation requirements are concerned, the Court reasoned that the acquiescence of two copractitioners has no rational connection with a patient's needs and, furthermore, unduly infringes on the physician's right to practice.

Thus, by using a test related to patient needs, the Court in *Doe v. Bolton* struck down four preabortion procedural requirements, commonly imposed by state statutes. Those procedural requirements concerned: (1) residency; (2) performance of the abortion in a hospital accredited by the Joint Commission on Accreditation of Hospitals; (3) approval by a committee of the hospital's medical staff; and (4) consultations.

## The First Trimester

During the first stage or trimester of pregnancy, the state is virtually without power to restrict or regulate abortions; the decision to perform an abortion is between the woman and her physician. A state may require only that abortions be performed by a physician licensed in accordance with its laws. However, a woman's right to an abortion is not unqualified, since the decision to perform the procedure must be left to the medical judgment of her attending physician. The right that any woman has, in the first three months of pregnancy, is to seek out a physician willing to perform an abortion and, if such a physician is secured, to have the abortion performed without intervention by the state. The state has no compelling interest at this stage of pregnancy which would permit it to override the woman's right to privacy by means of legislation.

## The Second Trimester

In *Roe v. Wade,* the Supreme Court stated:
For the stage subsequent to approximately the end of the first trimester, the State, in promoting its interest in the health of the mother, may, if it chooses, regulate the abortion procedure in ways that are reasonably related to maternal health.

Thus, during approximately the fourth to sixth month of pregnancy the state may regulate the medical conditions under which the procedure is performed. The constitutional test of any legislation concerning abortion during this period would be its relevance to the objective of protecting maternal health.

## The Third Trimester

By the time the final stage of pregnancy has been reached, the Supreme Court reasoned that the state had acquired a compelling interest in the product of conception which would override the woman's right to privacy and justify stringent regulation, even to the extent of prohibiting abortions. In the *Roe* case the Court formulated its ruling concerning the last trimester in the following words:

> For the stage subsequent to viability, the State in promoting its interest in the potentiality of human life, may, if it chooses, regulate, and even proscribe, abortion except where it is necessary, in appropriate medical judgment for the preservation of the life or health of the mother.

Thus, a state may prohibit all abortions during the final stage of pregnancy except those deemed necessary to protect maternal life or health. The state's legislative powers over the performance of abortions increase as the pregnancy progresses toward term.

## Status of State Regulation

The effect of the Supreme Court's decisions in 1973 was to invalidate all or part of almost every state abortion statute then in force. The response of state legislatures to these decisions was varied. However, a number of state laws were enacted to restrict the performance of abortions as much as possible. Some of these laws restricted abortions to a greater extent than permitted by Supreme Court decisions.

Among the subjects considered in the state statutes are: the nature of the facilities in which abortions are performed; the consent of the husband of a married patient; the consent of a parent or guardian of a minor patient; the filing of detailed reports by physicians and institutions regarding abortions performed; the determination by medical consultation of the need for abortion to preserve the woman's life in the third trimester; and the medical care extended to any aborted fetus capable of life.

These statutes also specifically recognize the right of physicians and hospital personnel to refuse to participate in abortions, without discrimination for their refusal, and the right of hospitals to turn away abortion patients. It is noteworthy that the majority of the Court in *Doe v. Bolton* found no constitutional infirmity in the *Georgia* statutory provisions of this type, sometimes referred to as a "conscience clause." The Court stated that "obviously [they] are in the statute in order to afford appropriate protection to the individual and to the denominational hospital."

In *Friendship Medical Center, Ltd. v. Chicago Board of Health,* 505 F.2d 1141, (7th Cir. 1974) cert. denied 95 S.Ct. 1438 (1975), the court reviewed the holdings of *Roe v. Wade* and *Doe v. Bolton* in which the court based its decision on a woman's fundamental right of privacy. The court stated that whether this right of privacy be founded in the Fourteenth Amendment's concept of personal liberty and restrictions on state action or in the Ninth Amendment's reservation of rights to the people, it is broad enough to encompass a woman's right to decide whether or not to terminate her pregnancy. The right is not absolute and is subject to some limitations. At some point the state's interest in the protection of health and prenatal life and in the adherence to medical standards become dominant. Prior to the end of the first trimester, governmental concern with maternal health is not sufficient to overcome a woman's right to decide to abort a pregnancy.

At approximately the end of the first trimester, the state has a compelling interest which permits regulation of abortion procedure to the extent that the regulation reasonably relates to the preservation and protection of maternal health. The state may provide for requirements concerning issues such as the qualifications of the person who is to perform the abortion; the licensure of that person; the facility in which the procedure is to be performed; and the licensure of that facility. Prior to the end of the first trimester, the physician, in consultation with the patient, is free to determine, without state regulation, whether the patient's pregnancy should be terminated. The abortion may be performed free from interference by the state.

The court observed that the state and, under appropriate authorization, local governmental units have broad powers to establish and enforce standards to protect the health of those persons within their jurisdictions. Traditionally, exercise of police power need only bear some rational relationship to a legitimate governmental interest. Where fundamental rights are involved, regulations limiting those rights may be sustained only by a "compelling state interest." The court found the Chicago Board of Health regulations invalid since the Supreme Court clearly held that a state could not regulate abortions by regulations reasonably related to preservation and protection of maternal health until after the first trimester. *Roe* and *Doe* compel consideration of the fundamental right of privacy, at least during the first trimester of pregnancy, to be free from governmental regulations that have an effect on the abortion decision. After the decision to abort is made, that decision must be able to be effectuated by an abortion free of interference by the state.

Regulations which controlled in the first trimester, matters which the Supreme Court said could not be controlled, were held invalid.

The court observed that the mortality rate for legal abortion is as low or lower than for normal childbirth. Therefore, under the equal protection clause of the Fourth Amendment to the U.S. Constitution made applicable to the states by the Fourteenth Amendment, there is little justification for more extensive governmental regulation, based on health considerations, for abortion than for childbirth. Given the fundamental right status of a woman's right to terminate her pregnancy during the first trimester, the court could not allow regulations to stand which, in purporting to promote maternal health, were more expansive than regulations applied to other medical procedures of the same risk and complexity. Any regulations applicable to abortion in the first trimester must give effect to a woman's fundamental right to privacy, the right to decide to abort a pregnancy.

Probably only general regulations such as those concerning maintenance of sanitary facilities and meeting minimal building code standards are permissible. Other cases interpreting the constitutionality of state regulations have followed the reasoning of the court in *Friendship Medical Center, Ltd. v. Chicago Board of Health.* (For example, *Mobile Women's Medical Clinic v. Board of Commissioners of the City of Mobile,* 426 F.Supp. 33, (S.D. Ala. 1977); *Arnold v. Sendek,* 416 F.Supp. 22 (S.D. Ind. 1976) affirmed 429 U.S. 968 (1976);*Word v. Poelker,* 495 F.2d 1349 (8th Cir. 1974).

A woman is entitled to have an abortion without the consent of the father of her child, whether he is her husband or not. A *Florida* statute requiring, as a condition of abortion, the consent of the husband of a married woman and consent of the parents of an unmarried minor was held to be invalid in *Coe v. Gerstein,* 376 F.Supp. 395 (D. Fla. 1973). Affirmed 94 S.Ct. 2246.

In *June v. Smith,* 278 So.2d 339 (Fla. App. 1973) cert den. 415 U.S. 958, an injunction to prohibit an abortion filed by the father was denied by the court holding that the woman has the right during the first trimester to decide whether or not she desires an abortion.

In *Hodgson v. Lawson,* 542 F.2d 350 (8th Cir. 1976), a *Minnesota* statute providing that physicians performing an abortion of a potentially viable fetus are to use methods to reasonably assure the fetus's survival was held to impose restrictions not necessarily related to maternal health. Under the decisions of *Roe v. Wade* and *Doe v. Bolton,* such restrictions during the second trimester of pregnancy are unconstitutional.

The statutory requirement that the woman's consent be obtained after a full exploration of the abortion procedure and its effect has been held constitutional by the Supreme Court in *Planned Parenthood of Central Missouri v. Danforth,* 428 U.S. 52 (1976). The stress and emotional factors involved in deciding on an abortion sufficiently distinguish it from other medical decisions to permit state regulation insuring that the woman's consent is freely and intelligently given. Record keeping and reporting requirements which are directed toward the preservation of maternal health and respect the patient's confidence and privacy are permissible in any trimester of pregnancy. The state has the power to make and enforce regulations to insure that all abortions, like any other medical procedures, are performed under conditions that assure maximum safety to the patient. The regulation of abortions in abortion clinics beyond the regulation of similar surgical procedures in other medical clinics is permissible only if a difference in treatment is shown to be necessary because of particular characteristics of the abortion procedure. [See *Hodgson v. Lawson,* 542 F.2d 350 (8th Cir. 1976).]

## Federal Payments for Abortions

According to P.L. 95-205, federal financial participation is not available for performance of an abortion except under the following circumstances: (1) a physician finds and certifies in writing that, on the basis of the physician's professional judgment, the life of the mother would be endangered if the fetus were carried to term; (2) two physicians find and certify in writing that based on their professional judgment, the mother would sustain severe and long-lasting damage to her health if the pregnancy were carried to term; (3) signed documents are received from a law enforcement agency or public health service stating that the person to have the abortion was reported, within 60 days of the incident, to have been the victim of rape or incest and that the report included the name, address and signature of the person who reported the rape or incest. These documents must be retained for three years in accordance with 45.C.F.R. 74.20 et seq. However, such information must be safeguarded from improper disclosure.

Federal financial participation is available for drugs or devices to prevent implantation of the fertilized ovum and for medical expenses to terminate an ectopic pregnancy.

The rules governing federal financial participation in expenditures for abortions will be designated in three parallel sets of regulations: the first will be for programs administered under Title XIX of the Social Security Act (42 C.F.R. 449.100-449.109); the second for those administered under Title XX of the act (45 C.F.R. 228.92); and the third for programs and projects supported with funds appropriated to the United States Department of Health, Education and Welfare and administered by the Public Health Service (45 C.F.R., Part 50, Subpart C).

## REGULATION

The *Doe* and *Roe* decisions of the Supreme Court leave open the question of how far medical professionals may proceed in placing restrictions and prerequisites on those seeking abortions. The subject of both decisions is state regulation of the procedure. However, hospitals may be found to be instrumentalities of the state or to be associated with the state in such a manner as to be deemed engaged in state action. Civil liability may then result from a hospital's refusal to peform an abortion or from its imposition of requirements difficult to meet, if a patient can show that the hospital's action could be characterized as state action and that her rights were thereby abridged. Existing federal and state legal doctrine regarding both state action and the individual's right of access to facilities for treatment may require hospitals to provide opportunities for abortion. To what extent this holds true is not yet altogether clear.

In *Doe v. Bellin Memorial Hospital,* 479 F.2d 756 (1973), the U.S. Court of Appeals for the Seventh Circuit ruled that a voluntary hospital which received Hill-Burton funds did not surrender "the right it otherwise possessed to determine whether it would accept abortion patients." Neither did the court find receipt of such funds and other aspects of state regulation sufficient to make the hospital's abortion rules state action.

In *Doe v. Bridgeton Hospital Assn., Inc.,* 366 A.2d 641 (N.J. 1976), the court stated that a hospital rule or regulation should be related to the hospital's purposes and operational needs. Moral concepts cannot form the basis of nonsectarian, nonprofit, eleemosynary hospital's regulations where that hospital holds out its facilities to the public. The New Jersey statute that relieved hospitals of any civil or criminal liability for refusing to provide abortion services was held unconstitutional in its application to nonsectarian, nonprofit hospitals. The federal constitutional right to an abortion is clearly established and for the state to frustrate this right violates a constitutional guarantee.

Hospitals owned or operated by governmental bodies may well be required to allow abortions that are not illegal under valid state laws because their activities are regarded as state action. However, this would not mean that physicians or hospital personnel, as individuals, would be required to participate in the abortion procedures.

All hospitals must restrict abortions in conformity with valid state legislation and must meet the reporting, personnel, and other requirements of such laws to avoid criminal liability. It appears that at least nongovernmental hospitals will have considerable discretion in establishing abortion policy and that such policy matters will be the subject of considerable concern

# Chapter 16

# Sterilization and Artificial Insemination

Sterilization is the termination of the ability to produce offspring. Sometimes, sterilization is the primary and desired result of a surgical operation; sometimes, it is a secondary consequence of an operation to remove a diseased reproductive organ or to cure a particular malfunction of such an organ. Most sterilizations involving reproductive organs that are not diseased are effected by vasectomy in men and salpingectomy in women. A vasectomy merely shuts off the flow of a portion of the seminal fluid. Not only is it a success in an overwhelming number of cases, but a reversal operation is sometimes successful. A salpingectomy blocks the passage between the ovary and the uterus, reducing the likelihood that pregnancy will occur through a natural reopening of the passage. An operation to reverse a salpingectomy is rarely successful.

## EUGENIC STERILIZATION

The term "eugenic sterilization" refers to the sterilization of persons within certain classes or categories described in statutes, without the need for consent by, or on behalf of, those subjected to the procedures. Persons classified as insane, mentally deficient, feebleminded, and, in some instances, epileptic are included within the scope of the statutes. Several states have also included certain sexual deviates and persons classified as habitual criminals. Such statutes are ordinarily said to be designed to prevent the transmission of hereditary defects to succeeding generations, but several recent statutes have also recognized the purpose of preventing procreation by individuals who would not be able to care for their offspring.

Approximately half the states have laws authorizing eugenic sterilization. The decision in *Wade v. Bethesda Hospital*, 337 F.Supp. 671 (1971), strongly suggests that in the absence of statutory authority the state cannot order sterilization for eugenic purposes.

Eugenic sterilization statutes provide at least the following presterilization requirements:

1. A grant of authority to public officials supervising state institutions for the mentally ill or prisons and to certain public health officials to conduct sterilizations.

2. A requirement of personal notice to the person subject to sterilization and if that person is unable to comprehend the procedures involved, notice to the person's legal representative, guardian, or nearest relative.

3. A hearing by the board designated in the particular statute to determine the propriety of the prospective sterilization. At the hearing, evidence may be presented, and the patient must be present or represented by counsel or the nearest relative or guardian.

4. An opportunity to appeal the board's ruling to a court.

The procedural safeguards of notice, hearing, and right to appeal must be present in sterilization statutes to fulfill the minimum constitutional requirements of due process.

The image of castration is commonly evoked by the term "sexual sterilization." However, current statutes generally do not authorize castration and in fact, many laws specifically prohibit it. Furthermore, most eugenic sterilization statutes provide for vasectomy or salpingectomy. This prohibition against castration, along with provisions granting immunity only to persons performing or assisting in a sterilization that conforms to the law, is an added safeguard for persons subject to sterilization.

Civil or criminal liability for assault and battery may be imposed on a person who castrates or sterilizes another person without following the procedure required by law. However, provision of liability, in eugenic sterilization acts, for unauthorized sterilizations should not be construed as an indication that state policy is for or against sterilization per se. The fact that a law contains a liability provision is not a guarantee that liability will follow the sterilization of a person outside the group legally subject to eugenic sterilization if that person consents to the procedure.


## THERAPEUTIC STERILIZATION

If the life or health of a woman might be jeopardized if she became pregnant, the danger may be avoided by terminating her ability to conceive or her husband's ability to impregnate. Such an operation is a therapeutic sterilization, a sterilization performed to preserve life or health. It is the medical necessity for sterilization which renders the procedure therapeutic. Sometimes, a diseased reproductive organ must be removed to preserve the life or health of the individual. The operation results in sterility, although this was not the primary reason for the procedure. Such an operation technically should not be classified as a sterilization, since the sterilization is incidental to the medical purpose.

Necessary medical or surgical treatment which incidentally destroys the patient's power to procreate is not likely to be contrary to public policy in any state. No basis for distinguishing between such a procedure and one that could technically be called a therapeutic sterilization has ever been judicially recognized. Indeed such a distinction would not seem logical since the purpose of each is to preserve health and life. Therefore, there seems to be no likelihood that any state could impose a penalty for the performance of therapeutic sterilizations.

## STERILIZATION OF CONVENIENCE

An operation resulting in sterilization of the patient is termed a sterilization of convenience or contraceptive sterilization if no therapeutic reason for such an operation exists. Such operations may be considered in terms of both criminal and civil liability.

### Criminal Liability

There was a time when arguments were advanced concerning the illegality of sterilization of convenience, primarily because of provisions in eugenic sterilization laws. However, no authorities proscribe such procedures and, in light of current judicial decisions and legislation, the possibility that a criminal prosecution will result from voluntary, consensual sterilization is slight.

### Civil Liability

Although civil liability for performing a sterilization of convenience with appropriate consent appears unlikely, liability may be imposed if the procedure is performed negligently or without the necessary consent. Several states have enacted specific legislation concerning sterilizations of convenience. For example, the *Virginia* statute provides that upon written request of an adult and his or her spouse, and after giving a full explanation of the consequences of such an operation, a licensed physician may perform the sterilization 30 days after the request. This requirement for the consent of the spouse is inapplicable in particular circumstances specified in the statute.

The consent of the person who is to be sterilized or subjected to an operation that may incidentally destroy the reproductive function should be obtained before the operation is performed. Even if an operation is medically necessary, in the absence of consent the performance of a sterilization constitutes a battery, as does the performance of any surgical or medical procedure for which consent has not been obtained.

Several distinctive aspects of operations resulting in sterilization should be stressed. Ordinarily, the patient's consent is sufficient authorization for an operation; however, since sterilization affects the procreative function, the patient's spouse has an interest that could be legally recognized. Therefore, when the operation is primarily intended to accomplish sterilization, it is advisable to obtain the spouse's consent. However, when the procedure is medically necessary and sterilization is an incidental result, the patient's consent alone is sufficient.

Where it is foreseeable that an operation needed to cure a condition will incidentally destroy the ability to procreate, it is imperative that the effect on the reproductive function is made clear to both patient and spouse. Further, when sterilization is to be combined with another procedure, specific reference should be made to the sterilization. A specific consent form that spells out the effect upon the reproductive process is strongly recommended. Its use may lessen the likelihood that either patient or spouse would bring suit for the loss of reproductive ability. Sterilization of convenience on minor patients may raise particular questions regarding whose consent is necessary, and rules regarding minor consent must be carefully observed.

Malpractice suits have been brought against physicians who performed sterilization operations when the desired sterility was not produced and pregnancy resulted. Cases have held that an error in judgment, if reasonable care and skill in applying medical learning were exercised, does not render the physician liable for unfavorable results in treatment unless there is an express contract to that effect.

Grounds upon which recovery has been sought for the failure of a sterilization are negligence in performing the operation, breach of contract or warranty to successfully sterilize the patient, fraud, deceit and misrepresentation in statements made to the patients and spouse asserting that the operation would result in sterilization and that sexual intercourse without contraceptives would be safe.

In *Custodio v. Bauer,* 251 Cal. App. 2d 303, 59 Cal. Rptr. 463 (1967) 27 ALR 3d 884, the court discussed damages for an unsuccessful sterilization operation and concluded that there should be: reimbursement for any outlay for the unsuccessful sterilization operation; an award for proven physical complications and for mental, physical and nervous pain and suffering which the operation was designed to prevent; compensation to the wife and husband if the sterilization operation cripples the patient and causes inability to perform marital and conjugal duties; compensation for loss of services of the patient and for medical expenses; compensation for the change in family status if it can be measured economically and an award for wrongful death if the mother dies in childbirth from foreseeable complications of the pregnancy sought to be prevented by the sterilization operation.

As a result of the birth of a child, suits have been filed for negligent failure to diagnose a pregnancy, negligent performance of an abortion or sterilization, and negligent filling of a prescription for contraceptives. Damages have been awarded the parents for the expenses of the unsuccessful operation; the pain and mental suffering caused by the unexpected occurrence and continuation of the pregnancy; medical complications resulting from the pregnancy; the cost of the delivery of the child; lost wages; and loss of consortium.

Suits have been filed for an infant's "wrongful life" or "wrongful birth." Some courts have refused to award damages on the grounds that it is difficult, if not impossible, to evaluate "being versus nothingness." Other courts have held that damages should be awarded as in any other action for damages resulting from negligence. In *Anonymous v. Hospital,* 33 Conn. Supp. 126, 366 A.2d 204 (1976), the court stated that the safest course of judicial action is to allow the allegations of the complaint to stand and permit the defendants to argue, in mitigation of damages, the satisfaction, joy and companionship which normal parents derive from their child and which make economic loss worthwhile. In *Bowman v. Davis,* 356 N.E.2d 496 (Ohio 1976) the court awarded $450,000.00 to the parents and $12,500.00 to the father for expenses and loss of consortium following the birth of healthy twins after an unsuccessful sterilization. Some courts have held that the sanctity of human life precludes recovery in tort for "wrongful birth" due to negligence in performing a sterilization or abortion. [For a lengthy discussion of cases involving this issue see "Annotation Tort Liability for Wrongfully Causing One to be Born" by Gregory G. Sarns, in 83 ALR 3d 15 through 110 (1978).]

## Regulation of Sterilizations of Convenience

In *Custodio v. Bauer,* the court decided that therapeutic and contraceptive sterilization is a matter of individual conscience when not prohibited by statute. The court questioned whether states may control sterilization operations since the dissemination of contraceptive information to married persons is now constitutionally protected. Such operations were considered by the court not to be against public policy, although there is opposition by some to abortions.

The U.S. Court of Appeals for the First Circuit has ruled, in *Hathaway v. Worcester City Hospital,* 475 F.2d 701 (1st Cir. 1973), that a governmental hospital may not impose greater restrictions upon sterilization procedures than other procedures that are medically indistinguishable from sterilization with regard to risk to the patient or demand on staff or facilities. The court relied on the Supreme Court decisions in *Roe v. Wade* and *Doe v. Bolton* which accorded considerable recognition to the patient's right to privacy in the context of obtaining medical services. The extent to which nongovernmental hospitals may prohibit or substantially limit sterilization procedures is not clear, but it appears likely that such hospitals will be allowed considerable discretion in this matter.

At least one state, *Kansas,* has enacted legislation declaring that hospitals are not required to permit the performance of sterilization procedures and that physicians and hospital personnel may not be required to participate in such procedures or be discriminated against for refusal to participate. Such legislation, which is more frequent with regard to abortion procedures, is often referred to by the term "conscience clause" and was not found objectionable in Supreme Court decisions striking down most state abortion laws.

## LEGAL STATUS OF ARTIFICIAL INSEMINATION

Artificial insemination is the instrumental injection of seminal fluid into a woman to induce pregnancy. If the semen of the woman's husband is used to impregnate her, the technique is called homologous artificial insemination (AIH), but if the semen comes from a donor other than the husband, the procedure is called heterologous artificial insemination (AID).

Neither practice is specifically prohibited by statute or common law in any jurisdiction. Furthermore, there appears to be no risk of liability and no danger of criminal prosecution for the medical personnel or hospital, apart from possible liability for negligence in performing the procedure.

AID raises several problems which legislation has begun to consider. The first state to pass a comprehensive statute dealing with virtually all of these problems is *Oklahoma*. This statute provides guidelines for the physician and hospital to follow and resolves some of the questions arising from AID that have been litigated. Subsequent to the *Oklahoma* legislation, a few other states have passed laws dealing generally with the same issues.

The absence of answers to a number of questions concerning AID may have discouraged couples from seeking to utilize the procedure and physicians from performing it. Some of the questions concern the procedure itself; others concern the status of the offspring and the effect of the procedure upon the marital relationship.

There has been only a minimal amount of litigation involving artificial insemination. Legal issues which cause concern are the legitimacy of the child conceived, the child's inheritance rights, support obligations, commission of adultery, and the liability of the physician and donor.

## Consent

The *Oklahoma* statute resolves the issue of whose consent should be obtained by specifying that husband and wife must consent to the procedure. It is obvious that the wife's consent must be obtained because, without it, the touching involved in the artificial insemination would constitute a battery.

In addition to the wife's consent, it is important to obtain the husband's consent to insure against liability which might accrue if a court were to adopt the view that, without the consent of the husband, AID was a wrong to the husband's interest for which he could sustain a suit for damages. Because AID involves the impregnation of the woman with the semen of a man other than her husband, failure to obtain the husband's consent may raise the issue of whether the woman has committed adultery. Several courts have had to deal with this question in divorce proceedings. Furthermore, the issue of adultery has a direct bearing on the legal status of the offspring.

The *Oklahoma* statute also deals with establishing proof of consent; it requires that the consent be in writing and that it be executed and acknowledged by the physician performing the procedure and by the local judge who has jurisdiction over the adoption of children, as well as by the husband and wife.

In states without specific statutory requirements, medical personnel should avoid liability by establishing the practice of obtaining the written consent of the couple requesting the AID procedure.

### Adultery and the Legal Status of Offspring

The *Oklahoma* statute resolves the questions which have arisen with respect to the legitimacy of a child conceived by means of AID, the duty of support owed an AID child by the nondonor husband, the effect of AID birth upon the child's right of intestate succession, and the right to custody of such child. The law declares that any child born as a result of AID performed in accordance with the statute's requirements is to be considered in all respects the same as a naturally conceived legitimate child.

In *People v. Sorensen,* 68 Cal. 2d 280, 437 P.2d 495, 24 ALR 3d 1093 (1968), the court held that where there is no statute prohibiting artificial insemination, a child conceived with semen from a third-party donor with the husband's consent is not the product of an adulterous relationship. The child was therefore found to be legitimate. Adultery is defined as voluntary sexual intercourse of a married person with a person other than the offender's husband or wife.

In *Doornbos v. Doornbos,* Unreported Super Ct. Cook County, No. 545, 149 81, app. dismd. 12 Ill. App.2d 406, 411, 25 ALR 3d 1108 (1963), the court held the mother to be guilty of adultery when artificial insemination was performed using semen of a third-party donor, whether the procedure was performed with or without consent of the husband. Thus, the child would be illegitimate.

The mother's allegation that she conceived by means of artificial insemination was not believed and she was found to be guilty of adultery in *Hoch v. Hoch,* Unreported, Cir. Ct. Cook County (1945 Ill.) 25 ALR 3d 1108.

The husband was required to pay child support in a case in which he had consented to AID in *Gursky v. Gursky,* 39 Misc. 2d 1083, 242 N.Y.S. 2d 406, 25 ALR 3d 1111 (1963), and the husband was given visitation rights with respect to a child so conceived in *Strnad v. Strnad,* 190 Misc. 786, 78 N.Y.S. 2d 390, 25 ALR 3d 1112 (1948).

Several states have enacted legislation declaring that children conceived by artificial insemination with the consent of the parents are to be considered legitimate and natural children. *California* has declared by statute that the husband of a woman who bears a child as a result of artificial insemination shall be liable for support of the child as though he were the natural father, if he consented in writing to the artificial insemination. This legislation adopts the position taken earlier by the *California* Supreme Court.

## Confidentiality of the Procedure

Another problem that directly concerns medical personnel involved in AID birth is that of preserving confidentiality. This problem is met in the *Oklahoma* statute, which requires that the original copy of the consent be filed pursuant to the rules for adoption papers and is not to be made a matter of public record.

## ETHICAL AND MORAL IMPLICATIONS OF ARTIFICIAL INSEMINATION

There are a variety of religious and ethical views concerning the propriety of artificial insemination, and various aspects of AID and, to a lesser extent, AIH have been questioned. However, the present state of the law does not appear to forbid AIH or AID, and a hospital would not be liable for permitting artificial insemination to take place upon its premises, if consent had been obtained from both husband and wife and if any special statutory requirements had been met. Physicians and nurses participating in the procedure would also not be subject to liability if the proper consent had been obtained, provided, of course, that negligence in performing the procedure is not involved.

# Chapter 17

# Autopsy and Donation

Nurses and other medical personnel involved in the operation of hospitals are often confronted with a variety of responsibilities concerning the handling of dead bodies. Failure to fulfill these responsibilities may result in liability.

## LEGAL PRINCIPLES REGARDING DEAD BODIES

Consideration of the legal duties in regard to the utilization, handling, and disposition of dead bodies cannot be divorced from the legal questions involved in determining when death occurs. In many legal contexts, such as on deciding rights to the property of the deceased person, the determination of death does not involve the hospital or its personnel. However, where hospital personnel and physicians are to take action inconsistent with maintaining the life of the patient, risks of liabilty for the hospital and its personnel are necessarily present. New technology, specifically medical advances in methods for artificially sustaining life and transplanting vital organs, requires consideration of processes and criteria for determining when death occurs.

Until recently, the courts had considered the determination of when death occurred to be peculiarly within the competence of the medical profession and based upon the prevailing opinion within the profession regarding the criteria to be applied. The fact that the decision-making process has important implications for society has led to serious consideration of possible benefits to be derived by providing physicians with more specific and objective guidelines. These guidelines would provide the physician with a set of publicly accepted processes and criteria to apply in making professional determinations.

Some steps have been taken to develop such guidelines for the medical profession. Safeguards for the patient and the physician with regard to the processes for determining death are evident in the Uniform Anatomical Gift Act. The Act recognizes the need to avoid any conflict of interest on the part of a physician by stipulating that the determination of the time of death cannot be made by a physician who is a member of a transplant team. A similar provision is contained in the Report of the Ad Hoc Committee to be used by a physician in determining death. Legislatures in several states have enacted laws setting forth criteria and processes relating to medical activities to be used in determining the moment of legal death and in related matters.

## Interests in Dead Bodies

The rule now uniformly recognized in the United States is that the person entitled to possession of a body for burial has certain legally protected interests. Interference with these rights can result in liability. Damages awarded in cases where liability is predicated upon interference with the rights of a surviving spouse or near relative with respect to the body of a decedent are based upon emotional and mental suffering that results from such interference. Thus, for damages to be awarded, the conduct of the alleged wrongdoer must be sufficiently disturbing to a person of ordinary sensibilities to cause emotional harm. Cases involving wrongful handling of dead bodies may be classified into four groups: mutilation of a body; unauthorized autopsy; wrongful detention; and miscellaneous wrongs such as unauthorized sale, refusal or neglect to bury, or unauthorized use or publication of photographs taken after death.

In many states, intentionally mutilating a dead body is a punishable crime and is also a basis for civil liability. Obviously, such acts could be said to cause substantial emotional suffering on the part of those who had loved and respected the decedent. Similarly, an unauthorized autopsy may be disturbing to persons who have an aversion to the procedure, although autopsies have become an accepted and necessary aspect of hospital practice. Thus, where an autopsy is performed without statutory authorization and without the consent of the surviving spouse or a relative whose duty it is to dispose of the decedent's remains, liability has been imposed.

Refusal to deliver a dead body to a person who demands and is entitled to receive custody has also resulted in liability. There do not appear to be any such cases directly involving hospitals, but if a hospital refused to deliver a body until the decedent's bill was paid or if it retained possession of a body after receiving a proper request for delivery, such refusal would constitute sufficient grounds for the predication of liability for interference with rights to a dead body.

Unintentional as well as intentional conduct interfering with rights to a body has resulted in hospital liability. The case of *Lott v. State,* 225 N.Y.S. 2d 434, 32 Misc. 2d 296 (1962), involved the mistagging of two bodies in a hospital, with the result that the body of a person of the Roman Catholic faith was prepared for Orthodox Jewish burial and a person of the Orthodox Jewish faith was prepared for Roman Catholic burial. This negligent conduct interfered with burial plans and caused mental anguish, for which liability was imposed.

## Right of Suit for Improper Action

Although several persons may suffer emotional stress and mental anguish because of indignities in the treatment of the body of the decedent, recovery for wrongful interference with the body and with proper burial of the body has generally been limited to the person who has the right to possession of the body for burial. Some state statutes delineate an order of the duty to bury the decedent. Others set forth an order of persons authorized to give consent to autopsy, from which the order of devolution may be established. In states without either provision, case law must provide the guidelines. Generally, the primary right to custody of a dead body belongs to the surviving spouse. Where there is no spouse the right passes to the children of the decedent, if any, and then to the decedent's parents.

## AUTOPSY

Autopsies, or post-mortem examinations, are conducted in order to ascertain the cause of a person's death, which in turn may resolve a number of legal issues. An autopsy may reveal whether death was the result of criminal activity, whether the cause of death was one for which payment must be made in accordance with an insurance contract, whether the death is compensable under workmen's compensation and occupational disease acts, whether death was the result of a specific act or a culmination of several acts. Autopsies are necessary to hospitals, physicians, and medical science because, aside from providing answers to these specific questions, the information gained from autopsies increases medical knowledge. Autopsies are also a source of information about the medical practice in the hospital. Hospitals have been sued successfully for harm resulting from the performance of unauthorized autopsies, where the hospitals failed to take adequate precautions to prevent such autopsies.

## Autopsy Consent Statutes

Recognizing both the need for information that can be secured only through the performance of a substantial volume of autopsies and the valid interests of relatives and friends of the decedent, most states have enacted statutes dealing with autopsy consent. Such legislation seems intended to have a twofold effect: first, to protect the rights of the decedent's relatives; second, to guide hospitals and physicians in establishing procedures for consent to autopsy.

Most autopsy consent statutes can be classified into two groups. One group consists of the statutes that establish an order for obtaining consent to autopsy based upon the degree of familial relationship. Provisions of this type furnish the most precise guidelines to the physician and hospital, enabling them to determine without resorting to other statutes or decisions, who the proper person is to contact for autopsy authorization.

The statutes of the second group contain provisions enumerating those persons from whom consent may be obtained but do not provide an order of priority among them. These laws state that consent is to be obtained from any one of the enumerated persons who has assumed custody of the body for burial. In some states with such statutes, there are no additional statutes concerning the devolution of the duty to bury and the right to custody. In these states a hospital must rely upon case law to determine whether a person who requests custody of a body for burial is entitled to such custody and is therefore the proper person from whom consent to autopsy should be obtained. Furthermore, the assumption of custody of the body by a person enumerated in the statutes must be clear before consent to autopsy can be relied upon.

In states which have autopsy consent statutes as well as statutes setting forth the order in which the duty of burial and right to custody of the body devolve upon the relatives of the decedent, the two statutes taken together indicate the proper person from whom consent is to be obtained. In states without autopsy consent statutes, other statutes relating to the duty to bury and right to custody of a body for burial or to donation of bodies or body parts may prove helpful in determining which of the decedent's relatives may give effective authorization for autopsy.

## Authorization by the Decedent

Approximately one-half of the autopsy consent statutes provide that the deceased may authorize an autopsy upon his remains. Ordinarily such consent must be in writing. While there should be no problem regarding the validity of the decedent's authorization in such states, as a practical matter it may be difficult to obtain consent because it is undesirable to bring the subject to the attention of most hospital patients. Furthermore, there may be legal as well as practical problems in obtaining authorization for an autopsy from a patient before death if the state does not provide by statute for such authorization. If an autopsy is desired, it would probably be simpler and more effective to obtain authorization from the relative or some other person who assumes the legal responsibility for burial, rather than from the patient before death.

Some states have no specific provision for authorization of autopsy by the deceased, but do permit donation of a person's body or parts thereof to hospitals, universities, or other institutions that operate eye or tissue banks, for use in the advancement of medical science, or for transplantation procedures. A court might construe the donation statute as authorizing the decedent to consent to an autopsy because one purpose, among others, for the performance of autopsies, is to advance medical science.

In states where there is neither an autopsy consent statute nor a statute permitting donation that may be construed to include autopsy, it is unwise to rely solely upon the authorization of a decedent to perform an autopsy. This is especially true where relatives of the deceased who assume custody of the body for burial object to an autopsy. Although many cases have upheld the wishes of a decedent with respect to the place of interment or the manner of disposition of the remains, whether by burial or cremation, the courts may not afford the same weight to a deceased's wishes concerning autopsy. In such instances, compelling reasons presented by certain kin of the decedent, especially the surviving spouse, may prevail over the wishes of the decedent.

## Authorization by Persons Other Than the Decedent

Two closely related concepts are concerned in determining who may authorize the performance of an autopsy. One of these has developed in litigation when a corpse has been mutilated and a person has been permitted to bring an action to recover damages. Such cases ordinarily determine an order of priority with respect to the person who may bring an action. The second concept is that of responsibility for burial of the deceased body and is the basis from which the right of an individual to bring an action for mutilation of a dead body arises.

The order of responsibility for burial is ordinarily the same as the order for preference for bringing an action for mutilation, since the latter arises from the former. The person upon whom the duty to bury the deceased is imposed has the right to custody of the body and the right to recover for mutilation of the corpse and is thus the person from whom authority to perform an autopsy should be obtained.

Where custody of the body has been assumed by the first person in the preference order, that person's consent is sufficient to authorize the autopsy and prevent liability for mutilation of the corpse. If consent to the autopsy is refused, performance of the autopsy could lead to liability, even if some other relative of the deceased sought to authorize it.

What if the first person in order of preference is deceased or mentally incompetent, or is unwilling or unable to assume the responsibility for burial of the body, or fails to do so? It is then necessary to determine who has such responsibility and the concomitant right to authorize an autopsy. Fortunately, in many states the order of responsibility for burial is set forth in statutes, and the right to authorize an autopsy is given to the person who has assumed custody of the body for burial.

Several statutes that specifically deal with authority for autopsies indicate who can give authorization when the first person in order of priority is unavailable. Such statutes enable the hospital to determine whose consent is sufficient, and the chance of a successful suit by anyone claiming superior rights in the body is practically nonexistent if the statutory provisions are followed.

In the absence of statutes furnishing a preference order with respect to responsibility for burial or for consent, the order usually followed is: surviving spouse, children of the deceased, parents, brothers and sisters, grandparents, uncles and aunts, and then cousins.

When consent for an autopsy has been obtained from a relative who assumed custody of the deceased's body, a court would be likely to consider such consent sufficient and not hold a hospital or physician liable for mutilation of the body in the event that a closer relative, who had been unavailable or who would not assume custody for the burial, were to bring an action against the hospital after an autopsy was completed. A court may find that a surviving spouse's unwillingness to assume responsibility for burial is sufficient to permit the right to custody of the body to devolve upon a relative who *is* willing to assume such responsibility. But if the spouse is unable to assume the responsibility of burial for financial or similar reasons, the court probably would not recognize the right of the other relative to bring an action for an unauthorized autopsy.

## Scope and Extent of Consent

Legal issues may arise as a result of performing an autopsy even if consent has been obtained from the person authorized by law to grant such consent. If autopsy procedures go beyond the limits imposed by the consent, or if the consent to the autopsy is obtained by fraud or without the formal requisites, liability may be incurred. It is a fundamental principle that a person who has the right to refuse permission for the performance of an act has, in addition, the right to place limitations or conditions on consent.

It is especially important that the hospital and its personnel adhere to any limitations or conditions placed upon the permission for autopsy because if such limitations are exceeded, the physician or hospital has no defense on the grounds of emergency or medical necessity. The principle involved in limiting the scope of an autopsy has been expressed as follows:

> One having the right to refuse to permit an autopsy to be held has the right to place any limitations or restrictions on giving consent thereto, and one who violates such stipulation renders himself liable, as, for example, where he mutilates the body, removes portions contrary to directions, or fails to return severed portions for burial. [72 Am. Jur. 2d *Dead Bodies,* § 32 (1965)].

While consent to autopsy may also encompass authorization for removal of body parts for examination, a separate question may arise concerning disposal of tissues and organs upon completion of the examination. The question is whether the hospital and its personnel may dispose of such material in a routine manner or use it for their own purposes, or whether the hospital must return the tissue and organs to the body before burial. In *Hendriksen v. Roosevelt Hospital,* 297 F. Supp. 1142 (1969), permission had been granted for a complete autopsy including an examination of the central nervous system by a scalp incision. Yet the court held that liability might be imposed upon the hospital if the plaintiff could show that all the internal organs had been permanently removed from the body. Pursuant to a *New York* statute requiring the authorization of the next of kin, consent was given for dissection; however, the court held that this statute should be narrowly construed and that separate consent would have to be obtained to retain the internal organs of the decedent.

Consent given with the understanding that organs and tissue could be removed and retained for examination would seem to authorize the hospital to dispose of such materials in a suitable manner or to utilize them after the autopsy. However, the *Hendriksen* decision raises doubts on this matter. Where the party giving consent expressly stipulates that parts severed from the body are to be returned to the body for burial, conduct deviating from this provision may result in liability. Also, it would appear that consent to autopsy does not include authorization to mutilate or disfigure the body. Therefore, if autopsy should involve the removal of exterior body parts and if the physical appearance of the body could not be restored without return of such parts, the hospital may be subject to liability for exceeding the scope of the authorization if the removed parts are not returned.

## Fraudulently Obtained Consent

A long-accepted principle establishes that consent obtained through fraud or material misrepresentation is not binding and that the person whose consent is so obtained stands legally in the same position as if no consent had been given.

This principle can apply to autopsies when facts are misrepresented to the person who has the right to consent in order to induce his consent. If a physician or hospital employee states as fact something known to be untrue in order to gain consent, the autopsy would be unauthorized and liability may follow.

## DONATION OF BODIES FOR MEDICAL USE

Recent developments in medical science have enabled physicians to take tissue from persons immediately after death and use such tissue for transplantation in order to replace or rehabilitate diseased or damaged organs or other parts of living persons. Progress in this field of medicine has created the problem of obtaining a sufficient supply of body parts to carry out those techniques. Throughout the country there are eye banks, artery banks, and other facilities for the storage and preservation of organs and tissue which can be used for transplantation and for other therapeutic services.

Organs and tissue that are to be stored and preserved for future use must be removed almost immediately after death. Therefore, it is imperative that an agreement or arrangement for obtaining organs and tissue from a body be completed before death or very soon after death in order to enable physicians to remove and store the tissue properly.

Every state has enacted legislation to facilitate donation of bodies and body parts for medical uses. Virtually all the states have based their enactments on the Uniform Anatomical Gift Act, drafted by the Commissioners on Uniform State Laws, but in some states there are deviations from this Act or additional laws dealing with donation.

## Summary of the Uniform Anatomical Gift Act

Any individual who is of sound mind and 18 years of age or older is permitted to dispose of his or her own body or body parts by will or other written instrument for medical or dental education, research, advancement of medical or dental science, therapy, or transplantation. Among those eligible to receive such donations are any licensed, accredited, or approved hospital, accredited medical or dental school, surgeon or physician, tissue bank, or any specified individual who needs the donation for therapy or transplantation. The statute provides that when only a part of the body is donated, custody of the remaining parts of the body shall be transferred to the next of kin promptly following removal of the donated part.

In cases of a donation made by a written instrument other than a will, the instrument must be signed by the donor in the presence of two witnesses, who, in turn, must sign the instrument in the donor's presence. If the donor cannot sign the instrument, the document may be signed at the donor's direction and in the presence of the donor and the two signing witnesses. Delivery of the document during the donor's lifetime is not necessary to make the donation valid. A donation by will becomes effective immediately upon the death of the testator, without probate, and the gift is valid and effective to the extent that it has been acted upon in good faith, even if the will is not probated or is declared invalid for testamentary purposes.

In the absence of a contrary intent evidenced by the decedent or of actual notice of opposition by a member of the same class or a prior class in the preference order, the decedent's body or body parts may be donated by the following persons in the order specified: surviving spouse, adult child, parent, adult brother or sister, decedent's guardian, or any other person or agency authorized to dispose of the body. A donation by a person other than the decedent may be made by written, telegraphic, recorded telephonic, or other recorded consent.

The statute provides several methods by which a donation may be revoked. If the document has been delivered to a named donee, it may be revoked by a written revocation signed by the donor and delivered to the donee, by an oral revocation witnessed by two persons and communicated to the donee, by a statement to the attending physician during a terminal illness that has been communicated to the donee, or by a card or piece of writing that has been signed and is on the donor's person or in the donor's immediate effects. If the written instrument of donation has not been delivered to the donee, it may be revoked by destruction, cancellation, or mutilation of the instrument. If the donation is made by a will, it may be revoked in the manner provided for revocation or amendment of wills. Any person acting in good faith reliance upon the terms of an instrument of donation will not be subject to civil or criminal liability unless there is actual notice of the revocation of the donation.

The time of death shall be determined by a physician in attendance at the donor's death, or a physician certifying death, who shall not be a member of the team of physicians engaged in the transplantation procedure.

## UNCLAIMED DEAD BODIES

Persons entitled to possession of a dead body must arrange for release of the body from the hospital, for its transfer to an embalmer or undertaker, and for its final disposal. The recognition by the courts of a quasi-property right in the body of a deceased person imposes a duty on the hospital to make reasonable efforts to give notice to persons entitled to claim the body. When there are no known relatives or friends of the family who can be contacted by the hospital to claim the body, the hospital has a responsibility to dispose of the body in accordance with the law.

Unclaimed bodies are generally buried at public expense and a public official, usually a county official, has the duty to bury or otherwise dispose of such bodies. Most states have statutes providing for the disposal of unclaimed bodies by delivery to institutions for educational and scientific purposes. Thus, unclaimed bodies in the custody of public officials, such as coroners or administrators of governmental hospitals, are subject to use for such purposes. Pursuant to these statutes, the public official in charge of the body has a duty to notify the government agency of the presence of the body. The agency then arranges for the transfer of the body in accordance with the statute. If no such agency exists under the statute, the hospital or public official may be authorized to allow a medical school or other institution or person, designated by the statute as an eligible recipient of unclaimed dead bodies, to remove the body for scientific use.

When an unclaimed dead body is in the possession of a charitable or proprietary hospital, the hospital should notify the public official charged by law with disposing of unclaimed bodies. The public official then arranges for the ultimate disposition of the body, either by burial or transfer to an institution entitled to obtain it for educational and scientific use.

Certain categories of persons are usually excluded from these provisions permitting the distribution of bodies for educational and scientific use. For public health reasons the statutes do not usually permit distribution of the bodies of persons who have died from contagious diseases. Generally, the bodies of travelers and veterans are also not to be used for educational and scientific purposes.

While the majority of these statutes quite explicitly require that relatives be notified and set time limits for holding the body so as to allow relatives an opportunity to claim the body, strict compliance with the statutory provisions is often impossible because of the very nature of problems that arise in handling dead bodies and the required procedures themselves. Noncompliance in such instances would not appear to cause liability. An example of such a provision is the requirement that relatives be notified immediately upon death and that the body be held for 24 hours subject to claim by a relative or friend. The procedure of locating and notifying relatives may consume the greater part of the 24-hour period following death, and if relatives who are willing to claim the body are located, the body should be held for a reasonable time to allow them to arrange custody for burial. It should be recognized that literal compliance may prejudice the interests of relatives of the decedent.

Similarly, when a body remains unclaimed and the hospital has no way of ascertaining that the decedent was a veteran, delivering or disposing of the body for educational or scientific purposes pursuant to the statute would not appear to cause liability if it was later proved that the decedent was a veteran. Failure to adhere to the statute in such instances is not likely to result in liability.

In some instances, a hospital may be or may want to become a recipient of cadaveric material to be used for science or education. This may be true with respect to bodies of persons held by public officials and other hospitals, as well as the unclaimed bodies of persons dying within the recipient institution. In either case, if a hospital wishes to receive such materials it must comply with the statutory provisions relating to recipients. The hospital may be required to register as an eligible recipient or request that unclaimed bodies be delivered to it, and it may be required to post a bond to insure proper use and disposal of the body. In addition, the hospital may be required to maintain equipment and facilities for the preservation and storage of cadavers.

# Appendices

# Explanation of Admission Consent Form

An admission consent form should be signed as part of the admission procedure. The admitting office personnel should specifically inform the patient of the need for the form. Both inpatients and outpatients should be required to sign the admission consent form upon admission for treatment.

The signing of the admission consent form may be dispensed with when a pregnant woman, already in labor, presents herself at the hospital for delivery of a child, because arrival at the hospital may be considered a voluntary submission to the medical and hospital routines and procedures usually associated with delivery of a child. Dispensing with the signing of a consent form is suggested in this instance because the patient may be in such pain as to be actually unaware of what she is signing, thus making the signed consent of no greater consequence than her submission to medical attention.

It should be noted that this exception to the general rule requiring an admission consent form does not apply when the patient is not in labor when admitted. Where delivery is to be by means of cesarean section, or labor is to be artifically induced after admission, or the patient requires other special procedures or anesthesia, the admission consent form should be signed when the patient is admitted to the hospital. In some of these situations, a special consent form may be required.

**Paragraph 1—Authorizaton.** At the time of admission to the hospital, the patient is generally in a position to authorize only routine and customary services. Moreover, the act of voluntary admission to the hospital can be interpreted as implied consent for such services and a form is not actually necessary. The Special Authorization and Consent form should be used for any other procedures which are performed on the patient during hospitalization. A form signed upon admission, however, serves to alert patients to the fact that they will be undergoing various examinations and tests and it serves as documentation of voluntary admissions and general authorization.

## AUTHORIZATION AND CONSENT
## UPON ADMISSION TO HOSPITAL°

Patient: _____ Date: _____

Identification No.: _____ Time: _____ a.m.
p.m.

**Authorization.**

1.  I understand that my admission to this hospital is indicated because of my condition. I voluntarily authorize and consent to the customary examinations, tests and procedures performed on hosptial patients in my condition and to routine medical treatment ordered by my physician, Dr. _____.

**Rules.**

2.  I agree to abide by the rules of this hospital, including to the extent I am able, cooperation with physicians and hospital personnel in my care and treatment, and observance of the rights of other patients.
Patient's Signature _____

Note:   When the patient is a minor (under 18 years of age) or otherwise legally incompetent (unconscious or mentally incapable of understanding), the next of kin or legal guardian is legally responsible for authorizing medical and hospital services. However, any minor patient who can understand this form should be given the opportunity to sign it in addition to the legal representative.

Signature of Patient's Legal Representative _____
Printed Name: _____Relationship _____
Witness' Signature _____
Printed Name _____

---

* Reprinted with permission from David G. Warren, *Problems in Hospital Law*, 3rd Ed. (Germantown, MD: Aspen Systems Corporation, 1978), pp. 139-140. ©1978 Aspen Systems Corporation.

**Paragraph 2—Rules.** The time of admission may be the best opportunity to impress upon a patient that the hospital has rules and conditions which are designed to promote patient care and protect patient safety. It is well-known that patient cooperation is necessary for optimum results, and this paragraph emphasizes that point. It also encourages the patient to be mindful of other patients, including their safety and comfort. If the rules of the hospital are made available to the patient or are posted, the patient's cooperation in matters of hospital schedule, services, visitors and business matters may be improved by calling attention to them at the time of signing this form.

**Signature Block.** Lines are provided for signature by the patient or for signature of someone authorized to consent for the patient.

Space is provided for the signature of a witness. Although no witness is required to make the consent effective, obtaining a witness who can attest to the genuineness of the patient's signature and competency to sign the form is advisable. One witness is sufficient to prove the circumstances of the signing. Moreover, formalizing the signing of the consent form by having more than one witness may introduce a degree of solemnity that may affect the patient's morale.

# Explanation of Special Consent Form

The special consent form should not be completed in the admissions office of the hospital. Providing the necessary information and answers to the patient's questions requires knowledge of medicine that only a physician possesses. If a procedure that normally calls for the use of a special consent form is to be performed shortly after admission, the physician may be able to provide the information and procure the patient's consent in the physician's office.

Use of the special consent form presupposes a pattern for disclosure in the conversations between the physician and the patient so that necessary matters are covered. Without a disclosure pattern that provides the patient with the necessary information, the form offers few benefits, because it is the full disclosure documented on the form which provides the protection from possible liability.

With some modifications, the special consent form can easily be adapted for surgical diagnostic procedures such as exploratory operations, as well as for nonsurgical diagnostic procedures that require either general anesthesia or the injection of a foreign substance into the blood stream.

A signed special consent form should be procured before any of the following procedures are carried out:

1. Major or minor surgery which involves an entry into the body, either through an incision or one of the natural body openings.
2. All procedures in which anesthesia is used, regardless of whether an entry into the body is involved.
3. Nonsurgical procedures involving more than a slight risk of harm to the patient or the risk of a change in the patient's body structure.

These procedures would include diagnostic procedures such as myelograms, arteriograms, and pyelograms.

4. Procedures involving the use of cobalt and X-ray therapy.
5. Electroshock therapy.
6. Experimental procedures or experimental drug therapy.
7. All other procedures which require a specific explanation to the patient as determined by the medical staff. Any doubts as to the necessity of obtaining a special consent from the patient should be resolved in favor of procuring the consent.

The special consent form should be completed at the time the physician explains to the patient the diagnostic or therapeutic procedure to be performed.

### SPECIAL AUTHORIZATION AND CONSENT TO SURGICAL AND MEDICAL PROCEDURES*

Patient: _____Date: _____

Identification No. _____Time: _____ a.m. p.m.

**Cross out any provisions which do not apply or are not approved by the patient.**

1. *Patient's Condition and Recommended Procedures.* I understand from my physician that the diagnosis of my condition is as follows:

_____

Dr. _____ explained alternative courses of treatment and recommends the following surgical or medical procedures, which I hereby authorize Dr. _____ and assistants to perform: _____

_____

2. *Extension of operation.* I understand that during the course of surgery unforeseen conditions may be revealed and I authorize the additional surgical procedures that are indicated as being necessary for my condition in the best exercise of professional judgment, except these specific procedures: _____

_____

---

* Reprinted with permission from David G. Warren, *Problems in Hospital Law,* 3rd Ed. (Germantown, Md.: Aspen Systems Corporation, 1978), pp. 140-146. ©1978 Aspen Systems Corporation.

3. *Risks and consequences.* In addition to the usual risks of these surgical or medical procedures (for example, loss of blood, infection, cardiac arrest), I have also been made aware of special risks and consequences that are associated with these procedures including:

_____

_____

4. *Anesthesia.* I authorize the administration of customary and appropriate anesthesia by, or under the supervision of, Dr. _____

_____

I understand that there are always special risks involved with anesthesia. Special instructions: _____

5. *Photographs.* I authorize the hospital to make photographs for my medical records and, if I am not identified by name, for purposes of medical research or education.

6. *Observers.* I authorize the admittance of observers to the operating room, as approved by my physician.

7. *Disposal of tissues.* I authorized the hospital to examine and dispose of, or retain for medical purposes, any tissues or parts which are removed during the operation.

8. *No guarantee.* Although I expect the procedures to be performed with not less than the customary standard of care, I acknowledge that no guarantee has been made to me concerning the results.

9. *Questions.* I am aware that I may ask questions about these procedures but I do not request further explanation at this time. I hereby authorize these procedures.

Patient's Signature _____

Physician's Signature _____

Note: When the patient is a minor (under 18 years of age) or otherwise legally incompetent (unconscious or mentally incapable of understanding), the next of kin or legal guardian is legally responsible for authorizing medical services. However, any minor patient who can understand this form should be given the opportunity to sign it in addition to the legal representative.

Signature of Patient's Legal Representative _____

Printed Name _____Relationship _____

　Witness' Signature _____

　Printed Name _____

Time of the Consent. The Special Consent Form should be completed at the time the physician explains to the patient the diagnostic or planned therapeutic procedures. The exact time that the consent is procured is important. It provides evidence that the consent was procured at a time when the patient was competent to sign the consent and not under preoperative sedation. The time is particularly important when the form is signed on the same day that the procedure is carried out, because in such instances there may be an inference that the patient may not have been competent to consent at the time the form was completed.

Paragraph 1—Patient's condition and recommended procedures. A space is provided so that the condition that is to be treated can be explained and the need to treat the condition stated. The reason for placing the emphasis on the condition is grounded upon the fact that courts have found it easier to imply that a patient has consented to all reasonable steps to remedy the condition if it is clearly stated, though the method used may differ from the one explained.

When the form is used for a diagnostic procedure, the nature of the condition disclosed by the tentative diagnosis should be stated in the space provided.

Naming the physician who explained the alternative courses of treatment and the recommended procedure to the person signing the form reinforces the statement that an explanation took place. Placing the burden of explanation upon the patient's physician is consonant with the physician-patient relationship and guarantees that the procedure will be explained by one competent to do so. The description on the consent form should be written in simple language understandable to the layman, rather than in technical terminology. This kind of explanation of the procedure will help support the position that the patient received an explanation of the procedure that could be understood by a "reasonable person." Absent such an understanding, a patient's consent may be deemed ineffective.

If another procedure to treat the same or another condition becomes necessary at some later date during the patient's hospitalization, a second consent form should be procured. If it is known at the time consent is being initially procured that a series of procedures is indicated over a period of time, then the series can be described and consent to the entire course of treatment procured.

When the form is used for a diagnostic procedure, a description of the procedure to be used in arriving at a more definitive diagnosis should be stated in the space provided. It is also suggested that the physician explain to the patient and note on the form the most likely remedial procedures that would be called for if the tentative diagnosis is confirmed.

**Paragraph 2—Extension of operation.** This paragraph is inserted to negate the possible contention that the surgeon is limited to the specific procedures described in Paragraph 1, and it should provide authority for an extension or modification of the procedure or the performance of another medically indicated procedure. By providing explicit consent to additional or different procedures where indicated, complete reliance upon the implication of consent for these procedures stemming from consent to a specific procedure is avoided.

When the form is used for a diagnostic procedure, the physician should explain to the patient that the diagnostic procedure may reveal the need for remedial surgery at that time, in preference to a second surgical procedure at a later date. If the remedial surgery does not fall within an emergency situation or within the scope of the alternatives in Paragraph 2, then it should not be performed at this time.

Any specific procedures, such as removal of the ovaries, which the patient for any reason requests to exclude from a necessary extension should be inserted on the form.

**Paragraph 3—Risks and consequences.** This explanation must cover those risks and consequences that are attendant to the particular procedure or procedures that have been described in Paragraph 1. For example, a plastic procedure involving face and neck may carry the associated risk of facial or vocal cord paralysis. A colostomy results in the patient's bowel movement occurring from an opening on the abdomen. Courts have found consent lacking when consequences that ordinarily follow a procedure are not mentioned to the patient.

Certain risks are attendant to all surgical procedures. It is necessary to mention that these risks are inherent in any surgical procedure and may materialize without malpractice or lack of due care. Any special risks and consequences for this particular patient should be inserted on the form.

**Paragraph 4—Anesthesia.** If the surgeon selects the anesthetic and provides the explanation of it to the patient, the name of the surgeon should be inserted in the space provided. Hospitals in which the anesthesiologist is responsible for choosing the anesthetic and providing the explanation to the patient should disclose the name of the anesthesiologist and may even consider requiring that a separate consent form for anesthesia be used.

It should be noted that if a patient refuses to accept a specific anesthetic (e.g., no general, local only), a notation on the form reflecting that decision should be made and the specified anesthetic should not be used. Any special instructions the patient wishes to give about anesthesia should be inserted on the form.

**Paragraphs 5 and 6—Photographs and Observers.** It is well known that, especially in teaching hospitals, both photographs and observers are often involved in surgical procedures, but the patient should be given the opportunity to know about those events in advance. Authorizing them in these paragraphs waives the patient's right later to claim invasion of privacy.

**Paragraph 7—Disposal of Tissue.** To avoid questions about the property rights of tissues removed during surgery, a standard provision in operation consent forms authorizes the hospital to retain or dispose of them. This is not an adequate provision, however, for use in connection with organ transplant procedures or abortion procedures. A separate form should be used.

**Paragraph 8—No guarantee.** Courts have allowed patients to recover for breach of contract when they prove that the physician guaranteed the success of the operation or treatment but that it was unsuccessful. To avoid the possibility of a patient's relying on a false hope of guaranteed success, this paragraph should be part of an authorization form. Some state statutes now require any guarantee of success or cure to be in writing in order to be enforced against a provider. In *Sullivan v. O'Connor,* 296 N.E.2d 183 (Mass., 1973), a plastic surgeon had promised to fix the plaintiff's nose and enhance her beauty. The court decided there had been a breach of contract and allowed recovery of not only her out-of-pocket expenses but also damages for her worsened condition and resultant mental distress and for the pain and suffering involved in the extra corrective operation.

**Paragraph 9—Questions.** To promote as full an explanation as is appropriate for each patient, the opportunity for questions should be emphasized. A patient who is satisfied with an explanation and whose questions have been answered is more likely to give an authorization which will be upheld by the courts.

**Signatures.** Both the patient and the physician involved with the explanation should sign the form. It is always preferable for the physician who is to perform the procedures to be the one to explain the procedures to the patient. If circumstances require other physicians to explain the procedures, they should make it clear that they are acting on behalf of the performing physician, but sign their own names on the form. It is always inadvisable for a nurse or a physician assistant to obtain the patient's authorization, except perhaps for uncomplicated or less risky procedures, but even then, the patient should be offered the opportunity to discuss the procedure with the performing physician. From the hospital's viewpoint, the physician's signature is some measure of assurance that the serious legal consequences of an unauthorized operation in the hospital are being minimized.

**Patient's legal representative.** When the patient is a minor, unconscious, mentally incapable of understanding, or otherwise incapacitated, the next of kin or legal guardian is legally responsible for authorizing medical services for the patient. Since courts are increasingly recognizing the rights of mature minors, any minor who can understand the form should sign the form, in addition to the legal representative.

**Witness.** A witness not under the control of the physician should witness the signing and sign as a witness. Although not legally necessary for validity of the form, a witness is useful to add solemnity to the event. A witness who is a relative or friend of the patient may also assist the patient in understanding the explanation of the procedures and consequences of signing the form.

# Nurses' Professional Liability Policies and Medical Malpractice Statutes

## PROFESSIONAL LIABILITY PROTECTION OFFERED BY AMERICAN NURSES' ASSOCIATION*

The American Nurses' Association is offering to members a professional malpractice protection plan underwritten by National Union Fire Insurance Co., a member company of American International Companies.

Two limits of coverage are offered: $100,000/$300,000 provides $100,000 per occurrence or an aggregate of $300,000 per year. The $200,000/$600,000 provides $200,000 per occurrence or an aggregate of $600,000 per year.

American Nurses' Association and the underwriter believe these limits of coverage to be adequate today to meet the needs of registered nurse activities. Should increasing awards indicate a trend otherwise, the association and the underwriter will consider making a larger limit available.

The ANA plan provides protection for professional services rendered or services which should have been rendered ... including the administering of drugs or medicine.

It provides protection for errors and omissions while the insured is serving on formal boards or committees of the professional nursing organizations or any professional committee in the practice of the insured member's profession.

It provides protection for the performance of additional professional acts by the R.N. so authorized under the Nursing Practice Act of the state

---

* Reprinted from the Professional Liability Insurance Policy of ANA by permission of the American Nurses' Association, © 1978.

in which the nurse is licensed. Only two specialists are excluded from coverage under the ANA plan and they are the Nurse Anesthetist and full-time Radiation Therapist.

The plan provides protection for the nurse instructor for acts which students perform while under such supervision ... it provides protection for activities as a director or supervisor of nursing. It will not cover personal management or ownership activities. The plan does not cover the operation of a Nursing Home.

The ANA plan provides protection to all participants. However, participants must be licensed to practice registered nursing in the state of employment. Military and federal nurses are exempted under this provision.

Under the ANA plan the protection afforded by the agreement applies to occurrences provided they take place on or after the date the agreement is in force (the effective date the agreement is issued and continuously renewed) and provided the claim is first made against the member during the agreement period or within 60 days after the expiration of the agreement.

A feature of the plan is a money-back guarantee. If participants in the plan are dissatisfied with the plan after having read the contract, and return that "cancelled" contractual agreement to the administrator within ten days of receipt of the agreement, the full moneys paid for the protection will be refunded.

Coverage is not available in Indiana. At publication time, arrangements are being made to have individual coverage available in California and Ohio.

The annual fee for the 100-300 service is $22.25. The annual fee for the 200-600 service is $28.50.

A 6-month plan is available for Graduate Nurses. Maximum coverage is $25,000 per occurrence with a total of $75,000 in any one year. Protection may be renewed once. Graduate Nurses must be acting under supervision of a Registered Nurse or physician. The semi-annual fee for Graduate Nurse coverage is $12.50.

Insurance plans of American Nurses' Association are programs of Special Membership Services. A portion of the yearly fee is used to defray the administrative cost incurred by the association and the plan administrator. ANA membership dues money is not used to maintain insurance programs.

Address inquiries about the American Nurses' Association's Professional Liability Protection Plan to Special Membership Services, ANA, 2420 Pershing Road, 5th Floor, Kansas City, Missouri, 64108.

# A NURSE'S SAMPLE PROFESSIONAL LIABILITY POLICY

## Declaration of Contents

Insurer
THE X INSURANCE COMPANY
111 MAIN ST., CHICAGO, ILL.

Agent
SMITH & JONES CO., AGENTS
222 SOUTH ST., PITTSBURGH, PENNA.

Insured
MISS IDA GREEN
333 ELM ST., PITTSBURGH, PENNA.

Policy period
FROM JANUARY 1, 1969 TO JANUARY 1, 1970

Liability limits
Premium

each claim ....................................... $ 40,000
aggregate ....................................... $120,000
yearly .......................................... $7.00

Pending actions
The named insured represents that no claims, demands, or legal actions are pending against the name insured arising out of any actual or alleged error, mistake, or malpractice.

The insurer named in the declaration of contents contracts with the named insured, named in the declaration of contents, in consideration of the paying of the stated premium and in reliance upon the statements made in the declaration and subject to all of the terms of this policy:

## INSURING AGENT
1. Coverage
    A. Malpractice Liability—to pay on behalf of the insured all sums which the insured shall become legally obligated to pay as damages because of injury arising out of malpractice, error, or mistake in rendering or failing to render nursing services.

## DEFENSE AND SETTLEMENT
The insurance company under this policy shall:
   A. Defend any suit against the named insured alleging injury to persons and/or property and which is seeking damages that are payable under this policy.
   B. Make any settlement of any claim or suit as it determines expedient.

## POLICY PERIOD
This policy is applicable only to accidents occurring during the stated policy period.

## CONDITIONS

1. Notice of Occurrence—When the insured knows of any alleged accident covered herein, he shall notify the company as soon as possible.
2. Notice of Claim—When any claim is instituted against the insured, he must immediately notify the company in writing and forward every notice or summons he or his representative has received.
3. Assistance—The insured must assist the company upon the company's request and such assistance shall include attending all hearings and trials and the giving of evidence. The insured must also assist in making settlements upon request of the company.
4. Other Insurance—If the insured has other insurance against a loss included under this policy's coverage, this company will pay its pro rata share of the loss.
5. Assignment—The insured cannot assign any interest in this policy, unless he receives written authorization from a properly authorized representative of the company. Every other attempt to assign the insured's interest shall not be effective.
6. Subrogation—Whenever the company makes any payment under this policy, the company will be subrogated to all of the rights of the insured to recover against any other person.
7. Changes—No agent of the company may change any section of this policy unless he receives written authorization from the company.
8. Cancellation—The insured may cancel this policy at any time by returning the policy to any agent of the company.
9. Limits of Liability—The liability of this policy shall be limited by the declaration applicable to "each claim" on each claim or suit. The liability of this policy shall be limited by the declaration applicable to "aggregate" for the total liability of the company.

---

Signature of Agent                    Signature of Named Insured

---

Witness

---

Witness

## LOUISIANA MEDICAL MALPRACTICE STATUTES

### PART XX. MEDICAL MALPRACTICE COVERAGE [NEW]
*This section, enacted by Acts 1975, No. 477. § 1 as R.S. 40:1299.40, has been redesignated on authority of R.S. 24:253.*

§ 1299.37 State hospitals; medical malpractice coverage

Each state owned or state operated hospital in Louisiana may provide medical malpractice coverage to medical doctors, dentists and professional nurses

who are employed by such hospital or who donate services free of charge to such hospital or who have personal services contracts with such hospital to provide medical services. Such coverage shall only apply to those claims arising from services rendered by such medical doctors, dentists or professional nurses as a direct result of such employment, donation of services or contract for services. For the purposes of this Part the term "medical doctor" shall mean any person holding a valid certificate to practice medicine issued pursuant to R.S. 37:1273: the term "dentist" shall mean any person holding a valid certificate to practice dentistry issued pursuant to R.S. 37:751 through R.S. 37:763; the term "professional nurse" shall mean any person holding a valid certificate to practice nursing pursuant to R.S. 37:921, R.S. 37:971 or R.S. 37:972.
Added by Acts 1975, No. 477, § 1.

### PART XXI. MALPRACTICE COVERAGE: STATE EMPLOYED PHYSICIANS, DENTISTS AND PROFESSIONAL NURSES [NEW]
*This Part and Section, enacted by Acts 1975, No. 674, § 1 as Part XX, R.S. 40:1299.40, has been redesignated on authority of R.S. 24:253.*

§ 1299.38 State agency may provide malpractice coverage
Each agency of the state which employs physicians, dentists or professional nurses to provide medical services for or on behalf of such agency and each agency of the state to whom any medical doctor, dentist or professional nurse donates their services may provide such persons with medical malpractice coverage at no cost to such persons. For the purposes of this Part the term "physician" shall mean any person holding a valid certificate to practice medicine issued pursuant to R.S. 37:1273; the term "dentist" shall mean any person holding a valid certificate to practice dentistry issued pursuant to R.S. 37:751 through R.S. 37:763; the term "professional nurse" shall mean any person holding a valid certificate to practice nursing pursuant to R.S. 37:921, R.S. 37:971 or R.S. 37:972. The coverage provided for herein shall apply only to those actions arising from services rendered as a direct result of such employment or donation.
Added by Acts 1975, No. 674, § 1.

### PART XXI-A. MALPRACTICE LIABILITY FOR STATE SERVICES [NEW]

§ 1299.39 Definitions and general applications
A. As used in this Part:
(1) "Person" means a physician, dentist, registered nurse, licensed practical nurse, pharmacist, optometrist, podiatrist, physical therapist, acting in the course and scope of his employment, health care facility staff appointment, or assignment for or on behalf of the State, or a resident, intern, or a student of any discipline listed herein who is assigned as a part of his prescribed training when acting in the course and scope of his employment, staff appointment, or assignment for or on behalf of the State.
(2) "Physician" means a person with a license or permit to practice medicine in this State.

(3) "Patient" means a natural person who receives or should have received health care from a person covered by this part.

(4) "Tort" means any breach of duty or any negligent act or omission proximately causing injury or damage to another. "Tort" shall not include any intentional act. The standard of care required of every person covered by this Part in rendering professional services or health care to a patient shall be to exercise that degree of skill ordinarily employed, under similar circumstances by the members of his profession in good standing in the community or locality and to use reasonable care and diligence, along with his best judgment in the application of his skill.

(5) "Malpractice" means any unintentional tort or any breach of contract based on health care or professional services rendered, or which should have been rendered, by a health care provider, to a patient, and also includes such legal responsibility of a health care provider arising from defects in blood, tissue, transplants, drugs and medicines, or from defects in or failures of prosthetic devices, implanted in or used on or in the person of a patient.

(6) "Health Care" means any act or treatment performed or furnished or which should have been performed or furnished by any person covered by this part for, to, or on behalf of a patient during the medical care, treatment, or confinement of the patient.

B.  There is created a State Health Care Provider Fund. Said fund shall be administered by the Division of Administration of the Office of the Governor for the exclusive purpose of paying expenditures as provided in Sub-section C of this Section for defense of claims and for any judgments of a court or a compromise as provided therein.

C.  Notwithstanding any other provisions of the law to the contrary, any health care provider ("person" as defined herein) acting within the course and scope of his employment, health care facility staff appointment or assignment for or on behalf of the State to any health care institution whether or not he receives compensation for such services, shall be held liable for any amount of damages in excess of five hundred thousand dollars plus interest and costs for any injury or death of the patient due to any alleged act of malpractice within the course and scope of such employment, staff appointment, or assignment. The State shall pay from the State Health Care Provider Fund created by Subsection A of this section any costs of legal defense and damages awarded by judgment of a court or by a compromise after institution of a suit for a medical malpractice claim or claims against such health care provider ("person" as defined herein) not to exceed five hundred thousand dollars plus interests and cost.

D.  Any such judgment, settlement, or compromise, including any costs of legal defense, rendered against any health care provider, as defined herein, shall be paid by the state of Louisiana.

Added by Acts 1976, No. 66, § 1. Amended by Acts 1976, No. 660, § 1.

## PART XXII. UNIFORM CONSENT LAW [NEW]

*This Part, enacted by Acts 1975, No. 529 as Part XX, has been redesignated on authority of R.S. 24:253.*

§ 1299.40  Consent to medical treatment

A.  Notwithstanding any other law to the contrary, written consent to medical treatment means a consent in writing to any medical or surgical procedure or course of procedures which (a) sets forth in general terms the nature and purpose of the procedure or procedures, together with the known risks, if any, of death, brain damage, quadriplegia, paraplegia, the loss or loss of function of any organ or limb, of disfiguring scars associated with such procedure or procedures, (b) acknowledges that such disclosure of information has been made and that all questions asked about the procedure or procedures have been answered in a satisfactory manner, and (c) is signed by the patient for whom the procedure is to be performed, or if the patient for any reason lacks legal capacity to consent by a person who has legal authority to consent on behalf of such patient in such circumstances. Such consent shall be presumed to be valid and effective, in the absence of proof that execution of the consent was induced by misrepresentation of material facts.

B.  Except as provided in Subsection A of this Section, no evidence shall be admissible to modify or limit the authorization for performance of the procedure or procedures set forth in such written consent.

C.  Where consent to medical treatment from a patient, or from a person authorized by law to consent to medical treatment for such patient, is secured other than in accordance with Subsection A above , the explanation to the patient or to the person consenting for such patient shall include the matters set forth in Paragraph (a) of Subsection A above, and an opportunity shall be afforded for asking questions concerning the procedures to be performed which shall be answered in a satisfactory manner. Such consent shall be valid and effective and is subject to proof according to the rules of evidence in ordinary cases.

Added by Acts 1975, No. 529, § 1. Amended by Acts 1976, No. 407, § 1.


PART XXIII.  MEDICAL MALPRACTICE [NEW]
*This Part, enacted by Acts 1975, No. 817 as Part XX, has been redesignated on authority of R.S. 24:253*

§ 1299.41  Definitions and general applications

A.  As used in this Part:

(1)  "Health care provider" means a person, corporation, facility or institution licensed by this state to provide health care or professional services as a physician, hospital, dentist, registered or licensed practical nurse, pharmacist, optometrist, podiatrist, chiropractor, physical therapist or psychologist, or an officer, employee or agent thereof acting in the course and scope of his employment.

(2)  "Physician" means a person with an unlimited license to practice medicine in this state.

(3)  "Patient" means a natural person who receives or should have received health care from a licensed health care provider, under a contract, express or implied.

(4) "Hospital" means any hospital as defined in R.S. 40:2102; any "nursing home" or "home" as defined in R.S. 40:2009.2; or any physician's or dentist's offices or clinics containing facilities for the examination, diagnosis, treatment or care of human illnesses.

(5) "Commissioner" means the commissioner of insurance of this state.

(6) "Representative" means the spouse, parent, guardian, trustee, attorney or other legal agent of the patient.

(7) "Tort" means any breach of duty or any negligent act or omission proximately causing injury or damage to another. The standard of care required of every health care provider, except a hospital, in rendering professional services or health care to a patient, shall be to exercise that degree of skill ordinarily employed, under similar circumstances, by the members of his profession in good standing in the same community or locality, and to use reasonable care and diligence, along with his best judgment, in the application of his skill.

(8) "Malpractice" means any unintentional tort or any breach of contract based on health care or professional services rendered, or which should have been rendered, by a health care provider, to a patient, and also includes all legal responsibility of a health care provider arising from defects in blood, tissue, transplants, drugs and medicines, or from defects in or failures of prosthetic devices, implanted in or used on or in the person of a patient.

(9) "Health care" means any act, or treatment performed or furnished, or which should have been performed or furnished, by any health care provider for, to, or on behalf of a patient during the patient's medical care, treatment or confinement.

(10) "Risk manager" means an insurance company appointed by the commissioner to manage the authority.

(11) "Risk" means any health care provider which shall apply for malpractice liability insurance coverage under the provisions of Section 1299.46.

(12) "Insurer" means the authority or an insurance company appointed to manage the authority, or an insurer writing policies of malpractice insurance.

(13) "Authority" means the Residual Malpractice Insurance Authority established under Section 1299.46.

(14) "Proof of financial responsibility" as provided for in this Part shall be determined by the commissioner of insurance in accordance with regulations enacted under the Administration Procedures Act of Louisiana.

B. Wherever necessary to the context of this Part the masculine shall mean and include the feminine and the singular shall mean and include the plural.

C. No liability shall be imposed upon any health care provider on the basis of an alleged breach of contract, whether by express or implied warranty, assuring results to be obtained from any procedure undertaken in the course of health care, unless such contract is expressly set forth in writing and signed by such health care provider or by an authorized agent of such health care provider.

D. A health care provider who fails to qualify under this Part is not covered by the provisions of this Part and is subject to liability under the law without regard to the provisions of this Part. If a health care provider does not so qualify, the patient's remedy will not be affected by the terms and provisions of this Part.

E.   Subject to R.S. 40:1299.47, a patient or his representative having a claim under this Part for bodily injury or death on account of malpractice may file a complaint in any court of law having requisite jurisdiction. No dollar amount or figure shall be included in the demand in any malpractice complaint, but the prayer shall be for such damages as are reasonable in the premises.

F.   The provisions of this Part do not apply to any act of malpractice which occurred before September 1, 1975.

Added by Acts 1975, No. 817, § 1. Amended by Acts 1976, No. 183 §§ 1, 2; Acts 1976, No. 660, § 1.

### § 1299.42   Limitation of recovery

A.   To be qualified under the provisions of this Part, a health care provider shall:

(1) Cause to be filed with the commissioner proof of financial responsibility as provided by Subsection E of this Section.

(2) Pay the surcharge assessed by this Part on all health care providers according to R.S. 40:1299.44; and

(3) For self-insureds, qualification shall be effective upon acceptance of proof of financial responsibility by and payment of the surcharge to the commissioner of insurance. Qualification shall be effective for all others at the time the malpractice insurer accepts payment of the surcharge.

B.   (1) The total amount recoverable for any injury or death of a patient may not exceed five hundred thousand dollars plus interest and cost.

(2) A health care provider qualified under this Part is not liable for an amount in excess of one hundred thousand dollars for all claims of malpractice because of injury to or death of any one person.

(3) Any amount due from a judgment or settlement or from a final award in an arbitration proceeding which is in excess of the total liability of all liable health care providers, as provided in Paragraphs (1) and (2) of this Subsection, shall be paid from the patient's compensation fund pursuant to the provisions of R.S. 40:1299.44(C).

C.   Except as provided in Section 1299.44(C), any advance payment made by the defendant health care provider or his insurer to or for the plaintiff, or any other person, may not be construed as an admission of liability for injuries or damages suffered by the plaintiff or anyone else in an action brought for medical malpractice.

D.   Evidence of an advance payment is not admissible until there is a final judgment in favor of the plaintiff, in which event the court shall reduce the judgment to the plaintiff to the extent of the advance payment. The advance payment shall inure to the exclusive benefit of the defendant or his insurer making the payment. In the event the advance payment exceeds the liability of the defendant or the insurer making it, the court shall order any adjustment necessary to equalize the amount which each defendant is obligated to pay, exclusive of costs. In no case shall an advance payment in excess of an award be repayable by the person receiving it.

E.   Financial responsibility of a health care provider under this Section may be established only by filing with the commissioner proof that the health care provider is insured by a policy of malpractice liability insurance in the amount of at least one hundred thousand dollars per claim or in the event the health care provider is self-insured, proof of financial responsibility in excess of one hundred thousand dollars.

Added by Acts 1975, No. 817, § 1. Amended by Acts 1976, No. 183, § 3.

### § 1299.43   Blank.

### § 1299.44   Patient's compensation fund

A.   (1) Subject to the exceptions contained in Article VII, Section 3(A) of the Louisiana Constitution of 1974, all funds collected pursuant to the provisions hereof shall be paid into the state treasury and shall be credited to the Bond Security and Redemption Fund. Out of the funds remaining in the Bond Security and Redemption Fund after a sufficient allocation is allocated from that fund to pay all obligations secured by the full faith and credit of the state due and payable within any fiscal year, the treasurer shall, prior to placing such remaining funds in the state general fund, pay into a special fund, which is hereby created in the state treasury and designated as the Patient's Compensation Fund, in an amount equal to the total amount of funds paid into the treasury as a result of the collections provided for hereunder. The fund and any income from it shall be held in trust, and all of such funds and income shall be subject to use and disposition only as provided by this Section.

(2) In order to provide monies for the fund, an annual surcharge shall be levied on all health care providers in Louisiana qualified under the provisions of this Part. The surcharge shall be determined by the Louisiana Insurance Rating Commission based upon actuarial principles and shall not exceed twenty percent of the cost to each health care provider for maintenance of financial responsibility. The surcharge shall be collected on the same basis as premiums by each insurer, the risk manager and surplus lines agents. The commissioner of insurance shall collect the surcharge from health care providers qualified as self-insureds. The surcharge for self-insureds shall be the amount determined by the insurance commissioner in accordance with regulations enacted under the Administration Procedure Act of Louisiana to be the amount of surcharge which the health care provider would reasonably be required to pay were his qualifications based upon filing a policy of malpractice liability insurance.

(3) Such surcharge shall be due and payable within thirty days after the premiums for malpractice liability insurance have been received by the insurer, risk manager and surplus lines agents from the health care provider in Louisiana.

(4) If the annual premium surcharge is not paid within the time limited above, the certificate of authority of the insurer, risk manager, and surplus lines agents shall be suspended until the annual premium surcharge is paid.

(5) All expenses of collecting, protecting and administering the fund shall be paid from the fund. The functions of collecting and administering the fund shall

be carried out by the insurance commissioner and his employees, or the commissioner may contract to carry out said functions for an amount not to exceed the amount appropriated by the legislature. The function of protecting the fund, including all matters relating to the evaluating and settlement of claims and relating to the defense of the fund shall be carried out by the attorney general. The attorney general may enter into contracts with persons to perform services in connection with and relating to the defense of the fund for an amount not to exceed the amount appropriated by the legislature for this purpose. These expenses of the commissioner of insurance and the attorney general shall be paid from the fund by the state treasurer in accordance with law. The fund shall be a budget unit of this state. The legislature shall appropriate from the fund, sufficient monies for the carrying out by the insurance commissioner and the attorney general of the duties, functions and responsibilities imposed upon them in this Section, and shall also appropriate all remaining monies in the fund for use by the treasurer to pay final judgments, court approved settlements, and final arbitration awards in accordance with Paragraph (7) of this Subsection A, and in accordance with Subsection B of this section.

(6) If the fund exceeds the sum of fifteen million dollars at the end of any calendar year after the payment of all claims and expenses, the Louisiana Insurance Rating Commission shall reduce the surcharge provided in this Subsection in order to maintain the fund at an approximate level of fifteen million dollars.

(7) All claims from the patient's compensation fund shall be computed on December 31 of the year in which the claim becomes final. All claims shall be paid on or before January 15. If the fund would be exhausted by payment in full of all claims allowed during a calendar year, then the amount paid to each claimant shall be prorated. Any amounts due and unpaid shall be paid in the following calendar years.

B. The state treasurer shall issue a warrant in the amount of each claim submitted to him against the fund on December 31 of each year. The only claim against the fund shall be a voucher or other appropriate request by the commissioner after he receives:

(1) A certified copy of a final judgment in excess of one hundred thousand dollars against a health care provider; or

(2) A certified copy of a court approved settlement in excess of one hundred thousand dollars against a health care provider; or

(3) A certified copy of a final award in excess of one hundred thousand dollars in an arbitration proceeding against a health care provider.

C. If the insurer of a health care provider or a self-insured health care provider has agreed to settle its liability on a claim against its insured and claimant is demanding an amount in excess thereof from the patient's compensation fund for a complete and final release, then the following procedure must be followed:

(1) A petition shall be filed by the claimant with the court in which the action is pending against the health care provider, if none is pending in the parish where plaintiff or defendant is domiciled seeking (a) approval of an agreed set-

tlement, if any, and/or (b) demanding payment of damages from the patient's compensation fund.

(2) A copy of the petition shall be served on the commissioner, the health care provider and his insurer, at least ten days before filing and shall contain sufficient information to inform the other parties about the nature of the claim and the additional amount demanded.

(3) The commissioner and the insurer of the health care provider or the self-insured health care provider as the case may be, may agree to a settlement with the claimant from the patient's compensation fund, or the commissioner and the insurer of the health care provider or the self-insured health care provider as the case may be, may file written objections to the payment of the amount demanded. The agreement or objections to the payment demanded shall be filed within twenty days after the petition is filed.

(4) As soon as practicable after the petition is filed in the court the judge shall fix the date on which the petition seeking approval of the agreed settlement and/or demanding payment of damages from the fund shall be heard, and shall notify the claimant, the insurer of the health care provider or the self-insured health care provider as the case may be, and the commissioner thereof as provided by law.

(5) At the hearing the commissioner, the claimant and the insurer of the health care provider or the self-insured health care provider as the case may be, may introduce relevant evidence to enable the court to determine whether or not the petition should be approved if it is submitted on agreement without objections. If the commissioner, the insurer of the health care provider or the self-insured health care provider as the case may be, and the claimant cannot agree on the amount, if any, to be paid out of the patient's compensation fund, then the court shall determine the amount of claimant's damages, if any, in excess of the amount already paid by the insurer of the health care provider. The court shall determine the amount for which the fund is liable and render a finding and judgment accordingly. In approving a settlement or determining the amount, if any, to be paid from the patient's compensation fund, the court shall consider the liability of the health care provider as admitted and established where the insurer has paid its policy limits of one hundred thousand dollars, or where the self-insured health care provider has paid one hundred thousand dollars.

(6) Any settlement approved by the court shall not be appealed. Any judgment of the court fixing damages recoverable in any such contested proceeding shall be appealable pursuant to the rules governing appeals in any other civil court case tried by the court.

(7) For the benefit of both the insured and the patient's compensation fund, the insurer of the health provider shall exercise good faith and reasonable care both in evaluating the plaintiff's claim and in considering and acting upon settlement thereof. A self-insured health care provider shall, for the able care both in evaluating the plaintiff's claim and in considering and acting upon settlement thereof.

Added by Acts 1975, 817, § 1. Amended by Acts 1976, No. 183 § 4.

§ 1299.45 **Malpractice coverage**

A. Only while malpractice liability insurance remains in force, or in the case of a self-insured health care provider, only while the security required by regulations of the insurance commissioner remains undiminished, are the health care provider and his insurer liable to a patient, or his representative, for malpractice to the extent and in the manner specified in this Part.

B. The filing of proof of financial responsibilty with the commissioner shall constitute, on the part of the insurer, a conclusive and unqualified acceptance of the provisions of this Part.

C. Any provision in a policy attempting to limit or modify the liability of the insurer contrary to the provisions of this Part is void, except that a provision in a malpractice liability insurance policy approved by the insurance commissioner which limits the aggregate sum for which the insurer may be liable during the policy period shall be valid.

D. Every policy issued under this Part is deemed to include the following provisions, and any change which may be occasioned by legislation adopted by the legislature of the state of Louisiana as fully as if it were written therein:

(1) The insurer assumes all obligations to pay an award imposed against its insured under the provisions of this Part; and

(2) Any termination of this policy by cancellation is not effective as to patients claiming against the insured covered hereby, unless at least thirty days before the taking effect of the cancellation, a written notice giving the date upon which termination becomes effective has been received by the insured and the commissioner at their offices. In no event shall said cancellation affect in any manner any claim which arose against the insurer or its insured during the life of the policy.

E. If an insurer fails or refuses to pay a final judgment, except during the pendency of an appeal, or fails, or refuses to comply with any provisions of this Part, in addition to any other legal remedy, the commissioner may also revoke the approval of its policy form until the insurer pays the award or judgment or has complied with the violated provisions of this Part and has resubmitted its policy form and received the approval of the commissioner.

Added by Acts 1975, No. 817, § 1. Amended by Acts 1976, No. 183, § 5.

§ 1299.46 **Risk management; authority**

A. The purpose of this Section is to make malpractice liability insurance available to qualified risks as defined in this Part.

B. There is created the Residual Malpractice Insurance Authority. The Department of Insurance is designated as the authority for the purposes of this Part. The authority is empowered to engage in making malpractice liability insurance in this state.

C. The commissioner shall appoint a risk manager for the authority. Unless otherwise agreed between the risk manager and the commissioner the separate, personal or independent assets of the risk manager shall not be liable for or subject to use or expenditure for the purpose of providing insurance by the authority.

All contracts between the commission and the risk manager, and any amendment thereto, and any adjustments made in the compensation or duties of the risk manager permitted by such contracts shall require the approval of the Division of Administration.

D. In the administration and provision for malpractice liability insurance by the authority, the risk manager shall:

(1) Be subject to all laws and regulations of this state which apply to insurance. Except as provided by this Part the Residual Malpractice Insurance Authority shall not be subject to the taxes provided by the Louisiana Insurance Code.

(2) Prepare and file appropriate forms with the Department of Insurance.

(3) Prepare and file premium rates with the Department of Insurance.

(4) Perform the underwriting functions; and subject to approval of the commissioner, shall formulate underwriting standards for insuring health care providers who by reason of training, experience, claims history and other generally accepted underwriting standards are reasonable insurance risks.

(5) Dispose of all claims and litigations arising out of insurance policies.

(6) Maintain adequate books and records.

(7) File an annual financial statement regarding its operations under this Section with the Department of Insurance on forms prescribed by the commissioner.

(8) Obtain private reinsurance for the authority, if necessary.

(9) Prepare and file for approval of the commissioner, a schedule of agent's compensation; and

(10) Prepare and file a plan of operations with the commissioner for approval.

E. Unless otherwise agreed between the risk manager and the commissioner, the risk manager shall receive as compensation for its services a percentage of all premiums received by it under the terms of this Section, as determined by the commissioner. The compensation may be adjusted by the commissioner.

F. If a health care provider desires malpractice liability insurance under this Part, he shall forward his application to the risk manager.

G. If the risk manager declines to accept the risk, notice of declination, together with reasons, shall be sent to the applicant and the commissioner. The applicant shall have ten days from the date of notice to file an appeal for review by the commissioner. On appeal, the commissioner shall review the decision of the risk manager to determine whether the approved underwriting standards have been fairly applied by the risk manager and shall enter an appropriate order.

H. The surplus of premiums over losses and expenses received by the authority shall be placed in a segregated fund and shall be invested and reinvested by the risk manager with the concurrence of the commissioner in accordance with the insurance code of the state of Louisiana and investment income generated shall remain in the fund. These funds shall not be considered public or state funds.

I.  The authority may issue malpractice liability insurance policies only to health care providers who are residents of Louisiana and to corporations, foreign or domestic, with regard to health care facilities operated within Louisiana. Insofar as practical, only the claims experience of Louisiana health care providers shall be considered in the determination of rates for such policies. The rates for such policies shall otherwise be determined and approved according to the same procedures and principles as rates for malpractice liability policies issued by private insurers in Louisiana.

Added by Acts 1975, No. 817, § 1. Amended by Acts 1976, No. 183, § 6.

### § 1299.47   Medical review panel

A.  All malpractice claims against health care providers covered by this Part, other than claims validly agreed for submission to a lawfully binding arbitration procedure, shall be reviewed by a medical review panel established as hereinafter provided in this Section.

B.  No action against a health care provider covered by this Part, or his insurer, may be commenced in any court of this state before the claimant's proposed complaint has been presented to a medical review panel established pursuant to this Section and an opinion is rendered by the panel. By agreement of both parties, the use of the medical review panel may be waived.

C.  Except as provided in Paragraph 5 of this Subsection, the medical review panel shall consist of one attorney and three physicians who hold unlimited licenses to practice medicine. The attorney shall act in an advisory capacity and as chairman of the panel, but shall have no vote. The medical review panel shall be selected in the following manner:

(1)  All physicians engaged in the active practice of medicine in this state who practice in the same community or locality as does the health care provider against whom claim is made, whether in the teaching profession or otherwise, who hold a license to practice medicine in the state of Louisiana, shall be available for selection.

(2)  Each party to the action shall have the right to select one physician and upon selection, said physician shall be required to serve. The two physicians thus selected shall select the third physician panelist, and after diligent effort should no agreement be reached within ten days, then the third physician panelist shall be drawn by lot by the attorney member of the panel from among two names submitted by each of the panelists already selected.

(3)  Where there are multiple plaintiffs or defendants, there shall be only one physician selected per side. The plaintiff, whether single or multiple, shall have the right to select one physician and the defendant, whether single or multiple, shall have the right to select one physician.

(4)  A panelist so selected and the attorney member selected in accordance with Subparagraph (7) below shall serve unless for good cause shown he may be excused. To show good cause for relief from serving, the panelist shall present an affidavit to a judge of the appropriate district court, which shall set out the facts showing that service would constitute an unreasonable burden or undue

hardship. The court may excuse the proposed panelist from serving, and in such event a replacement panelist shall be selected within ten days.

(5) If there is only one party defendant, other than a hospital, all panelists except the attorney shall be from the same class and specialty of practice of health care provider as the defendant. If there are claims against multiple defendants, one or more of whom are health care providers other than a paragraph of this Subpart C, and Subparagraphs (1), (2) and (3) hereof, may also be selected from health care providers who are from the same class and specialty of practice of health care providers as are any of the defendants other than a hospital.

(6) Within ten days after notification of a proposed panelist by the plaintiff, the defendant shall select a proposed panelist.

(7) The parties may agree on the attorney member of the panel, or if no agreement can be reached, then the attorney member shall be drawn by lot from the list of attorneys qualified to practice and presently on the rolls of the Supreme Court of the state of Louisiana. Upon request the clerk of the supreme court shall draw five names at random from the list of attorneys who reside in the same geographic area as the parties, and the parties shall then each strike two names alternately, with the claimant striking first until both sides have stricken two names and the remaining name shall be the attorney member of the panel.

(8) Before entering upon their duties, each voting panelist shall subscribe before a notary public the following oath:

"I, (name), do solemnly swear/affirm that I will faithfully perform the duties of medical review panel member to the best of my ability and without partiality or favoritism of any kind. I acknowledge that I represent neither side and that it is my lawful duty to serve with complete impartiality and to render a decision in accordance with law and the evidence."

The attorney panel member shall subscribe to the same oath except that in lieu of the last sentence thereof the attorney's oath shall state:

"I acknowledge that I represent neither side and that it is my lawful duty to advise the panel members concerning matters of law and procedure and to serve as chairman."

The original of each oath shall be attached to the opinion rendered by the panel.

D.   The evidence to be considered by the medical review panel shall be promptly submitted by the respective parties in written form only. The evidence may consist of medical charts, x-rays, lab tests, excerpts of treatises, depositions of witnesses including parties and any other form of evidence allowable by the medical review panel. Upon request of any party, or upon request of any two panel members, the clerk of any district court shall issue subpoenas and subpoenas duces tecum in aid of the taking of depositions and the production of documentary evidence for inspection and/or copying. The chairman of the panel shall advise the panel relative to any legal question involved in the review proceeding and shall prepare the opinion of the panel as provided in Subsection G. A copy of the evidence shall be sent to each member of the panel.

E.   Either party, after submission of all evidence and upon ten days notice to the other side, shall have the right to convene the panel at a time and place agreeable to the members of the panel. Either party may question the panel concerning any matters relevant to issues to be decided by the panel before the issuance of their report. The chairman of the panel shall preside at all meetings. Meetings shall be informal.

F.   The panel shall have the right and duty to request and procure all necessary information. The panel may consult with medical authorities. The panel may examine reports of such other health care providers necessary to fully inform itself regarding the issue to be decided. Both parties shall have full access to any material submitted to the panel.

G.   The panel shall have the sole duty to express its expert opinion as to whether or not the evidence supports the conclusion that the defendant or defendants acted or failed to act within the appropriate standards of care as charged in the complaint. After reviewing all evidence and after any examination of the panel by counsel representing either party, the panel shall, within thirty days, but in all events within one hundred eighty days of the selection of the last panel member, render one or more of the following expert opinions which shall be in writing and signed by the panelists:

(1) The evidence supports the conclusion that the defendant or defendants failed to comply with the appropriate standard of care as charged in the complaint.

(2) The evidence does not support the conclusion that the defendant or defendants failed to meet the applicable standard of care as charged in the complaint.

(3) That there is a material issue of fact, not requiring expert opinion, bearing on liability for consideration by the court.

(4) Where Subsection (2) above is answered in the affirmative, that the conduct complained of was or was not a factor of the resultant damages. If such conduct was a factor, whether the plaintiff suffered: (a) any disability and the extent and duration of the disability, and (b) any permanent impairment and the percentage of the impairment.

H.   The filing of the request for review of a claim shall suspend the time within which suit must be instituted, in accordance with this Part, until ninety days following the issuance of the opinion by the medical review panel. The request for review of a claim under this Section shall be deemed filed when a copy of the proposed complaint is delivered or mailed by registered or certified mail to the commissioner, who shall immediately forward a copy to each health care provider named as a defendant at his last and usual place of residence or his office.

I.   Any report of the expert opinion reached by the medical review panel shall be admissible as evidence in any action subsequently brought by the claimant in a court of law, but such expert opinion shall not be conclusive and either party shall have the right to call, at his cost, any member of the medical review panel as a witness. If called, the witness shall be required to appear and testify. A panelist shall have absolute immunity from civil liability for all communications, findings, opinions and conclusions made in the course and scope of duties prescribed by this Part.

J.   Each member of the medical review panel shall be paid at the rate of twenty-five dollars per diem, not to exceed a total of two hundred fifty dollars, for all work performed as a member of the panel exclusive of time involved if called as a witness to testify in court, and in addition thereto, reasonable travel expenses. Fees of the panel including travel expenses shall be paid by the side in whose favor the majority opinion is written. If there is no majority opinion, then each side shall pay one-half of the cost.

Added by Acts 1975, No. 817, § 1. Amended by Acts 1976, No. 183, § 7.

### § 1299.48   Reporting of claims

A.   For the purpose of providing the various licensing boards of Louisiana health care providers, as defined by R.S. 40:1299:41(A)(1), with information on malpractice claims paid by insurers or self insurers on behalf of health care providers in this state, each insurer of such health care provider, and each health care provider in Louisiana who is self insured shall, within thirty days of the date of payment, provide a written report to the licensing board of this state having licensing authority over the health care provider on whose behalf payment was made, and each such report shall contain:

(1)   The name and address of the health care provider.

(2)   A brief description of the acts of omission or commission which gave rise or allegedly gave rise to the claim, and the date thereof.

(3)   The name of the patient and the injury which resulted or allegedly resulted therefrom.

(4)   The amount paid in settlement or discharge of the claim, whether paid by compromise, by payment of judgment, by payment of arbitration award, or otherwise; and

(5)   Where any judicial opinion has been rendered with regard to a claim, a copy of such opinions shall be attached to the report.

Provided, however, no report shall be required for compromise settlements of claims where the amount paid is one thousand dollars or less, except where such payments were made in satisfaction or compromise of judgment of court or of award of arbitrators.

B.   The provisions of this Section shall apply to all health care providers in Louisiana, whther or not such health care provider has qualified under the provisions of this Part.

C.   There shall be no liability on the part of any insurer or person acting for said insurer, for any statements made in good faith in the reports required by this Section.

Added by Acts 1976, No. 114 § 1.

### PART XXIV.   LOUISIANA MEDICAL CONSENT LAW [NEW]

*This Part, enacted by Acts 1975, No. 798, § 1 as Part XX, consisting of R.S. 40:1299.40 to R.S. 40:1299.46, has been redesignated on authority of R.S. 24:253.*

§ 1299.50  Short title

This Part shall be known as and may be cited as the "Louisiana Medical Consent Law."
Added by Acts 1975, No. 798, § 1.

§ 1299.51  Part not applicable to abortion and sterilization

The provisions of this Part shall not apply in any manner whatsoever to the subjects of abortion and sterilization, which subjects shall continue to be governed by existing law independently of the terms and provisions of this Part.
Added by Acts 1975, No. 798, § 1.

§ 1299.52  Part not applicable to care and treatment of mentally ill

The provisions of this Part shall not apply to the care and treatment of the mentally ill, which subject shall continue to be governed by existing law independently of the terms and provisions of this Part.
Added by Acts 1975, No. 798, § 1.

§ 1299.53  Persons who may consent to surgical or medical treatment

In addition to such other persons as may be authorized and empowered, any one of the following persons is authorized and empowered to consent, either orally or otherwise, to any surgical or medical treatment or procedures including autopsy not prohibited by law which may be suggested, recommended, prescribed or directed by a duly licensed physician:

(a) Any adult, for himself.

(b) Any parent, whether an adult or a minor, for his minor child.

(c) Any married person, whether an adult or a minor, for himself, and for his spouse.

(d) Any person temporarily standing in loco parentis whether formally serving or not, for the minor under his care and any guardian for his ward.

(e) Any female regardless of age or marital status, for herself when given in connection with pregnancy or childbirth.

(f) In the absence of a parent, any adult, for his minor brother or sister.

(g) In the absence of a parent, any grandparent for his minor grandchild.
Added by Acts 1975, No. 798, § 1.

§ 1299.54  Emergencies

In addition to any other instances in which a consent is excused or implied at law, a consent to surgical or medical treatment or procedures, suggested, recommended, prescribed or directed by a duly licensed physician, will be implied where an emergency exists. For the purposes hereof, an emergency is defined as a situation wherein, (a) in competent medical judgment, the proposed surgical or medical treatment or procedures are reasonably necessary, and (b) a person authorized to consent under Section 1299.43 is not readily available, and any delay in treatment could reasonably be expected to jeopardize the life or health of the person affected, or could reasonably result in disfiguration or impair faculties.
Added by Acts 1975, No. 798, § 1.

§ 1299.55   Construction of part

The provisions of this Part shall be liberally construed, and all relationships set forth herein shall include the marital, adoptive, foster and step-relations as well as the natural whole blood. A consent by one person so authorized and empowered shall be sufficient. Any person acting in good faith shall be justified in relying on the representations of any person purporting to give such a consent, including, but not limited to, his identity, his age, his marital status, his emancipation and his relationship to any other person for whom the consent is purportedly given.
Added by Acts 1975, No. 798, § 1.

§ 1299.56   Right of adult to refuse treatment as to his own person not abridged

Nothing contained herein shall be construed to abridge any right of a person eighteen years of age or over to refuse to consent to medical or surgical treatment as to his own person.
Added by Acts 1975, No. 798, § 1.

§ 1299.57   Consent to medical arbitration agreements

The persons authorized and enpowered in R.S. 40:1299.53(a) and (b) to consent to surgical or medical treatment or procedures for others as provided therein are also authorized and empowered, for and on behalf of such others, and without court approval, to enter into binding medical arbitration agreements.
Added by Acts 1976, No. 269, § 1.

§ 5628.   Actions for medical malpractice

A.   No action for damages for injury or death against any physician, chiropractor, dentist, or hospital duly licensed under the laws of this state, whether based upon tort, or breach of contract, or otherwise, arising out of patient care shall be brought unless filed within one year from the date of the alleged act, omission or neglect; or within one year from the date of discovery of the alleged act, omission or neglect; provided, however, that even as to claims filed within one year from the date of such discovery, in all events such claims must be filed at the latest within a period of three years from the date of the alleged act, omission or neglect.

B.   The provision of this Section shall apply to all persons whether or not infirm or under disability of any kind and including minors and interdicts.
Added by Acts 1975, No. 808, § 1. Amended by Acts 1975, No. 214, § 1.

# Appendix D

# State-by-State Summary of Nurse Practice Acts*

---

\* Adopted from Virginia C. Hall, "Summary of Statutory Provisions Governing Legal Scope of Nursing Practice in the Various States," in *The New Health Professionals*, A Bliss and E. Cohen, Eds. (Germantown, Md.: Aspen Systems Corporation, 1977). Reprinted with permission. © 1977 Aspen Systems Corporation.

## If Additional Acts Amendment, Criteria and Conditions Stated

| State | Type of Definition | Definition Includes Prohibition Against Acts of Diagnosis and Prescription | Rules and Regulations | Professional Opinion | Education and Training | If New Definition, Incorporated some or all of New York's | Prohibitions of Practice of Medicine in Nurse Practice Act | Exception for Nursing in Medical Practice Act | Physician Supervision of Nurse Practitioners | Degree of Supervision |
|---|---|---|---|---|---|---|---|---|---|---|
| Alabama | New & Additional Acts Amendment | No | Yes | — | — | Yes | No | No | Required for Nurse Anesthetist | Direct for 30 days, then protocol for midwife |
| Alaska | Traditional & Additional Acts Amendment | Yes (Applies to "medical" acts only and additional acts not subject to prohibition.) | Yes* | — | — | — | No | No | Collaborative relationship for Nurse-Midwife | |
| Arizona | Traditional & Additional Acts Amendment† | No | Yes* | Yes* | Yes | — | No | Yes (Under physician supervision) | Under direction of and in collaboration with | Presence required for Nurse Anesthetist |
| Arkansas | Traditional | Yes (Applies to "medical" acts only) | — | — | — | — | No | Yes (Also separate exemption for nurse acting under physician supervision) | Required for Nurse Anesthetist | Presence required |
| California | New | No | — | — | — | No | No | Yes (For persons lawfully practicing another profession) | | As defined by policies and protocols developed for specific setting |
| Colorado | New & Additional Acts Amendment | No | Yes** | No | Yes | Yes | No | Yes (Also separate exemption for persons acting under physician supervision) | Required | Defined in protocols |

| State | Legislation Type | | | | | | | | Exemption / Supervision | Remarks |
|---|---|---|---|---|---|---|---|---|---|---|
| Connecticut | New | No | — | — | — | — | — | Yes | Yes | Yes (Under physician supervision) | Not stated |
| Delaware | Traditional | Yes | — | — | — | — | — | No | No | | Not stated |
| District of Columbia | No Definition | — | — | — | — | — | — | — | Yes | | Not stated |
| Florida | Traditional & Additional Acts Amendment | No | Yes | — | — | — | — | Yes | Yes (Under physician supervision) | | Not stated |
| Georgia | Traditional | No | — | — | — | — | — | — | Yes (Also separate exemption for persons acting under physician supervision) | | Nurse Anesthetists function under direction of physician |
| Hawaii | Traditional | Yes (Applies to "medical" acts only) | — | — | — | — | — | No | No (?)[2] | | No specific legislation |
| Idaho | Traditional & Additional Acts Amendment | Yes | Yes (Applies to "medical" acts only and additional acts not subject to prohibition) | No | No | — | — | No | No | | None referred to but "practice policies" for individuals may so indicate |
| Illinois | Traditional | Yes (Applies to "medical" acts only) | — | — | — | — | — | No | Yes (For persons lawfully practicing another profession) | | No specific legislation |
| Indiana | New & Additional Acts Amendment | No | Yes*** | No | No | Yes | Yes | No | Yes | | Required for Nurse Anesthetist |
| Iowa | New & Additional Acts Amendment | No | — | — | — | Yes | Yes | Yes | Yes | | No specific regulations |
| Kansas | Traditional | Yes | — | — | — | — | — | No | Yes (Also separate exemption for persons acting under physician supervision) | | No legislation |
| Kentucky | Traditional | Yes (Applies to "medical" acts only) | — | — | — | — | — | No | Yes | | No legislation |
| Louisiana | New & Additional Amendment Act | Yes | Yes | — | — | Yes | No | No | Yes | | Required |

If Additional Acts Amendment, Criteria and Conditions Stated

| State | Type of Definition | Definition Includes Prohibition Against Acts of Diagnosis and Prescription | Rules and Regulations | Professional Opinion | Education and Training | If New Definition, Incorporated some or all of New York's | Prohibitions of Practice of Medicine in Nurse Practice Act | Exception for Nursing in Medical Practice Act | Physician Supervision of Nurse Practitioners | Degree of Supervision |
|---|---|---|---|---|---|---|---|---|---|---|
| Maine | Traditional & Additional Acts Amendment | No | No | No | Yes | — | No | No | Physician can delegate certain services | |
| Maryland | New & Additional Acts Amendment | No | Yes** | Yes* | Yes | Yes | No | Yes (For persons lawfully practicing another profession) | Not stated | |
| Massachusetts | Traditional & Additional Acts Amendment | No | Yes* | Yes** | Yes | Yes | No | Yes (Applies only to nurses performing "Additional acts") | No regulations | |
| Michigan | Traditional | Yes (Applies to "medical" acts only) | — | — | — | — | No | Yes (For persons lawfully practicing another profession and separate exemption for persons acting under physician supervision) | No specific legislation | |
| Minnesota | New | No | — | — | — | Yes | No | Yes (For persons lawfully practicing another profession) | No specific legislation | |
| Mississippi | Traditional & Additional Acts Amendent | Yes (Applies to "medical" acts only and additional acts not subjected to prohibition) | Yes* | No | No | — | No | No | Not stated | |

| State | | | | | | | | | | |
|---|---|---|---|---|---|---|---|---|---|---|
| Missouri | New | No | — | — | — | Yes | No | Yes | No specific legislation | |
| Montana | Traditional | Yes | — | — | — | — | No | Yes | No specific legislation | |
| Nebraska | New & Additional Amendment Act | Yes, Medicine | Yes | — | — | Yes | No | Yes (For persons lawfully practicing another profession—not applicable to prescription or administration of drugs) | Required | Specific to each approved expanded role |
| Nevada | Traditional & Additional Acts Amendment | Yes (Applies to "medical" acts only and additional acts not subject to prohibition) | Yes** | Yes* | Yes | — | No | Yes | Collaboration | As agreed in writing |
| New Hampshire | New & Additional Acts Amendment | Yes (Additional acts not subject to prohibition) | Yes* | Yes** | Yes | Yes | No | Yes | Collaboration | Nurse anesthetists function within physical presence of physician |
| New Jersey | New | No | — | — | — | Yes | No | Yes (Under physician supervision) | No specific legislation | |
| New Mexico | Traditional | Yes (Applies to "medical" acts only) | — | — | — | — | No | Yes (Plus separate exemption for nurse practitioners in certain settings) | Required | |
| New York | New | No | — | — | No | Yes | Yes | Yes (For persons lawfully practicing another profession) | No regulations | |
| North Carolina | Traditional & Additional Acts Amendment | Yes (Applies to "medical" acts only and excepts acts under supervision of physician) | Yes* | No | No | — | No | Yes (For nursing and those acts "otherwise constituting medical practice" which are permitted by regulations of medical and nursing boards) | Required | Telecommunications, predetermined plan for emergencies, review of practice |
| North Dakota | Traditional | No | — | — | — | — | No | No | No regulations | |

## If Additional Acts Amendment, Criteria and Conditions Stated

| State | Type of Definition | Definition Includes Prohibition Against Acts of Diagnosis and Prescription | Rules and Regulations | Professional Opinion | Education and Training | If New Definition, Incorporated some or all of New York's | Prohibitions of Practice of Medicine in Nurse Practice Act | Exception for Nursing in Medical Practice Act | Physician Supervision of Nurse Practitioners | Degree of Supervision |
|---|---|---|---|---|---|---|---|---|---|---|
| Ohio | Traditional | Yes (Applies to "medical" acts only) | — | — | — | — | Yes | Yes (For nurse anesthetists only, under physician supervision) | Required for nurse-midwife and nurse anesthetist | Nurse anesthetist must work in presence of physician |
| Oklahoma | Traditional | Yes | — | — | — | — | No | Yes (Under physician supervision) | No regulations | |
| Oregon | New & Additional Acts Amendment | No | Yes** | Yes* | Yes | Yes | No | Yes | Collaboration | |
| Pennsylvania | New & Additional Acts Amendment | Yes (Applies to "medical" acts only and additional acts not subject to prohibition) | Yes* | No | No | Yes | Yes | No | Required | Telecommunications, predetermined plan for emergency |
| Rhode Island | Traditional | No | — | — | — | — | No | No | No specific legislation | |
| South Carolina | Traditional | Yes (Applies to "medical" acts only) | Yes | — | — | — | No | Yes | Required | Near proximity, available for consultation |

| State | Act Type | | | | | | | | |
|---|---|---|---|---|---|---|---|---|---|
| South Dakota | New & Additional Acts Amendment | No | Yes | No | Yes | Yes | Yes | Not stated | As indicated in written protocols for specific situations |
| Tennessee | Traditional | Yes (Applies to "medical" acts only) | — | — | — | No | Yes (Plus separate exemption for nurses under physician supervision) | Required | |
| Texas | Traditional | Yes (Applies to "medical" acts only) | Yes | — | — | Yes | Yes | Required (for medical treatment) | |
| Utah | New & Additional Acts Amendment | No | — | — | Yes | No | Yes | Required | |
| Vermont | New & Additional Acts Amendment | Yes | No | Yes | Yes | Yes | Yes (Under physician supervision) | No regulations | |
| Virginia | Traditional (Additional Amendments to Medical Practice Act) | No | Yes | — | — | No | Yes (Includes specific reference to certain procedures, which must be performed under orders of physician, plus separate exemption for nurses acting under physician supervision pursuant to rules and regulations of Boards of Nursing and Medicine) | Must be available for consultation | |
| Washington | New & Additional Acts Amendment | No | Yes** | Yes* | Yes | No | No | Uses "scope of practice" as in statements by national associations | |

## If Additional Acts Amendment, Criteria and Conditions Stated

| State | Type of Definition | Definition Includes Prohibition Against Acts of Diagnosis and Prescription | Rules and Regulations | Professional Opinion | Education and Training | If New Definition, Incorporated some or all of New York's | Prohibitions of Practice of Medicine in Nurse Practice Act | Exception for Nursing in Medical Practice Act | Physician Supervision of Nurse Practitioners | Degree of Supervision |
|---|---|---|---|---|---|---|---|---|---|---|
| West Virginia | Traditional | No | — | — | — | — | No | Yes | Required | Nurse anesthetists in presence of physician, nurse-midwives according to ACNM standards |
| Wisconsin | Traditional | No | — | — | — | — | No | Yes (Under physician supervision)[4] | No specific legislation | |
| Wyoming | New | No | — | — | — | — | No | Yes (Under physician supervision) | Required | Telecommunications, referral and consultation, regular chart review, pre-determined plan for emergencies, protocols for medication |

[1] Arizona's additional acts amendment, unlike any other, describes substantively one such act: the dispensing of prepackaged, labelled drugs under certain limited, specific circumstances.

[2] Hawaii has a delegation provision which applies to "any physician-support personnel" and which could be construed as including nurses.

[3] Although Maryland's additional acts amendment does not mention physician supervision, the amendment could be interpreted as subordinate to the definition's general description of nursing as consisting of "independent" nursing functions and "delegated" medical functions, in which case any medical acts within the additional acts amendment would have to be delegated acts.

[4] North Carolina's additional acts amendment does not mention physician supervision, but it appears in a separate section from the definition and would appear to be subordinate to that provision of the definition which prohibits acts of medical diagnosis and prescription except under physician supervision.

[5] Oregon alone among the states with additional acts amendments which refer to professional opinion speaks only of nursing opinion, as opposed to medical and nursing opinion.

[6] Wisconsin's law in this regard is somewhat oblique, but it would appear that not only nurses but any persons are authorized to "assist" physicians.

*By Boards of Nursing and Medicine.

**By Board of Nursing.

***By Board of Nursing or "in collaboration with" Board of Medicine.

*Cumulative with rules and regulations.

**Independent of rules and regulations.

# State-by-State Summary of Child Abuse Laws

| State | Citation | Applies To |
|-------|----------|------------|
| Alabama | Ala. Code Tit. 26, Section 26-14-1 (1975) | Hospitals, clinics, sanitariums, doctors, physicians, surgeons, medical examiners, coroners, dentists, osteopaths, optometrists, chiropractors, podiatrists, nurses, school teachers and officials, peace officers, law enforcement officials, pharmacists, social workers, day care workers or employees, mental health professionals, any other person called on to render aid or medical assistance to any child, or any person. |
| Alaska | Alaska Stat. Sections 47.17.010 to 47.17.070 (1971) | Practitioner of healing arts, school teachers, social workers, peace officers and officers of the division of corrections, administrative officers of institutions, or any other person. |
| Arizona | Ariz. Rev. Stat. Ann. Section 13-842.01 (1976) | Physician, hospital, intern, resident, surgeon, dentist, osteopath, chiropractor, podiatrist, medical examiner, nurse, psychologist, school personnel, social worker, peace officer, or any other person responsible for the care of children. |
| Arkansas | Ark. Stat. Ann. Sections 42.807-42-818 (1975) | Physician, surgeon, coroner, dentist, osteopath, resident, intern, registered nurse, hospital personnel (engaged in admission, examination, care, or treatment), teacher, school official, social service worker, day care center worker, or any other child or foster care worker, mental health professional, peace officer, law enforcement official, and any other person. |
| California | Cal. Penal Code Sections 11161.5 to 11161.7 | Physician, surgeon, dentist, resident, intern, podiatrist, chiropractor, marriage, family or child counselor, psychologist, religious practitioner, registered nurse employed by public health agency, school or school district, superintendent or supervisor of child welfare, certified pupil personnel employee of public or private school system, principal or teacher, licensed day care worker, administrator of summary day camp or child care center, social worker, peace officer, probation officer. |

| Age Limit | Report To | Immunity Provision | Physician-Patient Privilege Eliminated | Penalty |
|---|---|---|---|---|
| 18 | Duly constituted authority— Chief of Police, Sheriff, Dept. of Pensions & Security or its designee but not an agency involved in the acts or omissions of reported child abuse or neglect. | Yes | Yes | Misdemeanor. Sentence 6 mos or $500.00 |
| 16 | Department of Health and Welfare, peace officer. | Yes | Yes | |
| 18 | Municipal or county peace officer or protective services of state dept. of economic security. | Yes | Yes | Misdemeanor |
| 18 | Person in charge of institution or his designated agent who shall report. District or State Social Services Division of the Department of Social and Rehabilitative Services. | Yes | Yes | Misdemeanor. Sentence 5 days and $100.00. Civil liability for damages proximately caused by failure to report. |
| 18 | Local police authority, juvenile probation department, county welfare department, county health department. | Yes | | |

| State | Citation | Applies To |
|-------|----------|-----------|
| Colorado | Colo. Rev. Stat. Ann. Sections 19-10-101 through 19-10-115 (1975) | Physician or surgeon including physicians in training, child health associate, medical examiner or coroner, dentist, osteopath, optometrist, chiropractor, chiropodist or podiatrist, registered nurse, licensed practical nurse, hospital personnel engaged in admission, care, or treatment, Christian Science practitioner, school official or employee, social worker, worker in a family care home or child care center, mental health professional, any other person. |
| Connecticut | Conn. Gen. Stat. Rev. Section 17-38a (1973) | Physician, nurse, medical examiner, dentist, psychologist, school teacher, principal, guidance counselor, social worker, police officer, clergyman, coroner, osteopath, optometrist, chiropractor, podiatrist, any person paid to care for children or mental health professional. |
| Delaware | Del. Code Ann. Tit. 16 Sections 1001 to 1008 (Supp. 1972) | Physician, any person in healing arts, medicine, osteopathy, dentistry, intern, resident, nurse, school employee, social worker, psychologist, medical examiner or any other person. |
| Florida | Fla. Stat. Ann. Sections 827.01 to 827.09 (1977) | Physician, dentist, podiatrist, optometrist, intern, resident, nurse, teacher, social worker, employee of a public or private facility serving children. |
| Georgia | Ga. Code Ann. Sections 74-109 to 74-11 (1977) | Social worker, teacher, school administrator, child care personnel, day care personnel, law enforcement personnel, any other person. |
| Hawaii | Hawaii Rev. Stat. Sections 350-1 to 350-5 (1968), As Amended, (Supp. 7) | Doctor of medicine, osteopathy, dentistry, or any of the other healing arts, registered nurse, school teacher, social worker, medical examiner, and any other person. |

| Age Limit | Report To | Immunity Provision | Physician-Patient Privilege Eliminated | Penalty |
|---|---|---|---|---|
| Child | Local law enforcement agency or the county or district department of social services. Receiving agency is to report to central registry. | Yes | Yes | Class 2 petty offense. Fine $200.00. Civil liability for damages proximately caused by failure to report. |
| 18 | State Commission of Social Services or local police department. | Yes | Yes | $1,000.00 or one year. |
| * | Division of Social Services of Dept. of Health & Social Services. | Yes | Yes | Maximum of $100.00 and/or maximum of 15 days imprisonment. |
| 17 | Person in charge of institution, Department of Health and Rehabilitative Services. | Yes | Yes | Misdemeanor of second degree. Sentence 60 days, $500.00, or both. |
| 18 | Person in charge of institution and county health officer, and child welfare agency designated by Dept. of Human Resources and police authority. | Yes | | Misdemeanor. Imprisonment less than 12 mos. |
| 18 | Person in charge of medical facility, Department of Social Services and Housing. | Yes | Yes | |

* 18 or mentally retarded.

| State | Citation | Applies To |
|---|---|---|
| Idaho | Idaho Code Section 16-1619 through 16-1629 (1976) | Physician, resident, intern, nurse, coroner, school teacher, day care personnel, social worker, any other person. |
| Illinois | Ill. Ann. Stat. Ch. 23 Sections 2051-2061 (1975) | Physician, hospital, surgeon, dentist, osteopath, chiropractor, podiatrist, Christian Science practitioner, coroner, school teacher, school administrator, truant officer, social worker, social services administrator, registered nurse, licensed practical nurse, director or staff assistant of a nursery school or a child day care center, law enforcement officer, or field personnel of the Illinois Department of Public Aid. |
| Indiana | Ind. Ann. Stat. Sections 12-3-4.1-1 to 12-3-4.1-6 (1973) | Any person. |
| Iowa | Iowa Code Ann. Sections 235A.1 to 235A.24 | Health practitioner, social worker, certified psychologist, certified school employee, employee of a licensed day care facility, member of the staff of a mental health center, peace officer, any other person. |
| Kansas | Kan. Stat. Ann. 38-716 to 38-756 | Persons licensed to practice healing art, dentistry, optometrist, engaged in postgraduate training programs approved by the state board of healing arts, certified psychologists, Christian Science practitioners, licensed social workers, every licensed professional nurse or licensed practical nurse, teacher, school administrator or other employee of a school, chief administrative officer of a medical care facility, every person licensed by the secretary of health and environment to provide child care services or employee of the person so licensed at the place where the child care services are being provided to the child, or any law enforcement officer. |
| Kentucky | Ky. Rev. Stat. Ann. Sec. 199.335 1964 As Amended 1970, 1972, 1974 | Physician, osteopathic physician, nurse, teacher, school administrator, social worker, coroner, medical examiner, and any other person. |

| Age Limit | Report To | Immunity Provision | Physician-Patient Privilege Eliminated | Penalty |
|---|---|---|---|---|
| 18 | Law enforcement agency, person in charge of the institution or designee. Law enforcement report to Department of Health and Welfare. | Yes | Yes | |
| Child | Dept. of Child & Family Services, local law enforcement agency. | Yes | Yes | None |
| Child | County department of public welfare, law enforcement agency. | Yes | Yes | Misdemeanor. Sentence 30 days, $100.00, or both. |
| 18 | Dept. of Social Services, law enforcement agency. | Yes | Yes | Misdemeanor. $100.00 or 10 days. Civil liability for damages proximately caused by failure to report. |
| Child | District court of county in which such examination or attendance is made, treatment is given, school is located or such abuse or neglect is extant or to the department of social and rehabilitation services. | Yes | Yes | Misdemeanor |
| 18 | Person in charge of institution, Department of Human Resources. | Yes | Yes | |

| State | Citation | Applies To |
|-------|----------|------------|
| Louisiana | La. R.S. 14:403 (1964) As Amended 1970, 1974, 1975, and 1977 | Any person, physicians, interns, residents, nurses, hospital staff members, teachers, social workers, other persons or agencies having responsibility for care of children. |
| Maine | Me. Rev. Stat. Ann. Tit. 22 Sections 3853-3860 (1975) As Amended 1977 | Any medical physician, resident, intern, medical examiner, dentist, osteopathic physician, chiropractor, podiatrist, registered or licensed practical nurse, Christian Science practitioner, teacher, school offical, social worker, homemaker, home health aide, medical or social service worker for families and children, psychologist, child care personnel, mental health professional or law enforcement official. |
| Maryland | Md. Ann. Code Art. 27, Sec. 35A- (1977) | Every health practitioner, educator, social worker, law enforcement officer who contacts, examines, attends, or treats a child. |
| Massachusetts | Mass. Ann. c. 119 Section 51A (1973) As Amended 1975 and 1977 | Physician, medical intern, medical examiner, dentist, nurse, public or private, school teacher, educational administrator, guidance or family counselor, probation officer, social worker or policeman. Any other person may report. |
| Michigan | Mich. Statutes Ann. Section 25.248 (1)-(Mich. Comp. Law Section 722.621) (1975) | Physician, coroner, dentist, medical examiner, nurse, audiologist, certified social worker, social worker, technician, school administrator, counselor or teacher, law enforcement officer, duly regulated child care provider. |
| Minnesota | Minn. Stat. Ann. Section 626.556 (1975) | Professional or his delegate engaged in practice of the healing arts, social services, hospital administration, psychological or psychiatric treatment, child care, education, or law enforcement. Any person may report. |
| Mississippi | Miss. Code Ann. Sections 43-24-1, 43-24-7, 43-21-11, 43-23-9, 43-23-3 (1977) | Licensed doctor of medicine, dentistry, intern, resident, registered nurse, psychologist, teacher, social worker, school principal, child care giver, minister, any law enforcement officer, and all other persons. |

| Age Limit | Report To | Immunity Provision | Physician-Patient Privilege Eliminated | Penalty |
|---|---|---|---|---|
| 18 | Parish child welfare unit, Parish agency responsible for protection of juveniles, local or state law enforcement agency. | Yes | Yes | Misdemeanor. Sentence 6 mos. and/or $500.00. |
| 18 | Person in charge of institution, Dept. of Health & Welfare. | None | Yes | Civil violation $500.00. |
| 18 | Local Dept. of Social Services, appropriate law enforcement agency. | Yes | | |
| 18 | Person in charge of institution, Dept. of Public Welfare, attorney for county and medical examiner if death occurs. | Yes | Yes | Maximum fine $1,000.00. |
| 18 | Dept. of Social Services, person in charge of institution. | Yes | Yes | Civil liability for damages proximately caused by failure to report. |
| Child | Local welfare agency, police department; deaths to medical examiner or coroner who will notify the local welfare agency or police department. | Yes | Yes | Misdemeanor |
| 18 | County Welfare Department which will thereafter make a referral to the person designated by the judge of the county youth court or family court. | Yes | Yes | |

| State | Citation | Applies To |
|---|---|---|
| Missouri | Mo. Ann. Stat. Sections 210.110 to 210.165 (1975) | Physician, medical examiner, coroner, dentist, chiropractor, optometrist, podiatrist, resident, intern, nurse, hospital and clinic personnel, health practitioner, psychologist, mental health professional, social worker, day care center worker or other child care worker, juvenile officer, probation or parole officer, teacher, principal or other school official, minister, Christian Science practitioner, peace officer, law enforcement official, other person with responsibility for the care of children. Any other person may report. |
| Montana | Mont. Rev. Code Ann. Sections 10-1300 to 10-1322 (1974) As Amended (1977) | Physician, nurse, teacher, social worker, attorney, law enforcement officer, any other person. |
| Nebraska | Neb. Rev. Stat. Supp. Sections 28-1501 to 28-1508 (1975) | Physician, medical institution, nurse, school employee, social worker, any other person. |
| Nevada | Nevada Rev. Stat. Sections 200.501 thru 200.508 | Physician, dentist, chiropractor, optometrist, resident and intern licensed in Nevada, Superintendent, manager or other person in charge of a hospital or similar institution, professional or practical nurse, physician assistant, psychologist and emergency medical technician, ambulance licensed or certified to practice in Nevada, attorney, social worker, school authority, teacher, every person who maintains or is employed by a licensed child care facility or children's camp. |
| New Hampshire | New Hampshire Rev. Stat. Ann. Sections 169.37 to 169.45 (1975) As Amended 1975 | Physician, surgeon, county medical referee, psychiatrist, resident, intern, dentist, osteopath, optometrist, chiropractor, psychologist, therapist, registered nurse, hospital personnel, Christian Science practitioner, teacher, school official, school nurse, school counselor, social worker, day care worker, any other child or foster care worker, law enforcement official, priest, minister, or rabbi or any other person. |

| Age Limit | Report To | Immunity Provision | Physician-Patient Privilege Eliminated | Penalty |
|---|---|---|---|---|
| 18 | Person in charge of institution, Missouri Division of Family Service, death to medical examiner or coroner who will report to the police, peace officer, prosecuting juvenile officer, Missouri Division of Family Services. | Yes | Yes | Misdemeanor. $1,000 and/or one year. |
| 18 | Dept. of Social & Rehabilitation Services, local affiliate, county attorney where child resides. | No | Yes | None |
| * | Dept. of Public Welfare, Police Department, town marshall, Office of Sheriff. | | | |
| 18 | Local office of Welfare Division of Dept. of Human Resources, any county agency authorized by juvenile courts to receive reports, any police dept. or Sheriff's office. | Yes | Yes | Gross misdemeanor. 1 to 20 years if substantial bodily harm occurs. (Could interpret to cover failure to report.) |
| 18 | Bureau of Child & Family Services, Division of Welfare, Dept. of Health & Welfare. | Yes | Yes | Misdemeanor |

---

* Minor child 18 or incompetent or disabled persons or 6 years old or under left unattended in a motor vehicle.

| State | Citation | Applies To |
|---|---|---|
| New Jersey | New Jersey Rev. Stat. Ann. Sections 9:6-8.1 to 9:6-8.7 (1974) | Any person. |
| New Mexico | N.M. Stat. Ann. Sections 13-14-14.1 to 13-14-14.2 (1973) | Physician, resident, intern, law enforcement officer, registered nurse, visiting nurse, school teacher, social worker, any other person. |
| New York | N.Y. Soc. Service Law Sections 411 to 428 (1973) | Physician, surgeon, medical examiner, coroner, dentist, osteopath, optometrist, resident, intern, registered nurse, Christian Science practitioner, hospital personnel, social services worker, school official, day care center director, peace officer, mental health professional, and any other person. |
| North Carolina | N.C. Cent. Stat. Sections 110-117 to 110-119 (1977) | Physician or administrator of a hospital, clinic or other medical facility to which children are brought. |
| North Dakota | N.D. Cent. Code Sections 50-25.1-01 to 50-25.1-14 (1975) As Amended, 1977 | Physician, nurse, dentist, optometrist, medical examiner or coroner, any other medical or mental health professional, school teacher or administrator, school counselor, social worker, day care center or any other child care worker, police, law enforcement officer, and any other person. |
| Ohio | Ohio Rev. Code Ann. Section 2151-42.1 (1977) | Attorney, physician, intern, resident, dentist, podiatrist, practitioner of a limited branch of medicine or surgery as defined in section 4731.15 of the Revised Code, registered or licensed practical nurse, visiting nurse, or other health care professional, licensed psychologist, speech pathologist or audiologist, coroner, administrator or employee of a child day-care center, or administrator or employee of a certified child care agency or other public or private children services agency, school teacher, or school authority, social worker, or person rendering spiritual treatment through prayer in accordance with the tenets of a well recognized religion. |

| Age Limit | Report To | Immunity Provision | Physician-Patient Privilege Eliminated | Penalty |
|---|---|---|---|---|
| 18 | Bureau of Child Services, Division of Youth and Family Services. | Yes | | Misdemeanor. (Disorderly person). |
| 18 | County Social Services Office of the Health & Social Services Dept. in the county of child's residence or Probation Services Office in Judicial District of child's residence. | Yes | Yes | Misdemeanor. $25.00 minimum and $100.00 maximum. |
| * | Statewide Central Register of Child Abuse and Maltreatment Local Child Protective Service, person in charge of institution. | Yes | Yes | Class A Misdemeanor. Civil liability for damages proximately caused by failure to report. |
| 18 | Director of Social Services of county where child resides, parents, other caretakers. | | | |
| 18 | Division of Community Services of the Social Service Board of North Dakota. | Yes | Yes | Class B Misdemeanor. |
| 18 | Person in charge of institution, Children Services Board or County Dept. of Welfare exercising the children services function or municipal or county police officer in county of child's residence or where abuse or neglect occurred. | Yes | | |

* Abused 16, maltreated 18

| State | Citation | Applies To |
|---|---|---|
| Oklahoma | Okla. Stat. Ann. Tit. 21 Sections 845-848 1965, As Amended 1977 | Physician, surgeon, dentist, osteopathic physicians, residents, interns, every other person. |
| Oregon | Ore. Rev. Stat. Sections 418.740 to 418.775 (1975) | Public or private official, physician, intern, resident, dentist, school employee, licensed practical or registered nurse, employee of Dept. of Human Resources, County Health Dept., Community Mental Health Program, County juvenile dept, licensed child caring agency, peace officer, psychologist, clergyman, social worker, optometrist, chiropractor, certified provider of day care or foster care, attorney, law enforcement agency, police department, sheriff's office, county juvenile department. |
| Pennsylvania | Pa. Stat. Ann. Tit. 11 Sections 2201 to 2224 (1975) | Any person who in the course of their employment, occupation, or practice of their profession contacts children, licensed physician, medical examiner, coroner, dentist, osteopath, optometrist, chiropractor, podiatrist, intern, registered nurse, licensed practical nurse, hospital personnel engaged in the admission, examination, care or treatment of persons, a Christian Science practitioner, school administrator, school teacher, school nurse, social services worker, day care center worker or any other child care or foster care worker, mental health professional, peace officer or law enforcement official. |
| Rhode Island | R.I. Gen. Laws Ann. Sections 40-11-1 to 40-11-17 (1976) | Physicians, and any person. |
| South Carolina | S.C. Code Ann. Sections 20-9-10 to 20-9-70 (1962) As Amended 1972, 1974, 1976 | Practitioners of healing arts, resident, intern, registered nurse, visiting nurse, school teacher, social worker, any other person. |
| South Dakota | S.D. Compiled. Laws Ann. Sections 26-10-11, 26-10-15 (1964) As Amended 1973, 1976 | Physician, surgeon, dentist, doctor of osteopathy, chiropractor, optometrist, podiatrist, psychologist, social worker, hospital intern or resident, law enforcement officer, teacher, school counselor, school official, nurse, or coroner. |

| Age Limit | Report To | Immunity Provision | Physician-Patient Privilege Eliminated | Penalty |
|---|---|---|---|---|
| 18 | County office of the Dept. of Institutions, Social & Rehabilitative Services where injury occurred. | Yes | Yes | Misdemeanor |
| 18 | Local office of Children's Services Division, law enforcement agency. | Yes | No | Fine $250.00. |
| 18 | Person in charge of institution or agency, Dept. of Public Welfare of the Commonwealth of Pennsylvania. | Yes | Yes | First failure to report is a summary offense, subsequent failure to report is a misdemeanor of the third degree. |
| 18 | Director of Social & Rehabilitative Services, law enforcement agency. | Yes | Yes | |
| 18 | County Dept. of Social Services, County Sheriff's office, Chief County law enforcement officer. | Yes | Yes | Misdemeanor. Sentence: 6 mos. and/or $500.00. |
| 18 | Person in charge of institution. | Yes | Yes | Class I misdemeanor. |

| State | Citation | Applies To |
|-------|----------|------------|
| Tennessee | Tenn. Code Ann. Sections 37-1201, 37-1212 (1973) As Amended 1975 | Any person. |
| Texas | Tex. Family Code Ann. Sections 34.01 to 34.06 (1975) | Any person. |
| Utah | Utah Code Ann. Sections 55-16-1 to 55-16-6 (1975) | Any person. |
| Vermont | Vt. Stat. Ann. Sections 1351 to 1355 (1974) As Amended 1975, 1976 and 1977 | Physician, surgeon, osteopath, chiropractor or physician assistant licensed or registered, resident physician, intern, or any hospital administrator, psychologist, school teacher, day care worker, school principal, school guidance counselor, mental health professional, social worker, probation officer, clergyman or any other person. |
| Virginia | Va. Code Ann. Sections 63.1-248.1 to 63.1-248.17 (1975) | Persons licensed to practice healing arts, residents, interns, nurses, social workers, probation officers, teachers, persons employed in a public or private school, kindergarten or nursery, persons providing child care for pay on a regular basis, Christian Science practitioner, mental health professional, law enforcement officer. Any person may report. |
| Washington | Wash. Rev. Code Ann. Sections 26.44.010 to 26.44.900 (1975) | Practitioner, professional school personnel, nurse, social worker, psychologist, pharmacist, employee of social or health services. Any person may report. |
| Wisconsin | Wis. Stat. Ann. Section 48.981 (1974) | Physician, surgeon, nurse, hospital administrator, dentist, social worker, school administrator. |

| Age Limit | Report To | Immunity Provision | Physician-Patient Privilege Eliminated | Penalty |
|---|---|---|---|---|
| * | Judge with juvenile jurisdiction Tennessee Dept. of Human Resources, Office of Sheriff, law enforcement official where child resides, person in charge of institution. | Yes | Yes | Misdemeanor. $50.00 and/or 3 months. |
| ** | State Dept. of Public Welfare, Agency designated by court to protect children, local or state law enforcement. | Yes | Yes | Class B Misdemeanor. |
| 18 | Local city police, county sheriff's office, Office of the Division of Family Services, person in charge of institution. | Yes | Yes | Misdemeanor |
| *** | Commissioner of Social & Rehabilitative Services. | Yes | | Fine $100.00. |
| 18 | Person in charge of institution or department, Department of Welfare of the county or city where child resides or abuse or neglect occurred, juvenile and domestic relations district court if an employee of the Department of Welfare is the one suspected of abusing the child. | Yes | Yes | First failure to report $500.00. Subsequent failure to report $100.00 to $1,000.00. |
| † | Law enforcement agency, Department of Social & Health Services. | Yes | | Misdemeanor |
| †† | County Child Welfare Agency, sheriff, city police department. | Yes | ††† | Sentence 6 months and/or $100.00. |

```
  * 18, reasonably presumed to be under 18
 ** 18 who has not been married
*** Under age of majority
  † 18, any mentally retarded person
 †† 18 (Section 48.02)
††† See Section 325.21
```

| State | Citation | Applies To |
|-------|----------|------------|
| West Virginia | West Va. Code Ann. Sections 49-6A.1 to 49-6A-10 (1977) | Medical, dental, mental health professional, Christian Science practitioner, religious healer, school teacher, or other school personnel, social service worker, child care or foster care worker, peace officer, law enforcement official. Any other person may report. |
| Wyoming | Wyo. Stat. Ann. Sections 14-28.1 to 14-28.13 (1974) | Physician, surgeon, dentist, osteopath, chiropractor, podiatrist, intern, resident, nurse, druggist, pharmacist, laboratory technician, school teacher or administrator, social worker, any other person. |
| District of Columbia | D.C. Code Ann. Sections 2-161 to 2-169 (1977) | Physician, psychologist, medical examiner, dentist, chiropractor, registered nurse, licensed practical nurse, person involved in the care and treatment of patients, law enforcement officer, school official, teacher, social service worker, day care worker, and mental health professional. Any person may report. |

| Age Limit | Report To | Immunity Provision | Physician-Patient Privilege Eliminated | Penalty |
|---|---|---|---|---|
| 18 | Local State Department Child Protective Services Agency, report deaths to medical examiner or coroner. | Yes | Yes | Misdemeanor. Sentence 10 days and/or $100.00. |
| 19 | Person in charge of institution, Department of Health & Social Services, Division of Public Assistance & Social Services. | Yes | Yes | |
| 18 | Person in charge of institution, Metropolitan Police Department of the District of Columbia, Child Protective Services Division of the Department of Human Resources. | Yes | Yes | Sentence 30 days and/or $100.00. |

# State-by-State Summary of Good Samaritan Laws

| State | A. Date of act or last amended act | B. Covers any emergency or accident | C. Covers only roadside accidents | D. Covers everyone | E. Covers in-state physicians | F. Covers out-of-state physicians | G. Covers in-state nurses | H. Covers out-of-state nurses | I. Does not cover acts of gross negligence or willful misconduct | J. Covers only gratuitous services |
|---|---|---|---|---|---|---|---|---|---|---|
| Alabama | 1975 | X | | | X | X | X | X | | X |
| Alaska | 1967 | X | | X | | | | | X | X |
| Arizona | 1972 | X | | X | X | X | X | X | X | X |
| Arkansas | 1963 | X | | X | X | | | | X | X |
| California | 1963 | X | | | X | | X | | | |
| Colorado | 1975 | X | | | X | X | X | X | X | X |
| Connecticut | 1971 | X | | | X | X | X | X | | X |
| Delaware | 1974 | X | | X | X | | | X | X | X |
| District of Columbia | 1965 | X | | | X | X | X | X | X | X |
| Florida | 1965 | X | | X | X | X | | | X | X |
| Georgia | 1962 | X | | X | X | | | | X | X |
| Hawaii | 1974 | X | | X | | | | | X | X |
| Idaho | 1965 | | X | X | | | | | X | |

| State | A. Date of act or last amended act | B. Covers any emergency or accident | C. Covers only roadside accidents | D. Covers everyone | E. Covers in-state physicians | F. Covers out-of-state physicians | G. Covers in-state nurses | H. Covers out-of-state nurses | I. Does not cover acts of gross negligence or willful misconduct | J. Covers only gratuitous services |
|---|---|---|---|---|---|---|---|---|---|---|
| Illinois | 1973 | X | | | X | X | X | X | X | X |
| Indiana | 1971 | X | X | | | | | | X | X |
| Iowa | 1969 | X | X | | | | | | X | X |
| Kansas | 1976 | X | | X | X | X | X | X | X | X |
| Kentucky | None | | | | | | | | | |
| Louisiana | 1964 | X | | | X | X | X | X | X | X |
| Maine | 1977 | X | | X | X | | | | X | X |
| Maryland | 1977 | X | | X | X | X | X | X | X | X |
| Massachusetts | 1969 | X | | | X | X | X | X | X | X |
| Michigan | 1967 | X | Covers ambulance driver and attendant, police, firemen | | | | | | X | |
| Minnesota | 1971 | X | | X | | | | | X | |
| Mississippi | 1976 | X | | | X | X | X | X | X | |
| Missouri | 1974 | X | Covers persons trained in emergency care | | | | | | X | |
| Montana | None | | | | | | | | | |
| Nebraska | 1963 | X | | | X | X | X | X | X | X |
| Nevada | 1975 | X | | X | X | X | X | X | X | X |
| New Hampshire | 1977 | X | | X | X | X | X | X | X | X |
| New Jersey | 1968 | X | | X | X | X | X | X | X | |
| New Mexico | 1972 | X | | X | | | | | X | X |
| New York | 1971 | | | | X | X | | | X | |
| North Carolina | 1975 | | X | X | | | | | X | |
| North Dakota | 1977 | | X | X | X | X | X | | X | X |
| Ohio | 1977 | X | | X | | | | | X | X |
| Oklahoma | 1974 | X | | | X | X | X | X | X | X |

| State | A. Date of act or last amended act | B. Covers any emergency or accident | C. Covers only roadside accidents | D. Covers everyone | E. Covers in-state physicians | F. Covers out-of-state physicians | G. Covers in-state nurses | H. Covers out-of-state nurses | I. Does not cover acts of gross negligence or willful misconduct | J. Covers only gratuitous services |
|---|---|---|---|---|---|---|---|---|---|---|
| Oregon | 1967 | X | | | X | X | X | X | X | X |
| Pennsylvania | 1965 | X | | | X | X | X | X | X | |
| Rhode Island | 1969 | X | | | | | X | X | X | X |
| South Carolina | 1964 | X | | X | | | | | X | X |
| South Dakota | 1976 | X | | | X | | X | | X | |
| Tennessee | 1976 | X | | X | X | X | X | X | X | |
| Texas | 1964 | X | | X | | | | | X | X |
| Utah | 1975 | X | | | X | | X | | X | |
| Vermont | 1968 | X | | X | | | | | X | X |
| Virginia | 1977 | X | | X | | | | | X | X |
| Washington | 1975 | X | | X | | | | | X | X |
| West Virginia | 1967 | | X | X | X | X | | | X | X |
| Wisconsin | 1975 | X | | | | | X | | X | |
| Wyoming | 1961 | X | | X | X | | | | X | X |

# Glossary of Legal Terms

**Abortion:** The termination of pregnancy or inducement of miscarriage with intent to destroy a fetus.

**Administrative agency:** An arm of government which administers or carries out legislation; for example, the Workmen's Compensation Commission.

**Admissibility (of evidence):** Worthiness of evidence that meets the legal rules of evidence and will be allowed to be presented to the jury.

**Affidavit:** A voluntary sworn statement of facts, or a voluntary declaration in writing of facts, that a person swears to be true before an official authorized to administer an oath.

**Agency:** The relationship in which one person acts for or represents another; for example, employer and employee.

**Allegation:** A statement that a person expects to be able to prove.

**Appellant:** The party who appeals the decision of a lower court to a higher jurisdiction.

**Appellee:** The party against whom an appeal to a higher court is taken.

**Assault:** An intentional act which is designed to make the victim fearful and which produces reasonable apprehension of harm.

**Assignment:** A transfer of rights or property.

**Attestation:** An indication by a witness that the documents of procedures required by law have been signed.

**Battery:** The touching of one person by another without permission.

**Best evidence rule:** The legal doctrine requiring that primary evidence of a fact (such as an original document) be introduced, or at least explained, before a copy can be introduced or testimony giving concerning the fact.

**Bona fide:** In good faith; openly, honestly, or innocently; without knowledge or intent of fraud.

**Borrowed servant:** an employee temporarily under the control of another. The traditional example is a nurse employed by a hospital who is "borrowed" by a surgeon in the operating room. The temporary employer of the borrowed servant will be held responsible for the act of the borrowed servant under the doctrine of *respondeat superior.*

**Civil Law:** The law of countries such as Germany and France which follow the Roman system of jurisprudence in which all law is enacted. It is also the portion of American law which does not deal with crimes.

**Closed shop contract:** A labor-management agreement which provides that only members of a particular union may be hired.

**Common law:** The legal traditions of England and the United States where part of the law is developed by means of court decisions.

**Concurring opinion:** *See* Opinion of the court.

**Confidential information:** *See* Privileged communication.

**Consent:** A voluntary act by which one person agrees to allow someone else to do something. For medical liability purposes, consents should be in writing with an explanation of the procedures to be performed.

**Coroner's jury:** A special jury called by a coroner to determine whether the evidence concerning the cause of a death indicates that death was brought about by criminal means.

**Counterclaim:** A defendant's claim against a plaintiff.

**Crime:** An act against society in violation of the law. Crimes are prosecuted by and in the name of the state.

**Criminal law:** The division of the law dealing with crime and punishment.

**Decedent:** A deceased person.

**Defamation:** The injury of a person's reputation or character by willful and malicious statements made to a third person. Defamation includes both libel and slander.

**Defendant:** In a criminal case, the person accused of committing a crime. In a civil suit, the party against whom suit is brought demanding compensation to the other party.

**Deposition:** A witness' sworn statement, made out of court, which may be admitted into evidence if it is impossible for the witness to attend in person.

**Directed verdict:** The verdict returned by a jury when the judge directs the jury to return a verdict in favor of one party because the evidence or law is so clearly in favor of one party that it is pointless for the trial to proceed further.

**Discovery:** Pretrial activities of attorneys to determine what evidence the opposing side will present if the case comes to trial. Discovery prevents attorneys from being surprised during a trial and facilitates out-of-court settlement.

**Dissenting opinion:** *See* Opinion of the court.

**Emergency:** A sudden unexpected occurrence or event causing a threat to life or health. The legal responsibilities of those involved in an emergency situation are measured according to the occurrence.

**Employee:** One who works for another in return for pay.

**Employer:** A person or firm that selects employees, pays their salaries or wages, retains the power of dismissal, and can control the employees' conduct during working hours.

**Expert witness:** One who has special training, experience, skill, and knowledge in a relevant area, and who is allowed to offer an opinion as testimony in court.

**Federal question:** A legal question involving the U.S. Constitution or a statute enacted by Congress.

**Felony:** A crime of a serious nature usually punishable by imprisonment for a period of longer than one year or by death.

**Good samaritan law:** A legal doctrine designed to protect those who stop to render aid in an emergency.

**Grand jury:** A jury called to determine whether there is sufficient evidence that a crime has been committed to justify bringing a case to trial. It is not the jury before which the case is tried to determine guilt or innocence.

**Grand larceny:** The theft of property valued at more than a specified amount (usually fifty dollars), thus constituting a felony instead of a misdemeanor.

**Harm or injury:** Any wrong or damage done to another, either to the person, or to the person's rights or property.

**Hearsay rule:** A rule of evidence that restricts the admissibility of evidence which is not the personal knowledge of the witness. Hearsay evidence is admissible only under strict rules.

**Holographic will:** A will handwritten by the testator.

**In loco parentis:** The legal doctrine providing that under certain circumstances the courts may assign a person to stand in the place of parents and possess their legal rights, duties, and responsibilities toward a child.

**Independent contractor:** One who agrees to undertake work without being under the direct control or direction of an employer.

**Indictment:** A formal written accusation of crime brought by a prosecuting attorney against one charged with criminal conduct.

**Injunction:** A court order requiring one to do or not to do a certain act.

**Interrogatories:** A list of questions sent from one party in a lawsuit to the other party to be answered.

**Judge:** An officer who guides court proceedings to ensure impartiality and enforce the rules of evidence. The trial judge determines the applicable law and states it to the jury. The appellate judge hears appeals and renders decisions concerning the correctness of actions of the trial judge, the law of the case, and the sufficiency of the evidence.

**Jurisprudence:** The philosophy or science of law upon which a particular legal system is built.

**Jury:** A certain number of persons selected and sworn to hear the evidence and determine the facts in the case.

**Larceny:** The taking of another person's property without consent and with the intent to deprive the owner of its use and ownership.

**Liability:** An obligation one has incurred or might incur through any act or failure to act.

**Liability insurance:** A contract to have someone else pay for any liability or loss thereby in return for the payment of premiums.

**Libel:** A false or malicious writing that is intended to defame or dishonor another person and is published so that someone besides the one defamed will observe it.

**License:** A permit from the state allowing certain acts to be performed, usually for a specific period of time.

**Litigation:** A trial in court to determine legal issues, rights, and duties between the parties to the litigation.

**Malpractice:** Professional misconduct, improper discharge of professional duties, or failure to meet the standard of care of a professional which resulted in harm to another.

**Mayhem:** The crime of intentionally disfiguring or dismembering another.

**Misdemeanor:** An unlawful act of a less serious nature than a felony, usually punishable by fine or by imprisonment for a term of less than one year.

**Negligence:** Carelessness, failure to act as an ordinary prudent person, or action contrary to the conduct of a reasonable person.

**Next of kin:** Those persons who by the law of descent would be adjudged the closest blood relatives of the decedent.

**Non compos mentis:** "Not of sound mind"; suffering from some form of mental defect.

**Notary public:** A public official who administers oaths and certifies the validity of documents.

**Nuncupative will:** An oral statement intended as a last will made in anticipation of death.

**Opinion of the court:** In an appellate court decision, the reasons for the decision. One judge writes the opinion for the majority of the court. Judges who agree with the result but for different reasons may write concurring opinions explaining their reasons. Judges who disagree with the majority may write dissenting opinions.

**Ordinance:** A law passed by a municipal legislative body.

**Perjury:** The willful act of giving false testimony under oath.

**Petit larceny:** The theft of property usually valued at below fifty dollars and classed as a misdemeanor.

**Plaintiff:** The party to a civil suit who brings the suit seeking damages or other legal relief.

**Police power:** The power of the state to protect the health, safety, morals, and general welfare of its citizens.

**Privileged communication:** A statement made to an attorney, physician, spouse, or anyone else in a position of trust. Because of the confidential nature of such information, the law protects it from being revealed, even in court. The term is applied in two distinct situations. First, the communications between certain persons, such as physician and patient, cannot be divulged without the consent of the patient. Second, in some situations the law provides an exemption from liability for disclosing information where there is a higher duty to speak, such as statutory reporting requirements.

**Probate:** The judicial proceeding which determines the existence and validity of a will.

**Probate Court:** A court with jurisdiction over wills. Its powers range from deciding the validity of a will to distributing property.

**Proximate:** In immediate relation with something else. In negligence cases, the careless act must be the proximate cause of injury.

**Real evidence:** Evidence furnished by tangible things, such as weapons, bullets, and equipment.

**Rebuttal:** The giving of evidence to contradict the effect of evidence introduced by the opposing party.

**Regulatory agency:** An arm of the government which enforces legislation regulating an act or activity in a particular area; for example, the Federal Food and Drug Administration.

**Release:** A statement signed by one person relinquishing a right or claim against another person, usually for a valuable consideration.

**Res gestae:** All of the surrounding events which become part of an incident. If statements are made as part of the incident they are admissible in court as *res gestae,* as an exception to the hearsay rule.

**Res ipsa loquitur:** "The thing speaks for itself." A doctrine of law applicable to cases where the defendant had exclusive control of the thing which caused the harm and where the harm ordinarily could not have occurred without negligent conduct.

**Respondeat superior:** "Let the master answer." The legal doctrine which holds the employer responsible for the legal consequences of the acts of the servant, or employee, while acting within the scope of employment.

**Shop book rule:** If books are kept in the usual course of business they may be introduced in court so long as they are properly authenticated and held in proper custody.

**Slander:** An oral statement made with intent to dishonor or defame another person when made in the presence of a third person.

**Standard of care:** Those acts performed or omitted that an ordinary prudent person would have performed or omitted. It is a measure against which a defendant's conduct is compared.

**Stare decisis:** "Let the decision stand." The legal principle indicating courts should apply previous decisions to subsequent cases involving similar facts and questions.

**State statute; statutory law:** A declaration of the legislative branch of government having the force of law.

**Statute of limitations:** A legal limit on the time allowed for filing suit in civil matters, usually measured from the time of the wrong or from the time when a reasonable person would have discovered the wrong.

**Subpoena:** A court order requiring one to appear in court to give testimony.

**Subpoena duces tecum:** A subpoena that commands a person to come to court and to produce whatever documents are named in order.

**Subrogation:** The substitution of one person for another in reference to a lawful claim or right.

**Suit:** A court proceeding in which one person seeks damages or other legal remedies from another. The term is not usually used in criminal cases.

**Summons:** A court order which directs a sheriff to notify the defendant in a civil suit that a suit has been filed and when and where to appear.

**Testimony:** The oral statement of a witness given under oath at a trial.

**Tort:** A civil wrong. Torts may be intentional or unintentional.

**Tortfeasor:** One who commits a tort.

**Trial court:** The court in which evidence is presented to a judge or jury for decision.

**Uniform act:** A model act concerning a particular area of the law created by a nonlegal body in the hope that it will be enacted in all states to achieve uniformity in that area of law.

**Union shop contract:** A labor-management agreement making continued employment contingent upon joining a union.

**Verdict:** The formal declaration of a jury's findings of fact, signed by the jury foreman and presented to the court.

**Waiver:** The intentional giving up of a right, such as allowing another person to testify to information that would ordinarily be protected as a privileged communication.

**Will:** A legal declaration of the intentions a person wishes to have carried out after death concerning property, children, and estate.

**Witness:** One who is called to give testimony in a court of law.

**Written authorization:** A consent given in writing specifically enpowering someone to do something.

# Case Index

263

# Index